SOME ITEMS MAY HAVE
SHIFTED
IN FLIGHT

Richard Weston-Smith

Published by Brainstorm Creative Inc.

Wellhereweare.com

ISBN: 9780578855615

Editor: Malcom Croft

Cover art and interior graphics: Harry Harrison
Cover design and typography: Mark Witherspoon
Proofing Editor: Hugh Barker
Interior layout: Euan Monaghan

For Kirsten, the best of companions both in travel and in life

CONTENTS

*"I may not have gone where I intended to go,
but I think I have ended up where I needed to be."*

Douglas Adams, *The Long Dark Tea-Time of the Soul* (1988)

PROLOGUE

London, Autumn 2018.

A nurse walked me from my room down the hospital corridor, to what I imagine looked like the bridge of the *Heart of Gold* spaceship in *The Hitchhiker's Guide to The Galaxy*. Bright blue light saturated the entrance to the "Hybrid Theatre" as the glass doors swooshed open in a way Douglas Adams would have particularly admired. I was ushered into the prep room.

The floor had been painted an especially improbable shade of neon green. I was busy pondering the reason for this alarming colour choice, as the delightfully chatty anaesthetist talked me through the epidural and other things she was going to…

* * *

I awoke to find myself mysteriously back in the hospital room I had left five hours earlier, the only immediately noticeable difference being that my tongue no longer appeared to be attached to my brain and I had an urgent but unfulfillable need to blow a massive fart. Tubes connected me to several machines that went "beep" at annoyingly regular intervals, and my wife Kirsten hovered about, trying to get me to drink some liquid or other. The feeling of having been "minimally invaded" by a five-armed robot is a curious one. I was vaguely conscious that deep rummaging had occurred in hitherto un-rummageable places. It is exactly the same technology that allows a drone flying at 25,000 feet over Afghanistan to blow an ISIS Landcruiser into smithereens, while being flown by pilot named Chuck, sitting in a windowless converted shipping container on the outskirts of Las Vegas.

Looking under the sheets, I saw a tube had been recklessly inserted where one should normally avoid inserting anything – especially something of such startling girth. Well, hello Mr. Catheter. Clearly this entire procedure involves a lot of firsts for me, I thought, as I vigorously pumped the button labelled "PRESS HERE FOR INTRA-VENOUS HEROIN". Immediately feeling much better, it was all Kirsten could do to restrain me from enthusiastically hopping on a quick conference call with some clients and replying to some emails.

"Heroin and conference calls are a really bad combination, darling," she pointed out gently.

"Don't be ridiculous," I said. "I feel marvellous!" and promptly fell fast asleep for six hours.

As you are about to discover, I have been on many journeys in my life, but this was a journey of a different kind: a journey that resulted in several important things unexpectedly shifting in flight, so to speak. This was a journey through prostate cancer. Specifically, mine. It is a journey I wouldn't wish on anyone but, despite its evident seriousness, it was not without its fair share of hilarious moments.

I had been a symptomless 59-year-old male who had, quite randomly, decided to see my doctor for an overdue general health check, blissfully unaware that deep inside me a virulent cancer was exploding out of my nether regions in not-so-slow-motion. As you might well expect, things had gone progressively downhill from there. It had been a complex, challenging six months of juggling work, travel, research, and tests, while trying to maintain an outward impression of normality, when all was very far from normal. During the process, it had been discovered that I also had an early-stage lung cancer that, left undetected, would probably also have killed me in in a few more years.

Kirsten, an ever present and vital part of the journey, selflessly undertook to do hours of research into doctors, hospitals, procedures, chat forums and ground-breaking new techniques in the field. She intelligently sorted and analysed all this information, spoke to numerous medical professionals, and delivered succinct and useful summaries. I had no desire to do any of this, preferring to focus on trying to lead as normal a life as possible and continue my work through it all. Her help was invaluable.

Six months after diagnosis, with surgery only recently behind me, Mr. Catheter and I went for a walk along the river in Battersea Park, southwest London. By all accounts I seemed to be well on the way to recovery, although walking involved adopting the posture of an octogenarian man with a very bitey ferret down his trousers, which happens to be asleep, but could wake up at any moment and, on waking, would likely to be both hungry and agitated. The importance of walking in a way that would not disturb said ferret cannot be overstated. Things were a little fragile in my nether regions. To put it in architectural terms, what I had been through was the equivalent of an extensive basement remodel, with all the attendant risks of collapse and upsetting the neighbors. Of course, walking in public places carries enhanced risks, such as being greeted by a bouncy young chocolate Labrador who has decided you might just possibly have a ferret in your crotch that requires urgent investigation, and to whom the concept of asking permission is entirely foreign.

As I walked, reflecting on my circumstances, I began to see my life through a very different lens. I was both altered and unchanged, in equal measures. I had no regrets, nor did I bemoan my misfortune. On the contrary – *I was still here* – having dodged not one but two bullets, thanks to a single blood test. Suddenly and acutely aware of the tenuous hold we all have on life, I began to consider the extraordinary things I had done, the opportunities I had been given, the people I had met, and the places I had been. These had been important milestones in my life, these stories, these travels, these adventures. It struck me that I had not appreciated every detail of them as I could and should have, especially in recent years, increasingly encumbered as we have been by iPhones, social media, and the relentless connectivity that is now the ever-twitching superstructure of our lives.

And then it came to me. I realised how vital a part of me all this travel had been, and how diminished I would be as person, had I not had these experiences. With precious few photographs and almost nothing in writing, I felt suddenly compelled to revisit my experiences before they inevitably became obscured by the gathering clouds of advancing years. I wanted to shout from the rooftops, *"For God's sake, get a grip people! A selfie tells you nothing 30 years later. Appreciate every golden moment and – most importantly – the bits in between. Keep a journal, write it down, let none of it escape!"* I realised I should probably set an example and damn-well write it down myself.

So, I did.

* * *

"Memories are like a box of old toys; taken out,
wondered at, and then soundlessly put away."
Ian Weston Smith, 1918–2005

THE JOY OF TRAVEL
From golden age to internet age

I looked down at my hand with amazement. It was my father's hand, wrinkled and leathery, with a network of prominent veins, busily freckled and darkened by age and sun, but nevertheless firmly attached to my wrist. I stared at my father's hand, turning it this way and that, before quickly checking my other one to find it was also one of his. At the tender age of 17, this was either a sign that I needed to find a hospital, or excellent news because I had eaten a magic mushroom, and it was starting to work. Welcome to Wonderland.

Wonderland, at this precise moment, was Tully, North Queensland, where I had been sent to work on a cattle station for a year. At the time it was a common practice among upper middle-class British families to dispatch their male offspring on a gap year. Back then, this had an entirely different meaning to now. Today, a gap year is an extended globe-trotting boondoggle for sons and daughters, often funded entirely by their parents. I know, I have funded a few. It involves little to no work, exhaustive documentation on social media, almost constant inebriation, lost passports, occasional arrest or hospitalisation, and spontaneous beach sex with anything sporting a pulse and a moped – preferably both.

Back in the '70s, a gap year, if you were fortunate enough to do such a thing, involved sending a son (rarely, if ever, a daughter) to the farthest-flung point on the planet your connections could facilitate. The process began with a letter to family, friends, and business associates in Australia, South America, Africa and Siberia, requesting they arrange some useful, highly strenuous employment on a ranch, station, farm, illegal emerald mine, or *estancia*. Furthermore, it was desirable that one's co-workers be tough and unforgiving, the local fauna venomous, the climate blisteringly hot, the food mediocre, the hours long, the pay minimal, and that you be shouted at a lot. If it could be arranged for someone to occasionally throw rocks at you, or for you to work your passage out there on a cargo steamer and, while en route, for you to be further abused by a bunch of merchant seamen, so much the better. It was expected – and indeed desired

— that being the lowest form of life in whatever particular hellhole had been arranged for you would imbue you with inner strength, character, fortitude and a respect for authority, and generally blow away the privileged cobwebs of a British public-school[1] education.

In the only similarity to today's gap year, it was also quietly hoped you would sow your wild oats. This is a charming euphemism for having enthusiastic, table-thumping sex as often as possible, so any resulting infectious or procreational "issues" could be dealt with at arm's length, if at all. Then one could return home with a nice tan and a sexy scar or three, to be hitched to an attractive debutante called Emma, her parents being comfortably reassured that any strange sexual proclivities would have already been given a thorough test drive and put quietly away in a sturdy vault.

Unfortunately, the sort of remote, inhospitable places one ended up in for a gap year in 1977, usually had a total population of less than 20, few of whom were recognizably female. If there were any women, they were either eye-wateringly unattractive, married to the boss, or only available for a limited time in exchange for a large slice of your pathetic pay check. More often than one would imagine, all three applied. So, in reality, after such prolonged celibacy, Emma was in for unexpectedly frequent and largely experimental tinkering.

As my first real experience of global travel, my time on the storied King Ranch cattle station made a lasting impression on me. Having been brought up in the gently rolling softness of Hampshire and Oxfordshire, my family had ventured no further afield than the Mediterranean for holidays, where my most thrilling memory was occasionally being allowed a small glass of retsina. So, Australia was a new, exciting world into which to be catapulted. In what seemed like the blink of an eye, I had travelled to the other side of the planet, ridden 2,000 miles in a truckers' convoy across Australia, and ended up astride

---

1 In Great Britain, "Public School" actually means private, or boarding school. It is just another attempt by the British to thoroughly confuse foreigners by using contradictory language, in the same way that when we say, "With all due respect" we actually mean, "You are a complete idiot".

a horse at a remote outpost of the then-largest cattle ranch in the world, with a magic mushroom in my sandwich (more on that later).

As I stared up into the sky from horseback, feeling a million miles from everything safe and familiar, it was the contrails of jets, crossing high above, that were my tenuous daily connection to my home, my girlfriend, my family, my friends, in fact everything I had known throughout my mere 17 years on earth. Where were the people in that aircraft going? Perhaps to London? It was a comfort for me back then, and, as travel became an increasingly regular part of my adult life, the contrails above or behind me became a recurring thread of connectivity between places new, and home far away.

* * *

Exactly when travel became an integral, frequent part of my world, rather than the exception, is unclear; in the same way that you can't quite pinpoint *exactly* when a pair of new shoes became comfortable. But having lived in England, Australia, South Africa, and California, I have had more opportunities than most to travel. I have also been conflicted for most of my adult life about where "home" actually is. Travel is a wonderful gift, regardless of where you leave from or return to, whether for business or pleasure, in economy or first class, by train or on a bus. For those of us fortunate enough to spread our wings and soar to new lands and cities, travel opens our minds to other worlds, feasts our eyes on wondrous sights, and offers us unexpected experiences, education, friendships and memories that stay with us and become part of us.

Rarely do things go entirely according to plan, but it is sometimes these diversions, distractions, detours and disasters that make a trip memorable. Overhead baggage isn't the only thing that shifts in flight. Over time, travel subtly transforms and informs us, imparting to our character a unique patina, like that of a well worn leather wallet. From time to time, it changes us dramatically. Occasionally, it alters the course of our lives forever.

Regrettably, many of us now have a superficial appreciation of the gift of travel. We are often quick to criticise the lines at check in, the attitude of staff, the security, the lack of space, the quality of the food, the discomfort and the delays. We tend to rush about, returning home with a few selfies in front of assorted attractions, and remember little of the myriad of tiny details that make a trip epic – the expression "can't see the wood for the trees" is often appropriate. We are all guilty of this to one extent or another, and I have certainly grumbled and rushed from time to time. But as the years passed by and I racked up more and more miles on my odometer of life, complaining about these petty things began to sound like the unconscionable bleating of an entitled teenager. I know, I was one once. So, let's pause for a moment and reflect on how we got to this point when, until only recently, we all took travel for granted.

* * *

One of the first transcontinental flights of America, from New York to Pasadena, was made in 1911 by Calbraith Perry Rodgers. He had been tempted by a $50,000 prize offered by William Randolph Hearst to the first person to complete the journey in less than 30 days. It was a huge amount of money at the time. Rodgers took off on September 17 and landed in Pasadena on November 5. Those among you who are mathematically inclined will have already worked out that this took him 49 days; 19 longer than the wager allowed. This was largely due to the 70 stops he had had to make, and the time taken to rebuild the aircraft each time he crashed. Nevertheless, so great was his achievement that 20,000 people turned out to see him land.

Then, in the late 1920s and early 30s, there were the great Zeppelin Airships, able to fly a lucky few in astounding luxury over great distances. So bright was their future thought to be, that in 1929 the investment group responsible for building the Empire State Building announced that the height of the building would be increased by 200 feet. This was to allow a mooring mast for airships to be installed. It was imagined that passengers would exit the airship down a gang-plank and could be on the street in a matter of minutes. There even exists a pre-Photoshop, faked image of the Airship *Los Angeles* docking at the Empire State Building. In truth, the only docking ever to take place did not happen until September 1931, when a privately owned airship, piloted by Lieutenant William McCraken, docked for just three minutes, in a 40-mile-per-hour wind. The *New York Times* reported that "Traffic was tied up in the streets below for more than a half hour as the pilot jockeyed for position in the half gale about the tower, 1,200-feet above the ground." In reality, ferocious updrafts and other dangers prevented the mooring mast from being commercially feasible and no airship ever docked there again. The mast remains, a monument to the fleeting airship age.[2]

The airship age ended spectacularly badly when the Hindenburg went up in flames, but it wasn't long before the huge Boeing 314 Clipper seaplanes replaced them, with the range to cross the Atlantic and Pacific oceans in a couple of hops. Only twelve of these particular aircraft were built, nine of which constituted the famous Pan Am Clipper fleet. Able to land in any city with a sheltered harbour, they opened up the world, albeit only to the very wealthy and government employees. More on that later.

Commercial aviation received a huge leg-up from the Second World War, and thanks to necessarily rapid advances in both design and technology, everything started to race ahead. There were jet engines, pressurised cabins and all manner of things that would speed you to your destination in comfort. Flight attendants were valued more for their ability to mix cocktails and delicately spoon caviar than to memorize safety procedures. The era of air travel for the masses was off to a strong start, and air travel became increasingly available and affordable all over the world. Technology made it possible. Volume made it economically viable.

---

2 You will discover a lot more about airships in the story "A Medium Risk of Extortion" on page 289.

Skip ahead just 30 years, to the late 1980s and early 1990s – before we carried the sum of human knowledge, a multimedia communications centre, a travel agent, a department store, the Albert Hall, and a film studio around with us in our pocket. Even though we had Concorde and 747s, aviation technology had begun to plateau after the huge leaps made over the previous three decades.

Flying aside, the experience of road travel and transportation, and holidaying abroad, was very different indeed from what we know now. Those of you reading this who were born after 1990 will probably be amazed by some of what I am about to say.

Maps were printed on paper, and one needed to know how to actually interpret them, rather than having directions read to you in strangely unsettling accent of your choice. They were designed to fold using a highly complex, single-use analogue algorithm that was impossible to replicate. This ensured that as soon as you unfolded a new map, you would never again be able to re-fold it so that it lay flat. It would forever look like a piece of poorly executed origami, hastily stuffed into the outside pocket of your holdall.

Cash was king, and money belts a standard piece of kit, especially if you were going anywhere slightly dodgy, such as Swindon or Fresno. Credit cards were widely unacceptable in many countries, so in addition to cash, you needed "Traveller's Cheques". These were supposedly a safe way to carry large amounts of money, and could be quickly replaced if stolen, which they frequently were.

Communication was by landline, and until the early 1980's international calls often needed to be booked in advance at a specific time, through an operator. It was not uncommon to have to wait overnight to get a slot. The quality of the call, transmitted mostly through undersea cables, was terrible. Even when mobile phones started to arrive at the end of the 1980s, coverage was patchy at best and not international at all. If you had managed to use your phone abroad, on returning home you would receive a bill equal to the cost of the jet fuel that had got you there. Documents were mostly sent and received by fax, for which privilege hotels charged a small fortune.

One would often choose hotels from the *Michelin Guide*, or one of the directories that could be found in every hotel room, such as *Relais & Châteaux*, *Small Luxury Hotels of the World*, or *America on $1A Day*, depending on your budget. These were actual books, made from dead trees, and you had to carry them with you if you wanted to refer to them. I would spend hours flicking through these glossy catalogues of dreams, making a mental note of beautiful hotels I hoped to stay in one day.

To book a trip, you either picked up the phone and spoke to the hotel or airline directly, or you called your travel agent, whose number was branded on your prefrontal cortex and could be remembered no matter how inebriated, ill, lost or mugged you became. A physical paper ticket, interleaved with carbon paper[3], would then be mailed to you, delivered by a courier or, in cases of extreme emergency, collected at the airport. If you lost your ticket, it was like losing your passport; it was a dark day in hell. In many countries, there was a time when the main street of every small town had a bricks-and-mortar travel agent, or possibly two. They were ubiquitous and necessary, because although you could call an airline direct to buy a ticket, there was no other practical way to book holidays, hotels, cruises or complicated business trips, except by chatting to someone named Sylvia who had "the knowledge" and a lot of sexy brochures.

Travel agents did everything for us that we now largely do ourselves. If you travelled frequently on business or pleasure, they knew as much about you as your spouse – often more. They knew where you lived and worked, your credit card details, the names, birthdays, passport, and frequent flyer numbers of your entire family and most of your business associates. They had a history of where you had been, how you had got there and where you had stayed. They knew where you were planning on going next, what sort of hotels you stayed in, which rooms you preferred, what you liked to eat and whether or not you had been

---

3   Carbon paper transferred the pressure of a pen or typewriter key to imprint a copy on the paper below. Even today, in the header of emails, the abbreviation "cc" stands for "carbon copies".

arrested. They usually had close relationships with certain airlines and hotel chains and could get you upgraded or given special status. For very good customers, they would send a limo to pick you up – at their cost. For this reason, many people wanted to marry their travel agents.

Travellers could take pretty much as many suitcases as they wished and – incredible to us now – change, transfer, cancel, postpone or refund their tickets at will, for free. This is one of the reasons that the 1990s are referred to by some as the "second golden age of air travel". Security was rudimentary, but there were posters on display at check-in, informing people that guns, fireworks, machetes, radio-active waste, live tigers and dynamite were frowned upon as carry-on items. Nowadays, you cannot bring on a tube of toothpaste without a major brouhaha. Furthermore, every seat had an ashtray and smoking was not only permitted but encouraged. The cabin crew would come through the cabin and sell you 200 Marlboro, a Zippo lighter and a bottle of Remy Martin at the drop of a hat. Fully three quarters of the passengers smoked, so, for the few that did not, it was most unpleasant. It is interesting to note that when smoking was banned on airplanes in the early 1990's, the airlines were surprised to get an unexpected bonus. They found they could reduce the rate at which air was circulated through the cabin. This resulted in an energy reduction that cumulatively saved them millions of dollars a year in fuel costs.

With mobile phones in their infancy and email a pipedream, one could literally disappear, sometimes for weeks on end. People were almost impossible to reach (except through their travel agent), and the only news friends received about them was if they were eaten by an alligator, or a postcard from Bangalore dropped on the doormat, usually after they had been home for several weeks.

Remember the humble postcard? No trip of ours was complete until I heard the words "Darling, I have to get some postcards." I would sigh and reluctantly agree that, yes, we should send some post-cards to friends and family. An inordinate amount of time was taken spinning the racks to select the right card. Would Pamela prefer the one of the grape harvest with the well-hung young farmer who looks vaguely like Brad Pitt, or the safer and more generic basket of lavender? Perhaps John would like a Hell's Angel on a Harley? A choice was carefully made that best represented where we were, and a subject we thought would provide the most enjoyment to the recipient. So, we would head back to our accommodations to write a few witty and descriptive lines on the back. Three weeks later, a small card with a photo and a trivial personal message would be stuck on Pamela's fridge in Kincardine O'Neil, where it would stay until they moved to a new house or the magnet holding it decomposed.

In the nineties, 20 million postcards were sent every year. They were positively zipping around the planet. For a time I even used the humble postcard as an ingenious marketing device for my company, one that enabled me to reach clients who were too busy to take my calls. Whenever we were travelling or working abroad, I would buy 250 postcards from a very surprised and grateful postcard vendor in that city. Distributing them to my team, I would ask each of them to write something such as, *"Hello from Venice! We are busy filming a project here and thought of you. Love from all of us at Brainstorm!"* or something upbeat like that. I would then send them to all my key prospects. On returning to the U.S. they would invariably take my call, and all loved the novelty of getting an unexpected postcard from somewhere exotic. A postcard is one-to-one and demonstrates thought and effort. It says, "We are thinking of you. Wish you were here… you are important to us." They are always appreciated, often treasured, rarely thrown away. We still send postcards, even in this electronic age, although the global number sent annually is down to a paltry 5 million. Who figures out these statistics?

Straightforward things we now take for granted, like navigating foreign exchange and calling family members to let them know you are not being held hostage by the Caribbean Revolutionary Alliance, were all monumental challenges. It amazes me that even today people still call or text their loved ones to say, "I have arrived safely!". This may have been desirable under certain circumstances, such as when taking a six-month scientific voyage to Antarctica in a papyrus boat, powered by hamsters. But why would we still do this, when about half a million people are estimated to be up in the air at any given moment of the day or night, whizzing around at 500 miles per hour? Until Covid temporarily halted travel, nearly six million people were flying somewhere, every single day, on 230,000 flights. You have considerably more chance of being killed falling out of bed than dying in a plane crash, and, in the incredibly rare instances where a plane does go down, it's going to be on CNN long before you get a phone call. Calling to let your loved ones know you have arrived safely is like calling them every morning to confirm that you have survived getting out of bed and are now setting off to get a cup of coffee. No call? No air disaster on CNN? Then you can rest assured your loved one is sitting in the bar, sucking on their second Mai Tai.

* * *

And then along came the Internet. The Internet and the travel industry were made for each other, and it was love at first sight, much to the chagrin of travel agents. The Internet not only ushered in an era of do-it-yourself bookings, but also provided all the knowledge and resources you could possibly need to research your choices. Suddenly, the world really was at our fingertips. *Click.*

But it didn't happen overnight. At first, to go online you had to "dial in" using a special phone number and a landline, through a separate box that you carried with you called a modem, which was designed to work only sporadically and make a despicable noise. Web pages would appear very, very slowly, in slices, if you were lucky. Portable computers were about as portable as a large coffee-table book and had a battery life of no more than 12 minutes. We thought all this was terrific progress.

There were several years, from about 1994 to 2000, that were very much clicks-and-mortar. This transition period was referred to by travel agents the "the Apocalypse", as customers had the ability to book themselves a ticket from London to Milan, via Vancouver, and then dump it on their travel agent to try and sort out the complete dog's-breakfast they had created. Finally, there was the period of pre-extinction, during which the phrase most commonly heard in a travel agents office was, *"Well, sir, if you can see it on the Interthingy for £27 less, then piss off and buy it yourself!"* After that there was darkness and much wailing and gnashing of teeth, and no one wanted to marry a travel agent anymore.

But, for the average punter, a new world had dawned. Slowly but surely, every tiny detail you could possibly imagine about your trip emerged on the Internet, with photos and reviews and booking forms. What sorcery is this? Hurrah!

Click.

By 2010, sites had sprung up to automatically scuffle around all the other sites and instantly direct you to the best deal.

Click, click.

Complex itineraries could be created from the comfort of your own sitting room, which allowed for the approval of your spouse. Indeed, many spouses discovered they could book and pay for holidays quite independently of their partners, at a frequency and level of luxury that caused an alarming spike in domestic disturbances.

Click, click, click.

Generally, this was all marvellous; henceforth people travelled, and business boomed for hotels, airlines and tour guides named Valentino. One *click* to Timbuktu! *Click, click, clickety-click.*

Until, someone tried to actually change a ticket, and Accident & Emergency departments all over the world were overwhelmed by a sudden spike in injuries caused by people banging their heads against a fridge.

Now, at a moment's notice, any destination we can think of is within our reach.

But all this fabulousness costs money, as it always has. We grumble about the cost almost as vociferously as when the airline we have bought a ticket on goes out of business and leaves us sleeping in the departure lounge of Barcelona airport for three days.

Let's look at the economics: a flight from Los Angeles to Sydney, for example, is 14 hours long. On a 361 seat Boeing 777-300 ER[4], the airline would spend about $140,000 in fuel alone. Add in $31,000 for taxes, landing fees, and other provisioning services, $9,500 for food and drink and $9,600 for staff costs, and you come to a total of $190,000. That is an average hard cost of over $500 per seat. Add to that the overhead of running a massive company, leasing and maintaining the aircraft, and covering all the employee, ground, insurance, aircraft depreciation, landing and terminal costs. So, it is understandable that charges for ticket changes, baggage and other extras have become necessary for an airline to make money. For us, a few empty seats make a flight more bearable. For an airline, they make it unprofitable. That's why we suddenly find ourselves asleep on a bench in Barcelona.

To make each and every flight happen, an army of pilots, cabin crew, baggage handlers, ticket agents, air traffic controllers, mechanics, fuel technicians, logistics experts, caterers and meteorologists all work together like a well-tuned orchestra to ensure our 400-million-dollar aircraft gets us to our destination successfully at 500 miles per hour. It is nothing short of astonishing that we can take a seat in a metal tube, watch movies, eat a modest meal, go to sleep and wake up a few hours later, halfway around the world. The journey that took Calbraith Perry Rodgers 49 days in the infancy of flight, now takes a little over five hours, so one really shouldn't have a sense of humour failure every time there is a 20-minute delay, or we don't like our chicken fricassee.

* * *

Although we are sensitive about airlines cramming ever more people into their planes, we blithely take hundreds of people along for the

---

4 From *The Cost of Flying: What Airlines have to Pay to Get You in the Air* by Justin Hayward, Simple Flying, December 2020.

ride – sometimes thousands. Social media and global connectivity have allowed our friends and family to come too, whether they like it or not. For many of our virtual passengers, this involves suffering an endless stream of irritating selfies, in which we make goofy faces at them from Martinique or Marbella. And this is exactly how the real experience of travel has started to be eroded. As we take our social media followers on our travels, we are, through the same digital umbilical cord, still attached to the place from whence we came. We are still inundated with news, concerns, questions, invitations, comments and demands from home – and now, more than ever, social media. How difficult it is to voluntarily sever that connection. The more attached we are to home, the less attentive we become to our destination, despite the effort and expense we have made to get there. Do we even see and appreciate these destinations properly anymore? Do we notice the glimpses of a distant view between trees, or the carved stone gargoyle on the corner of a building? Do we think to stop at the little roadside bistro, and experience local flavours and hospitality, or are we more concerned about reaching the next Four Seasons hotel, with its comfortable predictability and international menu? Are we taking only fleeting glances around us, before we fire off an Instagram post, check (and re-check) how many likes it gets, and then promptly get distracted by an email from the office about the impracticality of Felicity's marketing budget?

For me, every time I fly, I take the time to enjoy just gazing out of the window for hours, watching the landscape relentlessly unfold like a conveyor belt, 30,000 feet beneath me. You never quite know what's coming up next. Even in incredibly remote areas, I occasionally spot a small dirt road leading to a distant settlement of some kind. I am always struck by the fact that it is almost certain one could walk into whatever rudimentary shop serves that lonely, dusty little community and buy a Coca-Cola. Almost anywhere in the world, this drink is within arm's reach of desire. I think of the incredible distribution network this giant company has built over the surface of the earth as a metaphor for the way travel has evolved. We can now go almost anywhere we want with relative ease, but it is increasingly difficult to find those special places, unspoiled by commerce and crowds.

Whether it is a single journey, or a collection of journeys to a variety of places over a period of time, the places we have travelled to become part of our soul; it is that part of mine that this book represents. Many of these stories have a thread of experiences that are no longer possible, in a landscape that no longer exists. Some tell of people and cultures now changed beyond recognition; of friends who have moved on, of momentary encounters and fleeting glimpses; each is a precious memory that can later be fondly recalled, but never repeated. And so this book is about loss in a way; not sadness, but the idea of why it's so important to see the unique value of an experience before it is gone forever.

I hope these stories will encourage in you a mindfulness with respect to your own journeys. With our heads buried in our smart-phones, digitally tethered to some other place, it is all too easy to miss the moments of magic our journey has to offer. As the glorious, unspoiled corners of the world become harder and harder to find, it is now more important than ever to put away our little handful of pixels, cast our eyes around, and drink in the rich, transformative elixir of travel at every opportunity.

Since my first forays from the comfort and security of home, I have always travelled with an open mind and a sense of humour. Now, by sharing some of the surprising, fun, dangerous, unexpected, fortunate, regrettable, nostalgic and amusing experiences I have had, I hope they might inspire you to travel better, see the wood for the trees, and cherish every moment of your own – or at least look up from your bloody iPhone for a couple of minutes.

Bon voyage!

Richard Weston-Smith,
Santa Barbara, June 2021

HONG KONG
The Mile High Club

It was early September 1977, and I was settling down into my seat on the British Airways 747-200, watching little rivulets of drizzle stagger and race their way down the window. I wondered what adventures lay ahead. I was 17, it was my first long haul flight, and I had never been on such a huge aircraft, packed with people of all shapes and sizes, all a-chatter with excitement. As we pushed back from the gate at Heathrow and everyone began to settle down, an announcement came over the PA system. "Would passenger Mr. Weston Smith please identify himself to one of the cabin crew." As a callow youth and inexperienced flyer, I was somewhat taken aback to be suddenly singled out from 375 other passengers. Was this normal? Was I in trouble? As I was A.D.D., highly inquisitive, and fond of experimentation, trouble and I were childhood friends. Rather timidly, I waved my hand in the air, and, after a few moments, a smartly uniformed attendant walked towards me with a scowl of annoyance.

"Mr. Weston Smith?"

"Er, yes," I responded, timidly.

"You have received a message," said Ms. Congeniality. "The Captain asked me to give you this." She reached across two swively-eyed spinsters and handed me a folded piece of paper. The Captain? Bloody hell! I opened the note, which read mysteriously: *"Don't eat anything! May cause stomach failure. Ralph."* I looked back at Ms. Congeniality, rather hoping an explanation might be forthcoming, but from her raised eyebrows it was clear she was expecting one from me. We gazed at each other for a moment, as confusion swirled through my head. Getting none, she smiled sarcastically, saying, "I think you will find the food on British Airways to be excellent," and stomped off to go and tell the man a few rows down that now was not a good time to light a cigarette.

* * *

I was sitting on this plane because, some months earlier, quite out of the blue, my father had announced that he had successfully arranged for me to spend a year on a cattle station in Australia. He had old Army friends and business colleagues down under who had, unbeknownst to me, been working diligently to find me a suitable position. I was to be a Jackaroo, the lowest form of life on the station, given full board and lodging, and paid a couple of hundred dollars a month. It was presented to me as a fait-accompli, not a choice, as he handed me a ticket and told me how very lucky I was. He correctly saw this as a wonderful opportunity and adventure, for which I should be enthusiastically grateful. I saw it as forcible separation from the love-of-my-life, and presented as much indignant ingratitude and myopic teenage stroppiness as I could muster.

Eventually resigned to my fate, I had been working up to my departure with some trepidation. There had been discussions and decisions about clothing, correct footwear, suitable hats, sunscreen, and other things it was thought I would need for a year on a cattle station, most of them would turn out to be quite spectacularly wrong. My apprehension was to some extent assuaged by a lot of partying, which I justified because I had just finished school and was going away for a year. My father scowled his disapproval, given my final exams had been the academic equivalent of a multi vehicle pile-up.

Nevertheless, the summer of 1977 turned out to be epic. Presented with a heady cup of new-found freedom, I drank greedily. With my beautiful, charismatic girlfriend Kirstie[5], with whom I was smitten, at my side, it was a bitter-sweet summer of love, laughter and indolence, embellished with long sunny days, and hot, hot nights. The agony of leaving her was made all the more acute by the seemingly eternal flame of young love.

In between the partying and general summer-of-luvviness, there were riding lessons. My mother had, with exceptional foresight, managed to locate an Australian named Greg, who ran a stable on the Berkshire Downs in Lambourn, close to where we lived. She explained to him that I was going to spend a year on a cattle station

---

5   Not Kirsten, my wife. Yes, weird, I know.

in Australia, and she had an inkling some sort of preparation might be helpful; I had barely been astride more than a Labrador in my life. This was despite the fact that both horse breeding and racing were in my blood. My grandfather was an expert horseman who had bred and owned *Royal Mail*, winner of the 1937 Grand National, the premier racing event of the year in the UK, which is generally regarded as the ultimate test of horse and rider. He died shortly thereafter while training to ride in the 1938 Grand National himself; no mean feat for a man well over six feet tall. He was also the only non-Italian to have ever ridden in Il Palio di Siena, the extraordinary annual horse race held in Siena, Italy, in which ten demonically possessed Italian horsemen gallop bareback, at breakneck speed, around the Piazza del Campo to win honour for their *Contrada*[6] and the undying admiration of all Sienese women. Not to be outdone, after his death, my grandmother determinedly continued breeding – horses – and eventually produced *Well to Do*, winner of the 1972 Grand National. This was all the more remarkable an accomplishment because she did not do it from some professional stable, but from two modest little paddocks at her home in Berkshire. So, it could be said that in not being a horseman I broke the mould, although that would shortly change.

Greg was very polite, in the way that certain Australians can be in female company, but rarely are when not.

"If he makes out to the lads on the Station that he can ride, that would probably be unwise," he told my mother cheerily. "But no worries, Mrs. Weston Smith, I'll teach him everything he needs to know."

"The very first thing they will ask you is if you can ride," he told me as soon as she was out of earshot, wagging his finger. "This is a fucking trick, mate. Do not, under any bloody circumstances whatsoever, tell them you can ride, not even a little bit. Do you understand me?" I nodded vigorously. "If you do," he continued, to underscore the point, "they'll put you straight on a horse that will fucking kill you." I became

6 A district, or a ward, within an Italian city.

unusually attentive. "When I have finished with you," he continued, throwing a 30-pound saddle at me, "you still won't be able to bloody ride – make no mistake about that – but you will be able to do two bloody important things: stay on a fucking horse at high speed, and open and close a fucking gate without getting off it. Right, let's go."

After a comprehensive, expletive-laden lesson on how to properly attach it to the horse, he heaved me straight into an Australian stock saddle. Considered the Recaro[7] rally seat of saddles, it was designed to allow the rider to stay put over rough terrain. It featured winglets to keep you in position on the downhill, as well as a high cantle and pommel to keep the rider comfortable for many hours of riding. However, on occasions it would not perform quite as intended. If the horse beneath you did something unexpected, such as slam on the brakes when you weren't paying attention, the pommel became your worst enemy. With the force of a crash-test dummy hitting a wall, it made contact with your testicles, leaving you speechless, gasping for air, and in eye-popping pain. All of this was profoundly unfamiliar and took a bit of getting used to, but Greg was a brilliant, charismatic teacher. True to his word, he showed me how to properly get on and off, stay rooted to the saddle at thundering speed, and smoothly open and close a gate without dismounting. One day I asked, "are you going to teach me the basics of mustering cattle?"

"Nah" he replied, "The horses'll teach you that."

He was full of sphincter-clenching stories of the Australian bush, and we spent many happy hours galloping across the Berkshire Downs, in all their glorious, soft, rolling, un-Australian magnificence until he felt confident that I would be able to hold my own for the first few crucial days. I decided I liked Aussies.

On our last ride out, Kirstie, who was an accomplished horsewoman, came too. It was a beautiful summer day, the air sticky with humidity as we galloped up onto the Downs. Enjoying distant

---

7   Long considered the premier seat for rally cars; once seated you barely move, regardless of how much the car is thrown about.

views to north and south, we had the most exhilarating time, even when the clouds opened and completely drenched us in a thunderous downpour. On returning to the yard and dismounting, Greg stretched out his hand.

"What are you going to tell them when they ask if you can ride?" he said.

"Never ridden a bloody horse in my life," I answered.

"You'll be 'right then, mate," he said, slapping me on the back. "Now fuck off!"

Kirstie looking glum at Heathrow Airport, before I left for Australia.

I drove home, rather proud of myself for having graduated with a degree in not riding. Kirstie nonchalantly peeled off her soaking-wet clothes one by one, tossing them into a soggy pile in the footwell. "That's better," she said, as several lorry drivers swerved wildly. Life was good; but as we know, all good things come to an end.

At Heathrow Airport, in the face of my imminent departure, Kirstie looked suitably glum. My mother, always randomly pragmatic, wandered off, returning a few minutes later with two gin and tonics, a Union Jack flag, and a copy of *Playboy* magazine. "Here you are darling," she said, "you might need these," adding, "but not all together" for clarification. Kirstie looked even more despondent.

Ralph was an old school friend of mine who had kindly joined us at Heathrow to see me off. He was a quite wonderfully mad Egyptian, the sort of mad friend who causes me to look back and wonder what a miracle it is that I am still walking around on this planet. We will explore that theme a little more, later on.

* * *

The engines of the 747 throttled up and, as it lumbered down the runway gathering speed, the drizzly raindrops on the windows slowly rotated from vertical drips to horizontal streaks, the green, green grass of home fell away beneath the aircraft and we rose up through misty clouds, undercarriage clunk-a-thumping as it folded itself back into the fuselage. My mind was in turmoil; I had told Ralph I was going to swallow a small piece of hashish before I boarded, to help me sleep on the flight. The remainder I had given to him, so as not to fall foul of the law. So why had he gone to the presumably considerable effort of getting this message to me? It had to be easier to get a message hand-delivered to the Queen of England than to a passenger on a taxiing 747.

Had Ralph also eaten some hash, and was he now writhing in agony somewhere below me in Wimbledon? Was it a joke? He must have known it was too late; that I had eaten it an hour ago. Short of having my stomach pumped by Ms. Congeniality at 30,000 feet, which I did not relish the idea of, there was little I could do about it. Besides, I was feeling just fine. Actually, very fine indeed. The giant plane banked slowly as we emerged from the clouds, and the rays of a magnificent sunset blasted a thousand colours across the sky and through my head. I started to notice that I was feeling pretty high all of a sudden. "Man, this is SO cool," I giggled loudly. The spinsters next to me shifted a little uncomfortably in their seats, whispering their disapproval of this unconventional utterance. Distant thunderheads erupted upwards, 10,000 -feet high, roiling shades of orange playing over them and shafts of creamy sunlight spearing every breach in their gigantic softness. "Wowwwww!" I exclaimed slowly as we levelled out. It was excellent hashish. Jesus, Ralph, "causes stomach failure"? On the contrary, this was epic! A mile-high high. I was in the moment, oblivious to both what I was leaving behind, and what adventure lay ahead. As we climbed above the clouds and darkness slowly enveloped the aircraft, a deep, peaceful sleep enveloped me.

I slept like a baby and woke just in time to experience the thrill of an e-ticket landing at Hong Kong's' Kai-Tak airport. In the American vernacular, e-ticket is derived from the old ticket system at Disneyland where the e-ticket rides were the fastest, newest, wildest, and most fun. Nowadays in America it is more commonly used to describe other exciting things, like a Himalayan bus ride or terrific sex.

Known as the "Kai-Tak heart attack," Hong Kong was, for a long time, one of the most challenging landings in the world for pilots, and either terrifying or exciting for passengers, according to their tolerance for danger. Due to the surrounding peaks, it was impossible for aircraft to do a straight-in approach to Hong Kong. So, in the early 1970s, someone came up with a fiendishly brilliant idea: program the instrument landing system to line up the aircraft to fly into the side of a mountain, then dodge it at the last minute. So, once cleared to land, the pilot headed across Victoria Harbour, until he[8]

---

8 It was almost always a man in those days, but thankfully we now we have many more female pilots. According to a 2001 study by researchers at the Johns Hopkins Bloomberg School of Public Health, male pilots are far more likely to land the plane with the undercarriage retracted, or to take off when they know perfectly well there is something wrong with it. This is known as the Biggles factor, after the fictional pilot and hero of the WWI adventure books.

reached "Checkerboard Hill," so-called because of its big orange and white checked marker. Flying at 200-miles per hour at only 650 feet, he then had to disengage the autopilot, completely ignore the automatic guidance system, and manually throw the plane into a sharp, visual, right-hand-turn for final approach. This instantly put all the alarms in the cockpit into "you-are-going-to-die!" mode and, banking precipitously, the colossal plane would turn 47 degrees. Coming out of the turn at just 140 feet off the ground, the pilot had mere seconds to line-up to the runway. Skimming hair-raisingly low over the top of apartment blocks and busy streets, the pilot would drop onto the runway, slamming on the reverse-thrusters to bring the aircraft to a juddering halt, before he and 375 passengers ended up in the harbour. This is universally known to be the most fun a pilot could have while fully clothed. What could possibly go wrong?[9]

To the authorities, this seemed like a good reason to classify Kai-Tak as the sixth most dangerous airport approach in the world and require pilots to have practiced the approach numerous times in a simulator before actually landing there. So, they did, and mine had, and it was a great relief to disembark via a jet-bridge, not the emergency slide. Woo-hoo! Hello, Hong Kong!

I had a fellow Brit on this adventure, who I was meeting in Hong Kong, a solidly built chap with a ruddy complexion and blondish curly hair named Chris. We didn't know each other at all before this adventure, and, although we weren't natural friends, we would get on fine. He was more the sporting type, a rugger-bugger, and a bit of a "lad." If anyone were to have put money on which of us would be more likely to survive a year on an Aussie cattle station, his muscular build, enthusiasm for sport and ruddy countenance would have made him the favourite by a long chalk. If he was, to coin a phrase, built like a brick shithouse, I was the grass hut to his shithouse – a strong wind would have blown me over. Of slight build and with a

---

9 In November 1993, a China Airlines 747 did end up in the harbour, miraculously with no loss of life.

dislike of athletics, it was evident to any observer that I would not last a week in such a rough, unforgiving environment. He met me at Kai-Tak Airport and took me to his father's apartment in the Mid-Levels, where we would stay for a few days to break the trip. The days that followed were a neon whirlwind of sightseeing, drinks parties, dinners and late nights at the Godown.

The Godown was a well-known nightclub off Chatham Road, owned by Bill Nash and run by Carole Allan, its name being a Malaysian word meaning "dockside warehouse". It was, for decades, a popular hangout of ex-pat bankers, journalists, traders and the rest, with the tables being served by attractive European secretaries earning some extra cash after their office day job. Bill was a former British Army officer and fluent Mandarin speaker; some said he worked for MI6. Chris's father knew the Godown well, and Chris had obviously made it his local while he was in Hong Kong, so I tagged along, and we instantly became part of the furniture. It was tremendous fun, and Carol took us under her wing, plying us with free drinks and making me feel like a regular. She was very kind, one might even say motherly, in a nightclubby sort of way. We caroused the evening away and stayed late, helping her close the place up most nights. Days inevitably started as late, as only teenagers and rock stars can start them, with a monumental hangover.

One night, wisely predicting that a year on a cattle station almost certainly meant no sex, Carol kindly (and in that nightclub-by-but-motherly sort of way) set me up with a "hostess" in a bar a few doors along from the Godown. I had absolutely no idea what she was up to when she said, "Come with me," before grabbing my hand and leading me off down the street.

"Where are we going?" I asked.

"Hong Kong surprise!" she replied mysteriously, weaving in and out of people on the crowded street. We soon arrived at a bar, where Carol was clearly known and welcomed. Some money changed hands, followed by a lot of chat and laughter in Cantonese that I didn't understand. I started to get the drift when this astonishingly beautiful girl, dressed in a mini skirt that left nothing to the imagination, walked straight up to me and kissed me directly on the lips.

"Have a good time sweetie!" said Carol, walking out of the door. I had only an innocent idea of what a "good time" meant, and she clearly didn't realize I was a simple boy from the home counties. I had exactly as much experience of sex with a hooker as the Archbishop of Canterbury, and chatting up a Chinese hostess in a Hong Kong bar was light years outside of my comfort zone. I immediately sat down, mainly because I needed something more reliable than my legs underneath me.

So, there she was, with her soft, smiling face and delicate almond eyes framed by midnight black, bobbed hair. Her naked legs were long, erupting from her thighs beneath a ridiculously short skirt that deliberately revealed very much more than was polite. For a country boy all this was, to say the least, rather a lot to take on board, let alone know how to handle. Clearly there were expectations, but I was beginning to feel that I was not up to the challenge. Uncomfortable with an offer that would have left many of my less genteel friends unphased, I really had no clue what to do. Sex was not on my agenda, especially as I was so recently separated from Kirstie that our relationship had been diminished by neither time nor distance. So, much to her amazement, I resorted to the classic British weapon; I decided to have a chat. Had a cup of tea been available, I would probably have ordered one of those too. And a biscuit.

"Honey, you handsome boy! My name Ling-Ling."

"Delighted to meet you... er... my name is Richard, um... and you are very beautiful. Do you live here?"

"You have nice leg," she said, sliding her hand very much further up one of them than was normal for a complete stranger.

"Wowww! Bloody hell, yes... well, er... I have only just arrived, but Hong Kong is a lovely city. I went up the Peak Tram today and..."

"You like me, honey?" she interrupted, running her perfectly manicured fingers through my hair as she edged closer still.

"Yes, I do, very much, but I er... am on my way to Australia and..."

"You want come up stair with me?" she whispered, nibbling lightly on my earlobe. "I have nice bed."

"Well, I am sure your bed is very comfortable and that's extremely kind of you, but I think it's a bit early for bed right now, er, maybe later?"

"We have fun time, honey!" she crooned, a hand doing some more rather startling exploration of my nether regions. "Oooo, you big boy!" she giggled.

She spoke only about 20 words of English, so our conversation was linguistically limited, as each of us attempted to lead it in entirely different directions. Her vocabulary was colourful, to say the least, and punctuated with much suggestive flashing of her underwear. She was indeed phenomenally pretty, but I was far too uncomfortable to take advantage of what she was clearly offering, and simply looked at her like a rabbit in a headlight.

Eventually, having used up whatever time or favours Carol had purchased on my behalf, she stood up, said, "You nice boy!", gave me a lingering kiss, and floated off to find a more responsive customer. Well, that was interesting, I thought, unsure if I had just missed a fabulous opportunity, or sensibly walked away from something I would have deeply regretted, both morally, and possibly medically. "Well, how was *that* sweetie?" asked Carol in a suggestive tone of voice, when I walked back into the Godown.

"Extraordinary!" I answered truthfully, and fortunately she was too busy to quiz me in any greater detail.

A few days later, bleary-eyed and sleep-deprived, Chris and I stumbled onto a British Airways flight to Melbourne. Hong Kong had been a thrill, and instilled in me a love of the city that has endured for much of my life[10].

My father, Ian, unable to secure my passage to Australia on a leaking Ukrainian iron-ore carrier, had devised a highly creative alternative. He was a kind and fair father, but strict; one who firmly believed that to become a man, I needed to toughen up. Given that he had gone to

---

10 At least until it was handed back to China and they completely buggered it up.

fight for his country at the age of 23, and had been injured in battle, captured and imprisoned for several years, I would eventually come to understand his motivation. So, after a few days in Melbourne, we had been instructed to report to the depot of IPEC Tenex, an overnight road-express service that covered most of Australia in the days before airfreight. We would be traveling the 2,200 miles up the east coast of Australia to Tully as passengers. To put this in perspective, as one always should in Australia, that is the same as driving from London to Istanbul. But without crossing a single border, or stopping much.

Aussies aren't especially fond of the British, or Poms, as they call them, unless they are immediate family. Most likely an acronym for Prisoners of Mother England (POME), it is commonly used as a derogatory term. For a trucker to be lumbered with two young Poms was not something he would have been especially happy about, preferring the company of his mates on the CB radio.

Greeted therefore with some resignation, we set off into the night with Davey, CB radio chirping away. Leaving the city behind us, we were gradually joined by other trucks, forming a small convoy as we headed north. The road was relentlessly straight. There were no street-lights, no moon, and the night was Vantablack.[11] A puddle of light from our headlights preceded us, but we could see nothing beyond it. Kangaroos occasionally bounded out of the blackness across our path but, as it was equipped with heavy steel "roo-bars", the truck was immune to a hit from a 200-pound kangaroo. Davey motored on through the night without flinching. He eventually warmed up a bit, but conversation was limited. Sleep came only fleetingly, and was mostly bouncy. For the first time I was struck by how very far away from home I was, and how strange the circumstances were in which I found myself. It was like a dream, being in the cab of a truck, driving through the Australian night. It made no sense in the context of my life to that point, yet was very real at that moment.

---

11 Vantablack, which was created by Surrey Nano Systems, absorbs up to 99.96 percent of visible light and, until recently, was the blackest known black.

The truck in which I travelled over 2,000 miles.

Through the huge, flat, bug-splattered windscreen, dawn came and went several times with a spectacular explosion of colour; at sunset, it played in reverse. The persistent roar of the massive diesel engine dulled our senses, ringing in our ears even when we stopped briefly for a burger, fuel, and a piss. Conversation was sporadic; our only entertainment the crackle and squawk of the CB radio and the unrolling landscape before us. We changed drivers in Dubbo (Bruce), and again in Brisbane (Snowy), heading up the coast through Rock-hampton, Mackay, Townsville (Jeff), and arriving, finally, at Euramo, a tiny settlement on the main north-south highway, just outside Tully, North Queensland.

Euramo consisted of a hotel "pub", a post-office and a motley collection of simple bungalows. Most had a basic wire mesh fence around them, and dogs running a well-worn path up and down the perimeter, barking furiously as we passed. Some were draped with voluminous passionfruit vines, their incongruously elaborate flowers closing up in the quickly fading light at the end of a dusty day.

Jeff rocked to a halt outside the hotel with a hiss of compressed air. "There you go, Poms; this is your stop." He wished us good luck; we thanked him, clambering down from the cab and pulling out our bags. Then, with a rapid ascension of gears, a belch of exhaust and a cloud of dust, the truck growled away into the fading evening light. The air was humid and hot. We were in a strange land, alone, long before the age of mobile phones. Hopefully our rendezvous, arranged by others far away and many months before, would happen as planned.

If not, we were fucked.

AUSTRALIA
The Bloody Pom

Night was closing in fast. Our only instructions were that we would be met in the hotel.[12]. Dragging our bags into the noisy bar, Chris and I looked around as the 50 or so patrons simultaneously stopped, turned, and stared at us. Suddenly, you could hear a pin drop. After a suitably awkward silence, a small, sun-ravaged man in flip-flops, wearing a battered bush-hat and dirty shorts, downed his beer, slid off his bar stool and padded towards us. "You must be the Poms," he said, stating the blindingly obvious. "Follow me."

Tully is mostly known for three things: a highly credible sighting of a flying saucer in 1966; being the wettest place in Australia; and as basecamp for the 2002 season of the UK's prime-time reality TV show, *I'm a Celebrity...Get Me Out of Here!* The latter accurately suggests that the jungle from which the ranch was carved out is the sort of place one would want to run screaming from, rather than stay and relax in, celebrity or not. I don't want to put you off, or incur the wrath of the lovely people at Tourism Tropical North Queensland (tag-line: *"Where the Rainforest Meets the Reef"*) but, before you take the tourist brochures at face value and go hiking in their utterly fabulous rainforest, you should at least consider some of the demented flora and fauna that will be lurking in wait for you.

Now, I know this is not the first time Australia has been called out for its hostile wildlife, but honestly, this stuff never gets old, nor does it cease to amaze – and you can't ignore it, because it will bite you. Speaking for the rest of the world, I apologise to the nation of Australia in advance, but it's just the way it is, and you are going to have to deal with it, even though it bores you, and you think we exaggerate. We don't.

In the nasty-small-buggers department: scorpions, ticks, leeches and mosquitos will be lining up to take a chunk out of you – and that's just a starter for ten.[13] Next up are the wild pigs. They make

---

12 A hotel in Australia is often just a pub/bar.

13 A friend of mine once found a leech on his eyeball after we had been swimming in a creek.

Attila the Hun look like a bunny rabbit, give no fucks whatsoever about anything, and will have a go at you even if you are armed with a flame-thrower, and a Gatling gun, sitting in a metal cage, perched atop a big yellow bulldozer. But the pigs have long been losers in competition with cassowaries to win the award for the most insanely terrifying land animal in Australia.

Cassowaries, vaguely related to the emu (and, one might be forgiven for thinking, the velociraptor), hold the title of "World's Most Dangerous Bird™". They have absolutely no sense of humour, can be close to seven-foot tall, have nasty, beady eyes, a blue neck, a four-inch-long razor-sharp talon on each foot, and can move at speeds of up to 50 miles per hour through dense bush. Fond of leaping at and disembowelling people who look at them, it is recommended that they be avoided at all costs. Hollywood would have a hard time dreaming up something more insanely scary. On the dirt roads accessing the beaches around Tully, one will frequently come across signs, warning that an imprudent encounter will ruin an otherwise bucolic day at the beach.

Next on the list are some of the most venomous snakes in the world. These include the Taipan (most deadly land snake[14]), Eastern Brown (second most deadly land snake), Death Adder (just bog standard deadly), Black Whip Snakes and Red-bellied Black Snakes (pretty bloody lethal), Brown Tree Snakes and a variety of beautifully patterned, 30-foot-long pythons who will affectionately but relentlessly squeeze the life out of you before attempting to swallow you whole. It is a well-known joke in North Queensland that the shortest possible time it will take you to get from wherever you are to a hospital, is about 35 minutes longer than it will take a snake bite to kill you. In some instances, you would be lucky even to get as far as your car.

Australia boasts an inventory of about 170 species of snakes, many with the most toxic venom this side of the Orion Nebula. Reassuringly – if anything in Australia can be reassuring – actual bites are

---

14 See "Running Out of Air", p 77.

relatively uncommon, and an efficient anti-venom network keeps fatalities to between four and six deaths a year.

For those who can handle snakes just fine, there are the spiders to contend with. These claim the title of the most widely distributed venomous creatures in Australia. The Funnel-web, *Atrax robustus* is, as its name implies, the most robustly dangerous spider in the world. It particularly enjoys life in the suburbs of Sydney, as do many humans. Like humans, they can be quite aggressive when threatened. Bear in mind that, "feeling threatened" to a Funnel-web can be triggered by something seemingly unthreatening to us, such as standing still and breathing. Although only a couple of centimetres in size, its fangs are more substantial than a Brown Snake and powerful enough to punch right through a toenail or, for that matter, Kevlar. Without the need to go into too much detail, there are an additional 40 species of Funnel-web spiders across Australia. The most dangerous is the northern tree Funnel-web spider, *Hadronyche formidabilis*, which can be as much as four to five centimetres long and is undoubtedly very *formidabilis* indeed. It spends its time in trees, the terrifying implications of which I need hardly spell out. This might explain why the northern part of Australia is sparsely populated by humans, or much else for that matter.

Huntsman spiders are both widespread and well known. They are the size of a dinner-plate, scary as fuck[15] and have a reputation for jumping out from behind the curtains or from under the loo-seat. Just let that sink in for a moment: jumpy, *and* the size of a dinner plate. And if that wasn't scary enough, with such long legs, they are very fast indeed, moving at up to three foot per second. I know what you are doing. You are measuring out about three feet in your mind. Let me help you: the distance from the ground to your waist is somewhere close to three feet. Now, say "one alligator". That's how long it would take a huntsman to get up your leg and scuffle about

---

15 This is an entirely appropriate use of the work "fuck", as you are about to discover.

in your naughty-bits. But wait, there's more! Some members of the species can actually do cartwheels and backflips as they are running.

In reality their venom is mild, and they are pretty harmless; their ability to do harm comes more from the drivers who flip down the sun visor at 75 miles per hour to discover a hairy, eight-eyed Huntsman six inches from their face. This can result in a range of accidents, from head on collisions and multi-car pileups, to solitary vehicles mysteriously suspended in the lower branches of eucalyptus trees. Unlike other spiders, Huntsman do not weave webs to catch their food. Instead, they sit and wait. When food comes along, they either pounce, or use their impressive acceleration to outrun their victims. They have a very flat body and can squeeze through surprisingly small gaps, such as into your car or under your bathroom door. Some types of Huntsman are even social, living in groups of as many as 300. The official line is that, despite their intimidating size, Huntsman spiders can be "useful around the house"; they apparently help with pest control by eating cockroaches. However, if you have both cockroaches and Huntsman spiders, then it is probably time to move house.

Up in North Queensland, there are crocodiles all over the place. It goes without saying that they are extremely bitey and can permanently ruin what would otherwise be a lovely barbie. Occasionally, a nasty cyclone blows through the tropical north, causing widespread flooding and allowing the previously creek-bound population of crocs to go float-about. They then start turning up in all sorts of places where they should not, including: the pub, the local library, and the produce aisle of the supermarket. North Queensland is the only place in the world where the weather forecast can contain the phrase "Heavy thunder showers and widespread flooding, with occasional crocodiles."

And if you thought that was all, then there is the plant life. In 90% of the country there is barely a bush. But in North Queensland's massive, steaming tropical rainforests, giant basket ferns, king ferns and fan palms, thickly intertwined, stand among wild mango trees, festooned with vines. Flocks of vividly coloured rainbow lorikeets and king parrots screech from one to another. All stunningly beautiful and mostly harmless, though often spiky. But this being Australia there are, of course, a couple of notable exceptions.

Ribbonwood is one of the world's rarest and most primitive flowering plants, dating back to over 110 million years. It's not so harmless; these huge trees hold large, brown fruits, and the seed is highly poisonous, making this one of the few fruits that no rainforest bird or animal can tolerate. The tree is commonly known as the Idiot Fruit, for reasons the Aboriginal population thought were entirely self-explanatory.

In England, patches of stinging nettles – into which it is popular for children to throw each other for amusement – can be found all over the countryside in summer. If you touch one, it will give you a sharp, tingling pain for ten minutes or so. Pain level: ouch/bugger. By contrast, in Queensland, they have the thirty-foot tall Stinging Tree, *Dendrocnide moroides*, which delivers searing, screaming, blinding agony that can stick around for months – even *years*. Pain level: being burnt with red-hot coals while also being lightly spritzed with drain cleaner. Every square inch of trunk, branches, fruit, and leaves are covered in thousands of tiny hypodermic-like hairs that pierce the skin and break off inside you, each delivering a dose of toxin. It is so toxic that even standing close to a one for more than a few minutes will trigger sneezing, breathing problems and nose bleeds. A brush with a stinging tree won't kill you (regrettably), but suicide will definitely be right at the top of your to-do list as you try to slide right out of your own skin. In fact, being gored by a rabid pig, chewed on by a crocodile or disembowelled by a cassowary would all be infinitely preferable to an encounter with this tree.

Consider ex-serviceman, Cyril Bromley, who was stung after falling into the tree while crossing a creek in North Queensland in 1941. He said the pain was so appalling they had to tie him to his hospital bed for three weeks, and no treatment helped to diminish the pain in the slightest. He also recounted how a fellow officer had understandably shot himself because the pain was so intense – after using a stinging tree leaf to wipe his arse. Botanist Ernie Rider, who was brushed lightly in the face and torso by the foliage in 1963, said:

> "For two or three days, the pain was almost unbearable; I couldn't work or sleep, then it was pretty bad pain for another fortnight or so. The stinging persisted for two years and recurred every time I had a cold shower. There's nothing to rival it; it's ten times worse than anything else you can imagine."

Anything this insanely toxic will inevitably attract the attention of the military. Sure enough, in 1968, Alan Seawright, a Professor of Pathology at the University of Queensland, got a call from the Chemical Defence Establishment at Porton Down (the top-secret laboratory that developed chemical weapons in the UK). They were interested in getting hold of some specimens. "Chemical warfare is their work, so I could only assume that they were investigating its potential as a biological weapon," said Seawright. "I never heard anything more, so I guess we'll never know."[16]

Stinging Tree toxins retain their ability to inflict pain for a ridiculously long time; even dried botanical specimens collected over 100 years ago can still sting. This must be one of the lesser known hazards of curatorship in a botanical museum. One of the few (and mostly pointless) treatments is said to be the application of hydrochloric acid to the skin[17]. One can only imagine what insane level of pain would make the "application of hydrochloric acid to the skin," a relief.

Queensland has venomous everything and is wet, to boot. But surely a bit of rain is nothing to get flustered about, you may be thinking; he probably means wet, like Wales. No. I don't. Not even

---

16 Source: Amanda Burdon, *Australian Geographic*, June 2009.

17 Hydrochloric acid is highly corrosive to the eyes, skin, and mucous membranes.

close. Wales is positively arid compared to Tully. The rain in Tully is more like an attack with a water cannon than a meteorological event. It is delivered with such force that you cannot see farther than about three feet, and it is painful because the drops are enormous, extremely close together, and traveling at terminal velocity from thousands of feet up. It is so wet that it is not unusual to get twelve inches of rain in 24 hours and so hot that dust will be coming off the roads 48 hours later. Tully gets a staggering average annual rainfall of 160 inches (13ft, or 4,000 mm for the metrically minded), with a record of 310 inches (7,900 mm). By comparison, Cardiff, Wales, known for being eternally moist, gets a piddling 40 inches (1152 mm) of rainfall annually, California, a miserable 21 inches, if you are lucky.

Tully is the only town in the world that has proudly erected a $90,000, 28-foot-tall golden gumboot, adorned with a green tree-frog, as a monument to celebrate its astonishing wetness. I would have loved to have been a fly on the wall in the committee meeting of the Tully Lions & Rotary Club:

"Order! Order! Gentlemen, the first item of business is the proposal by Mikey over 'ere that we should have some sort of monument erected to celebrate our fine town of Tully."

Cries of: "Hear hear!", "Bloody right!" and "Good on- on-ya Mikey!"

"Order! Order!"

"What has Tully got that makes us different?"

"Cane toads."

"Bananas?"

"Snakes!"

(Long pause for thought.)

"Bloody rain!"

All: "Rain!", "Yeah, strewth!", "Hear hear, mate!"

(Long pause for thought.)

"Well, ... how's about we erect a bloody great gumboot at the bottom of Main Street?"

"A boot?"

"Yeah, a bonza[18] boot, with a bloody spiral staircase up inside it!"

"Let's make it ruddy big – like 28 feet!"

"Bloody right! An' let's paint the bloody thing gold so no one can bloody miss it!"

"I think we should have a bloody tree frog on it somewhere too. Tree frogs are ripper."

"OK, so I propose the motion that we kick-in[19] for a bloody great golden boot with a staircase on the inside and a tree frog on the outside. What say you all?"

Cries of: "Bloody oath!", "We're on a good lurk![20]", "Nice one, Mikey!", "Motion carried!" and "Mines a 4X".

★ ★ ★

It was fully dark when Chris and I were dropped at the Jackaroo's quarters, having seen little of the countryside we were driven through for 45 minutes. After travelling for a few miles with tall sugarcane fields either side, we could not see much beyond the edge of the dirt-roads we were on, but several bridges suggested a landscape intersected by creeks. Twice I saw snakes, wriggling on the road, and once we thought we glimpsed a wild boar. Our driver was not inclined to conversation, emitting only the occasional beery belch, and a choice oath as he swerved to avoid a bouncing wallaby. Finally, we pulled up at a single storey, tin-roofed building, raised on stilts. It was deserted and dark.

"Here ya go, Poms, this is the Jackaroo's quarters. You're the only blokes here, so make yourselves comfortable, and report to the back door of the Station House up the road there at six."

---

18 Excellent, attractive or pleasing.

19 Fund.

20 On to a good thing.

The Jackaroo's Quarters, King Ranch, Tully River Station

Thanking him, we dragged our cases inside, the empty quarters echoing with our footsteps. Cautiously, I felt for a light switch and a bare bulb in the hallway sprang to life, illuminating our new home. Off a wide central corridor there were five basic bedrooms and a communal bathroom, with a large enclosed veranda at the far end. There, 47 species of venomous insect had instantly mounted an all-out assault on the mesh, in an attempt to come in and say hello to us. It was spartan, the rooms furnished with two single beds, each with an old, stained pillow but no sheets or bedclothes, a desk, and a chair. That was it. Either they weren't expecting us, or this was as welcoming as they were going to be. Jackaroos were the lowest form of life on an Australian Station; so, the arrival, welcome, sustenance, and comfort of a couple of Pommie Jackaroos who had been traveling on a truck for 2,000 miles were of absolutely no interest to anyone. We each picked a room, unpacked some essentials, set our alarm clocks, and went to sleep in our clothes. Outside, an army of crickets and cane toads held a competition to see how long they could keep us awake.

In the moments before I fell into a deep sleep, I reflected on the one thing I knew for sure: no one had any worries in Australia. Everyone I had met in the few days since my arrival had told me so. It was not entirely clear what irksome fretting they feared might possibly arise in the course of getting you a glass of water or ordering a sandwich, but it was very reassuring to know that none had occurred in either party. At some point in time, there must have been an endless variety of concerns in the execution of even the most mundane daily tasks, which would explain their need to constantly confirm everything had now been sorted out and was worry-free. Terrific place, Australia.

I had arrived.

* * *

The next morning, as instructed, Chris and I walked a short distance up the hill, affording us our first view of our new surroundings. The ground fell gently away, and I could see we were in a wide, lush valley, surrounded on three sides by distant forested mountains. The eastern side was open, where the rainforest transitioned to thick scrubland, the beach and, eventually, the Barrier Reef. Vivid paddock grasses contrasted with the darker greens of clumps of trees as they followed the course of creeks. A few ranch hands' houses stood here and there in the foreground, mostly stilted.

Close by, palm trees were dotted about the station house gardens, brightly coloured birds flitted from tree to tree, screeching, and a dog barked somewhere in the distance. The back door was flanked by a huge passion vine, heavy with fruit, its flowers complex and mesmerizing. I knocked cautiously. "Come on in, boys!" came a cheery voice from inside.

Cookie was the cook, and the only person we had met so far in Australia who seemed immediately and genuinely pleased to see us. With her broad smile and motherly[21] countenance, she stood at

---

21 Not at all in a nightclubby sort of way

the kitchen table, surrounded by an array of different baking bowls and ingredients. "Come and get some brekkie, and then you can tell me about your journey," she said, making us feel slightly less apprehensive. Breakfast was substantial; I had never seen anything like it: toast, fried eggs, beans and steak in abundance. Having not eaten since mid-afternoon the day before, we were hungry; wolfing it all down as Cookie quizzed us relentlessly. She was excited to hear everything about us, where we came from and how we had got there; it would all be fresh grist to the station's gossip mill. She explained to us that we should then make ourselves a sandwich for lunch from the cold meats she had laid out and take some cake for "smoko". Seeing our blank faces, she explained that smoko is an Aussie institution, meaning a mid-morning or afternoon break for a cup of tea, cake, and a cigarette or three.

The view from the Station House, over the
Jackaroo's quarters and the valley beyond.

Smoko was pretty much written into the constitution and considered an inalienable right of all labourers. So deeply entrenched in

Aussie life was it that, from time to time, disputes over it would spark industrial action. Smoko was mandatory, even when at war. On the fourth of July 1918, the Australian Army and U.S. infantry launched a relentless and ultimately successful attack against German positions in and around the town of Le Hamel, in northern France. It is recorded that Aussie troops punctuated their astonishing feats of bravery by downing arms each morning and afternoon for the hallowed break.[22] Neither enemy shellfire nor the imperatives of an Allied advance were about to interrupt smoko.

Cookie clucked and fussed around us, helping pack up all our food for the day. She was genuinely excited to have us Poms there to break her routine and provide new interest. We were certainly grateful for her attentions, and her food – especially her little passionfruit cupcakes. I can remember their exotically fragrant taste to this day, but have never been able to replicate them.

Our first assignment was to "The Shed" where the fleet of Toyota Land Cruisers, cattle trucks and heavy Caterpillar equipment was serviced and repaired by a small team of extremely skilled mechanics. This was a fairly gentle introduction to ranch life, most probably because they didn't know quite what to do with us. No one really wanted the hassle of having to train up and babysit a couple of green Pommie Jackaroos.

We had been dropped into an entirely strange culture, and had absolutely no clue about anything, which made us about as useful as a couple of capybaras in a brewery. We mostly did the easy, boring stuff, such as oil changes, or power-washing the thick rainforest mud off vehicles before they came into the shed. After a week or so, I was taught to do some basic welding and repair tires, all the while listening to the humorous banter of the mechanics as I gingerly tried to find my way around my new home. They were a friendly, good-humoured bunch, and they treated us well enough.

---

22 Source: Journal of the Royal New South Wales Lancers.

* * *

In 1853, riverboat captain Richard King purchased a flourishing oasis in the Wild Horse Desert of South Texas. Initial success and expansion were further fuelled by oil and gas royalties from the land, and the town of Kingsville quickly grew up in its centre. After World War II, expansion continued through a series of acquisitions in Kentucky, Pennsylvania, Mississippi, west Texas and Florida. Ranching operations eventually spread overseas, with land purchases in Argentina, Cuba, Brazil, Australia, Venezuela, Spain, Indonesia and Morocco. By the late 1970s, King Ranch owned millions of acres, and was the largest private landowner in the world.

If you tried to form the letter W out of a short piece of rope, you would have a Running W, the brand insignia of King Ranch. Some think it represents the diamondback rattlesnakes that were found all over the ranch, others the elegant horns of a Texas Longhorn bull. Over the course of 160 years, King Ranch led some of the first cattle drives, developed the Santa Gertrudis and Santa Cruz breeds of cattle, bred the finest Quarter horses and produced champion Thoroughbreds, all under its iconic "Running W" brand.

King Ranch's Tully River Station was developed in 1963 by Bob Kleburg, a descendant of the King family. Kleburg was offered a lease by the Queensland Government on 50,000 acres, and a huge program to clear the natural vegetation began. Back then, rainforest was considered plentiful, and only a few people, and no laws, gave a rats-arse about the demolition of this pristine rainforest for cattle ranching. Two giant Caterpillar D12 bulldozers dragged a length of massive ship's anchor-chain between them, tearing and clanking through the screaming virgin rainforest in a way that today fills me with horror. However, the nascent conservation movement was growing fast, and this was, thankfully, the last large-scale clear-felling of forests for pastoral purposes in North Queensland.

Nurtured by the tropical climate and rich loamy soil of the newly cleared land, grass grew incredibly fast, as did the livestock that fed on it. In the arid Australian outback, the rule of thumb was to allow 200 acres for each animal. At Tully, the ratio was an incredible 1:1. Within ten years, the ranch was supporting 30,000 head of cattle and had become the largest tropical cattle property in Australia. Cattle could be brought in from other stations in less fertile areas, quickly fattened up and made ready for market. The ranch became a well-oiled and highly profitable machine.

After a few weeks working at the shed, I was re-assigned to "The Stud", an outpost some ten miles distant from the main station house that was to become my home for the remainder of my stay. I left Chris behind at the Shed, which turned out to be a transformative move for me, but possibly the beginning of the end for him. As its name implies, the Stud was the part of the station responsible for breeding the Santa Gertrudis cattle. It was very capably run by Peter Cory, a tall, serious man with a permanently worried look on his face. An expert herdsman, naturally impatient, with a short fuse, he was not best pleased at being assigned a Pommie Jackaroo to babysit. To him, I was far more of a hindrance than a help. Jeff Nissan and Phil Bowen were his two Ringers.

A Ringer is a highly experienced horseman or stockman. In the early days of pastoral Australia, when the lines between properties were just marks on a map and the boundaries had no physical infrastructure, a routine evolved whereby there was just one annual muster. The hired hands of these ranching enterprises were faced with a monumental task. Cattle ranged free, becoming wild, and even roguish. After gathering a mob of cattle together who hadn't seen a human in 12 months, the best the stockmen of the day could do was to manage, not control. So, this is where the ringer bit comes into it: the stockman knew the cattle could rush (stampede) at any given provocation. To prevent the rush, they would haze the mob in a circular direction, not stopping them, but tiring them out to a manageable degree. So, they would control an unruly mob of cattle by "ringing" around them, hence the name.

Although the same age as me, they had both grown up in the outback and had been mustering cattle from an early age. Jeff was short and stocky, with a no-nonsense manner and an endearing smile. Phil came from the town of Roma, where his family ran a station. He was laid back, with a good sense of humour, and we got on well.

No one was even slightly interested in my real name. I was just called "Pom" or "the bloody Pom", by everyone[23], although I discovered that it was quite frequently expanded to "stupid Pom", "fucking Pom", or "stupid fucking Pom", usually by Peter. The Aussie accent up in North Queensland is broad and I had some trouble understanding them, and they me. I kept saying "What?".

"Hey Jeff, can you take the Cruiser and run over to Warrami to pick up some dip for us?"

"Sure Peter. I may need a hand."

"OK, well take the bloody Pom."

"Hey Pom, come on! We're goin' ta Warrami," he would yell, as one might to a spaniel.

"What?" I would respond, not having understood a word of what he said.

"Warrami, Pom… let's go!

"What?!"

"Jesus Christ," Peter was heard to mutter, "not only have they sent me a fucking Pom, they've sent me a deaf fucking Pom." It was not uttered with malice – the most mundane exchange usually contained a spectacular variety of foul language – but nor did it carry any respect. Respect was something the Aussies took very seriously, and I would have to earn it. For the time being, they seemed to regard me as one might a young cattle dog – good company, but untrained, and more often under their feet than not. Needless to say, there was an unspoken list of boxes I would need to check if I was to be accepted, on both a personal and professional level.

Sure enough, on my first morning at the Stud, as we sat around together having smoko, I was casually asked the all-important question.

---

23 In the entire time I was on King Ranch, I was never once called by my real name, by anyone.

"Hey Pom, can ya ride?" said Phil innocently, as he deftly rolled a cigarette with one hand.

I was instantly alert, and my heart skipped a beat. "Nope. Never ridden a horse in my life," I answered, as I had been trained to do, back in Lambourn.

"Bugger," said Jeff, giving Phil a sideways glance. I wasn't sure if the disappointment was because he now knew they now had the job of teaching me, or because they had all been denied some excellent entertainment. Probably a bit of both.

"Put him on Sergeant," said Peter, without looking up from his stock book.

Quarter horses originated in the United States in about the 1660s as a cross between native horses of Spanish origin and English horses. The fastest horses in the world over the quarter mile, their good nature and natural cow-sense made them a firm favourite in the prairies and ranches of the American west. They only came to Australia in 1954 but were quickly adopted as the work horse of choice on the stations. Quarter horses are seriously athletic, bred for speed, strength, and agility. They are also smart, and love what they do.

The naming convention of horses at the ranch was simple and effective, with the inspiration for a new name, as often as not, provided by the horse itself. One was called *Astronaut*, because if he decided to buck, you would be thrown so high you would need a space suit. *Whichaway* was a good horse but would occasionally have a complete sense of humour failure halfway through a muster, take the bit in his mouth and just bolt. No one ever knew which-a-way he would go. *Canardly*, was a mercurial, tricky ride, only for the experienced horseman. He occasionally bucked and performed to such an extent, that you can'ardly ride him. I suspect he was the horse I would have been put on, had I intimated I could ride. Thanks Mum.

Sergeant, so named because he always took command of a situation, was an old quarter horse, highly experienced at mustering cattle, and soft in both muzzle and temperament. Peter knew he would teach me much of what I needed to know. In hindsight, he was the equine equivalent of a Tesla – fantastic acceleration, breath-taking top speed, wonderful handling, air conditioning, great brakes, but needed to be recharged after three hours. Best of all, he had equine autopilot. Sergeant knew his trade so well that when a steer broke away from the mob of cattle we were herding, his ears would immediately prick up and I would feel him stiffen beneath me. With his eyes locked on the offending animal, I needed only to give him the slightest touch and he would launch like a guided missile.

The first few times it was utterly terrifying, and I held on for dear life as Sergeant thundered towards our target at full speed, the ground a blur below us. He would leap over tree trunks and holes that I could not even see until they were below us, deftly weaving between small trees and patches of tall elephant grass as he homed in on his target. Gauging the perfect angle, he would curve around and bring the beast back to the mob. I learned fast. If one tried to break away and dodge past us, with the lightest touch of the rein on his neck, Sergeant would deftly block its path, darting left, then right, then left again, in an elegant dance that confounded the animal. The much less intelligent and clumsy bovine didn't stand a chance against years of finely honed equine skill. I quickly learned to love the adrenaline rush that coursed through me each time we launched.

When we broke for a rest in the shade of a mango tree, Sergeant would allow me to lean up against his front legs for a quick power nap, and remain motionless, save for the occasional fly shudder. So, no one really had to teach me how to ride, they just had to teach me which button to press on Sergeant. He was, even to this day, the best horse I have ever ridden, and taught me all I know. In saying I could not ride, I had unknowingly checked the first and most important box, one that would define me in their minds above all else: I was not an arrogant bullshitting Pommie bastard. *Check.* Thanks Greg.

The yards, where we handled and processed all the cattle, were built of sturdy timber and designed to hold and separate cattle, or funnel them through a narrow chute that led to the dip. Ticks were a big problem in the tropical north, and the cattle needed to be fully immersed every few months to rid them of the parasites. In the middle of the chute was a metal "crush", so called because you could use it to squeeze and hold an animal, allowing it to be worked on. This minimised the risk of injury to both the animal and operator. I know I would make it exceedingly difficult for someone trying to de-horn, vaccinate, castrate and tag me, and considerable restraint would be necessary.

During my first month, we had some young bulls in the yard and had just put the first one into the crush. It stood there, straining and rocking against this sudden confinement, his massive balls slapping from side to side between his legs. I was standing by, waiting to see what happened next, when Phil whipped out a scalpel, reached between its legs, grabbed hold of one testicle and deftly made an incision in the sack. After pulling the testicles out, two more quick slices were made, and the severed testicles tossed into a bucket. Simultaneously, Jeff pierced its ear with a tag and stabbed it with a vaccination gun. It all took no more than ten seconds, and quite a lot of anguished mooing[24] before the crush was opened and the newly created bullock leapt forward and charged off down the chute. In moments, the next bull was ready on the crush. I was standing, aghast, trying to get my head around this sudden, savage bush surgery, when Peter handed me a scalpel and just said, "Cut 'em off, Pom."

"What?" I replied, as usual.

"Cut 'em off, Pom. Cut its bloody balls off!"

"Me? Aaaah, yes, right." I paused, as my stomach did a couple of back flips. "Will you show me how?" I had already learned that it was better to ask for help than to forge ahead and screw something up. When it came to matters of testicular removal, I needed no encouragement.

"Phil, show the Pom," said Peter.

---

24 Believe it or not, this is still considered to be the method least harmful to the animal's welfare, and with the fastest recovery.

Crouching beside me, Phil talked me through it step by step. I had never made an incision in anything alive, and a bull's balls constituted quite a leap in both life and veterinary experience. I was expecting to ride a horse; no one had told me about this. With my hand trembling, I did exactly as Phil told me, and soon there was a second pair of testicles in the bucket.

Cut the balls off a bull: *check*.

RWS working cattle in the Stud Yards

Chris Vicary, another ringer who worked at a different yard but was my current roommate, soon set up my all-important social initiation on Friday night.

"Hey, Pom, we're going to the pub tonight. You wanna come?" he asked, casually.

"Er, yeah Chris, that would be great, thanks.'

The Euramo pub, where other Chris and I had been dropped on the night of our arrival, was a working man's establishment through and through. The pubs I was used to back home were charming and amiable, with a crackling log fire, a friendly snuffling Labrador, comfortable chairs, and a homely feel. In Australia, it was all business – and bugger the fire. There were two large, functional rooms, with long bars, a number of Formica tables that could not easily be broken in a fight, and tiled floors that could be quickly hosed down if someone unexpectedly started blowing chunks. Decoration was non-existent, other than a few advertisements for Bundaberg Rum and 4X[25] beer. It was designed for one purpose only – to get alcohol inside customers as efficiently as possible. It was normal practice, if you were sitting at the bar, to put an amount of money down in front of you, and the barman would keep pouring you beers and taking money from your pile until it was gone, or someone dragged your pickled carcass home, whichever was first. Beer was always dispensed into frosted glasses that were taken from a chiller cabinet, to ensure the beer stayed cool for as long as possible.

There was a lengthy period, from 1916 to 1954 when Australian licensing laws required pubs to close at 6pm. Intended as an interim wartime restriction, with support from temperance groups it endured for 50 long years, through both World Wars, and multiple governments. At precisely 5:00pm each day, a tidal wave of workers would erupt from their places of employment and run as fast as they could to the nearest pub. Cleared of all seating, tables, and other furniture that might impede capacity, the pubs would quickly fill with a heaving mass of shouting men, all trying to drink as much as they possibly could in just 60 minutes. This was known as the "six

---

25 Castlemaine XXXX beer, known as 4X, was – and still is – the beer of
   Queensland.

o'clock swill". The only way the bar staff could dispense beer fast enough to sate the demand was by attaching a trigger to the end of a hose. This was called a Pluto gun, and a barman could fill a clutch of glasses being thrust at him by going from one to another in quick succession, without stopping. It was this invention that inspired today's soda guns, that dispense different sodas and water according to which button is pressed. Crushed up against the bar, six or ten deep, Aussie workers would drink as many beers as they could in one hour, becoming completely parrot-faced, before tumbling out onto the pavement and staggering home.

Having finished work, showered and changed out of our sweat and cow-shit splattered work clothes, we all piled into Chris's car and set off to the pub. I had never driven the road off the station during daylight, so was interested to see the lay of the land. The dirt road was mostly straight, only curving here and there to avoid a creek. Barbed wire fenced in the paddocks either side, eventually transitioning to tall fields of sugar cane as we left the station. The cane fields went on for miles, railway tracks criss-crossing the road here and there, with the occasional cane-train hauling its fresh-cut load to the local mill – one of the largest in Australia.

Arriving at the pub, I took my seat at a table and Chris ordered a round of drinks. Beer or rum & coke were the two drinks of choice among the station hands – and pretty much everyone else, it seemed. Friday nights were busy, and there was quite a crowd. Scattered among them were others from King Ranch. Ronny Reece and Squeaky Dave, kings of the pool table, who I knew from the Shed. Their specialty was to invite an out-of-towner to play with them, let him have a couple of wins, feign poor skills then offer a small wager on the next game. This would be skilfully escalated until they thought they had exploited their sucker enough, at which point they would offer double-or-nothing on the last game so they could save face. Of course, they always won.

The drinks flowed and different people bought rounds for the group, rather than everyone buying individually. This is known as a "shout", and I could tell when it was "my shout". I rose to the occasion in a timely fashion and threw in some extra bags of peanuts to show I was not stingy.

Not a mean bastard: *Check.*

The conversation mostly evolved around station life, horses, gossip, and Kim, the cute blonde publican's daughter who was serving behind the bar. As the evening wore on, we got drunker and more raucous, until I thought I might be coming to the limits of my capacity. At that moment, as if in sympathy, Vince, the local barfly, fell backwards off his stool and crashed to the floor. No one batted an eyelid.

"Last orders, gents!" yelled Keith, the publican.

"Ten bucks each guys," said Chris, putting out his hand. "I'll pick up some booze to take back." We all duly handed over our bills, and a few minutes later, Chris came back with a box, loaded to the brim with beers, a bottle of rum and some Coke. We all piled into the car and drove back to the Station. Fortunately, all but 300-yards of the journey was on private dirt roads, so there was no danger of us being stopped. Drunk as he certainly was, Chris was an excellent driver; had he run off the road, the only casualty would have been a few stems of cane or an itinerant wallaby. Back at the quarters, we set into part two of the night's drinking, supplemented with a joint or two. I have no recollection of how long it went on, or of much else. All I remember is that a couple of the others passed out before me.

Pom holds his liquor: *Check.*

I came around at about ten the next morning, lying flat in my back on the grass outside, with a monumental hangover, sunburn, and an empty bottle of rum nearby.

Pom's a generally good bloke: *Check*

Meanwhile, back at the Shed, built-like-a-brick-shithouse Chris, from the UK, couldn't hack it, and bailed out after two months. He failed all the checks miserably because it turned out he really, really hated snakes, heat, humidity, Australia, and Australians

– all of which were present in abundance. Unfortunately, he made the fundamental mistake of telling another station hand about the snakes, and within hours the word was out. Snakes started turning up everywhere Chris was, as if drawn by a tractor beam. It was like a snake convention. They were selected to be mostly harmless, but for someone who was ophidiophobic[26,] a ten-foot-long Carpet snake curled up on your bed can really screw with your head. The other lads found all this highly entertaining. Chris' biggest failing, however, was that he was constantly whingeing[27] – something Aussies cannot abide – and had done nothing to endear himself to them.

Having survived my initiation, both on horseback and in the pub, for the next eight months I had the most extraordinary experiences and adventures as a Pommie Jackaroo on King Ranch. Within a month, I had been made personally responsible for five horses, one of which was a young colt I had to train. Slowly but surely, I began to become a horseman. Peter helped me along by throwing rocks and yelling at me from time to time, but I had enormous respect for him and worked diligently to be as good a Jackaroo as I was able. The ringers taught me to lasso, crack a whip, burn bonfires three-storeys high and capture the snakes that slithered out of them. We would collect Taipans and Death Adders without a second thought and sell them to the anti-venom centre at the weekend. It wasn't long before I could mend fences, brew tea in a billy[28], round up horses on a dirt bike, and throw a Land Cruiser into a power-slide at the drop of a hat. I was taught to muster 500 head of cattle (not alone), and I could dip, brand, de-horn, castrate and vaccinate them as required.

---

26 Ophidiophobia: fear of snakes. The word is derived from the Greek words "ophis", meaning snake. Apparently, about a third of adult humans are ophidiophobic.

27 Complain persistently in a way that especially irritates Australians.

28 A saucepan or kettle, in which one brewed tea, usually over an open fire.

Having a smoke, shoeless and covered in cow-shit, after a long day
mustering and dipping cattle. No, I am not wearing socks. It's all shit.

As mandated by the rules governing gap years, the local fauna was
extremely venomous, the climate blisteringly hot, the food basic, the
hours long, the pay minimal, and I ended most days covered from
head to toe in cow-shit. Nevertheless, it was one of the best times
of my life. At weekends, which we had to ourselves, I slept on the
beaches of the Pacific and stargazed, or explored the rainforest. Phil,
Chris and I would often spend weekends up in Palm Cove, north of
Cairns, where his parents lived, or with friends up in Mareeba, on the
Atherton Tablelands. Our group usually consisted of the three of us,
plus a couple of local friends of Chris's who I got to know well. One
of them was Steve Lahtinen, a kind, gentle man who loved fishing,

and had worked on King Ranch for a while before I arrived. For most of the time I knew him, he wore a neck brace due to a gymnastic accident of some kind. The other was Ronnie Whiteman. "Little Ron", possessed of unhinged exuberance, humour and joie de vivre, was born with seven holes in his heart. He lived on a lifetime government disability pension, most of which he spent on weed because he said it made him feel much better. His doctors had told him he would probably not survive beyond his teens, but in his twenties he could still drink most of us under the table and had a medically impossible amount of energy. We didn't give it much of a thought at the time, but in hindsight I think he truly lived each day as if it were his last. Probably a wise strategy, under the circumstances. A few weekends were spent on the Station, hunting wild boar, breaking in young horses, tinkering with cars and spending evenings in the pub. Mischief and mayhem were constant companions. I became a crack shot, and learned all sorts of useful things, such as how to recognise which mushrooms were magic, and which would kill you.

The mushrooms – known as "Gold-tops" because of their gold-coloured cap – grew everywhere, fuelled by abundant manure and rain. On a relatively quiet day, or on the rare occasions when one had been sent off to do some solitary task that was not too demanding, I was taught that if one slipped a single small mushroom into one's sandwich, it would make the day more interesting. Everything looked more vivid, more attractive. I think today it would be called micro-dosing. It wasn't enough to impede one's ability to perform work – in fact it increased focus and general enthusiasm, accelerated thought processes and analysis, and just slightly enhanced everything. The result was life, colour corrected.

After about six months, we had just completed an arduous muster that involved winkling several recalcitrant bullocks out of a jungle creek they had been hiding in – bad stinging-tree territory. It had been a long morning, and as I finished counting the animals through the gate and patted my tired and sweaty horse, Peter rode up beside me. Oh shit, I thought, what have I done wrong now?

"What's the count, Pom?"

"325 head," I replied, and he noted it down on a little pad he always kept in his shirt pocket.

"You know, Pom, you're doin' alright. Keep it up." And with that he wheeled his horse and rode off. Peter was a man who dispensed compliments rarely, if ever, so this was high praise; it was as if he had just pinned a medal on me. I felt terrific. It had taken a long time coming, and I had screwed up a lot, but I was finally graduating from lowly Jackaroo and generally useless Pom, to something resembling a Ringer. *Check.*

At around the same time, we were at the Euramo pub one evening; it was my shout, and I was waiting at the bar minding my own business. One of the locals, who was pretty well dipped, decided to give me some grief, with a view to taking a swing at me.

King Ranch Ringers bringing cattle from the rail-head, sometime in the 1970's

"Little Ron"

From left to Right: Little Ron, RWS, Chris Vicary, Phil
Bowen, Chris's brother, Steve Lahtinen

"You'se a fucking Pommie bastard, aren't ya," mumbled Dickhead, slapping the bar.

"… and two bags of peanuts please, Kim," I continued, ignoring him.

"Aww, you Pommies think you're pretty fucking special, don'cha?" Dickhead continued, giving me a shove.

"Hey, leave the Pom be, you great oaf," chimed in Kim, dumping several beers in front of me.

"I'll tell you what," I said to him, keen to avoid getting clocked. "Why don't you stay here and have a nice chat with Kim, while I take these beers over to my mates?"

"Fuck you, Pommie bastard," said Dickhead, swaying a bit as he pulled back his arm to deliver a punch.

"Oi!! Dickhead!!" came a shout from somewhere in the room. Hearing his name, Dickhead paused for a moment to see where the insult had come from. Chris was striding towards the bar. He stopped about four feet away and said, matter of factly, "Don't fuck with the Pom!" The room went quiet. Dickhead swayed gently as he tried to process this unexpected support for his opponent.

"He'sh a fucking Pommie bastard!" said Dickhead, as if that was explanation enough.

"Yeah, that's right mate, he is, but he's our Pommie bastard, so if you want to fuck with him," he said, gesturing towards our table, "you're gonna have to fuck with all of us." I turned towards our table, as all of them pushed back their chairs and stood. Then, to my amazement, others around the room began to stand; every ringer, mechanic, dozer driver and ranch hand from King Ranch – about a dozen in all – slowly got to their feet, even those I barely knew. Dickhead's eyes and ears sent some blurry and grammatically flawed panic signals to his amygdala, which had a quick chat with his hypothalamus, and they both agreed he should just scratch his head and look stupid while they figured out where the emergency stop button was for his tongue.

"C'mon, Pom, lemme give you a hand with those beers," said Chris, and we scooped them up and walked away.

It was a seminal moment, my impromptu graduation ceremony, back in the very same bar where I had first alighted from the truck, many months earlier. I was now a fully qualified member of King Ranch's Tully River Station, worthy of their respect and support, and they were all prepared to go into battle for me. Bush Aussies don't make friends of foreigners easily, and regard new arrivals with a good deal of suspicion, but when they accept you, they are the best and most loyal friends you could ever have. At that split second, I realised I had been changed forever, I had become someone I had never could have imagined I would be.

I was one of them.

* * *

King Ranch's Australian operation was sold off in the late 1980s after the death of Kleburg. and Tully River Station was divided up and sold. The area now supports many small banana, pineapple and cane farms.

Today, the Running W still appears on prize-winning cattle, leather goods, and even a special U.S. version of the Ford F-150 pick-up truck. It remains an indisputable icon of the American ranching industry. After I left, I never saw my good friend Chris Vicary again. He was killed some years later in a motorbike accident in Western Australia, and I miss him terribly. Thanks to the Internet, Phil Bowen, Steve Lahtinen and I keep in touch regularly; they are still good mates. Peter Cory is retired, lives in Brisbane and provided some historical background for this story, which amused him. Turns out he was a pretty good bloke too. An extract from his letter of reference to me in 1978 contains the following glowing testimony:

> *"Richard started with less than no knowledge of stock... but managed to develop into a reasonable horseman."*

Never a truer word was spoken. And it was the only time he or anyone else in Australia ever called me by name.

HAWAII
Paradise Lost

I made my way through the milling, bright, noisy crowd at Honolulu Airport, in search of a locker in which to store my bags for a few hours. In those days, baggage lockers existed at all airports, mostly to satisfy the needs of drug dealers and terrorists, who found them to be anonymous, convenient, inexpensive, and secure storage facilities for large quantities of cash, bombs, and drugs. Most good movies in the 1960s and '70s included someone looking furtively about, while putting a holdall or envelope containing plot-critical material into a baggage locker. The key is later discovered on their dead body, at which point a frantic race ensues to find said locker, thwart the villains and save the planet. Only very occasionally were they used by ordinary travellers, such as myself.

I was evidently looking somewhat lost as I searched for the locker sign, when a dude (in the American vernacular, this can be translated as "a young man of about my age and disposition") approached me and asked if I needed any help.

"Hey, man, you lookin' for something?"

"Er, yeah, I've got a layover, and I'm looking for a place to store my bags," I explained.

"Ahh, cool! Yeah, over there, man." He pointed me to the baggage lockers, then held out his fist as if to pass me something.

"Hey, man, take this. Have a good time in Hawaii, man!" he said, lowering his voice conspiratorially and dropping something into my hand. "Aloha!"

I cautiously peeked down to see a small white joint. When I looked up, he had vanished into a heaving sea of hibiscus camouflaged shirts.

* * *

Flying from Sydney to Vancouver in 1978 required a stop in Hawaii to refuel, change planes, and generally support the Hawaiian economy. I was on my way back from my gap year on an Australian cattle station, and this was only my third long haul flight ever. It involved a six-hour layover in Honolulu, during which time I was required to clear customs and enter the United States. This was all very exciting. I was determined to make the most of the opportunity by taking a taxi into Honolulu to lay my eyes on the legendary Waikiki Beach and have a look around this mid-Pacific outpost of America. Waikiki, a name I knew only through the American TV series *Hawaii 5-0*, is a neighbourhood of Honolulu on the south shore of the island of Oahu. In the 1800s, the area was popular with Hawaiian royalty, who surfed there on very early forms of surfboards. By the 1880s, a few hotels had opened, and its popularity grew in leaps and bounds.

I was now excited to see this storied beach for myself. Hooray! On clearing customs, I was ejected into the arrivals area amid a sea of American tourists wearing loud Hawaiian shirts and flower leis. What fun it was to be in America for the first time. They talked loudly in American accents and had American looking children. This was fascinating! One of the extraordinary things about travel, that amazes me to this day, is that one minute you are in a place that is so reassuringly familiar that you take it for granted, and in mere hours you find yourself halfway around the world, in a completely different culture. While some cultures are clearly defined, like Japan or India, others are more blended. When I arrived in Australia, it struck me that there were strong elements of both England and America – or at least the America I had seen on TV. There were drive-in theatres and pick-up trucks and cowboys, for example. New Zealand, on the other hand, has Maori, with an enormous dollop of clotted cream and cucumber sandwiches. Now, here I was in America. But although it was definitely America – there was a sign and a smiley picture of Jimmy Carter that said so – it was Hawaii-America, with Hawaiian people who were also Americans and Americans who were definitely not Hawaiians.

Fresh off a cattle station, I was hardly traveling incognito. Cowboy boots and jeans were accented with a much-loved t-shirt, printed with some obscurely witty reference to weed that only I found amusing. My hair, having been allowed to grow freely in three dimensions for an entire year, was almost an afro, upon which perched an Akubra.

The Akubra is pretty much the gold standard of Australian head-wear. It is, in essence, a cowboy hat made of stiff felt. It could be steamed into all manner of fetching swoops and curls according to one's stylistic preference, to ensure the most effective guttering of rain or perceived attractiveness to the opposite sex, ideally both. Like a Barbour jacket in the UK, a Loden coat in Austria or a Stetson in the U.S., the Akubra is national treasure. It is worn by prime ministers, politicians, and businessmen as well as truckers, ranchers, ringers, cowhands, and even the humble Jackaroo.

Designed to be rainproof, dirtproof, aerodynamically stable at speed, and fully customizable, mine was also equipped with a cunning device that prevented it from ever blowing off. A thin leather band ran inside, from temple to temple. During normal use, it lay unseen against the brim, but in situations where one's forward velocity was likely to get interesting, you could momentarily tip the front of the hat upwards and allow the band to drop down half an inch onto one's forehead. In this position, the more upward pressure the wind applied to the brim, the more firmly the hat stayed in place. You could be thundering through the outback in pursuit of a way-ward cow or standing up in the back of a Ute[29] at 60 miles per hour, and the hat would remain as if welded to your head. Occasionally I would be unexpectedly and violently dismounted by a tree branch, but the hat would always stay on. Mine was not designed to blend in, as I had chosen one of a yellow-ochre colour that I later rather wished I hadn't, but it was equipped with a natty leather hat-band that I had woven myself, with some help from Phil and Chris. I thought it was terrific.

Excited about my mission to see Waikiki, but immediately para-noid about the gift I had just been given, I quickly located an empty locker and stuffed my bags inside. This was a surreal turn of events. Here I was, in America, and Hawaii, for the first time, with six hours to spare, on my way to check out Waikiki, and a complete stranger

---

29 Pick-up truck.

had just given me a joint. Marvellous! Or was it? Having watched way too many episodes of *Hawaii 5-0*, and imagining myself suddenly surrounded by Hawaiian-shirted undercover cops, guns drawn, I was convinced I had somehow been set up. So, I decided to conceal the joint in the back of my camera and leave it in the locker for half an hour. This was in the misguided belief that possession of a joint, inside a camera belonging to me, inside a locker often used for the storage of drugs that now contains only my belongings, and to which only I have the key, is somehow much better than possession of a joint in your pocket. Idiot.

By this point in time, I was a master study in why teenage boys are idiots. They have a fully developed body, adult strength, sexual maturity and are allowed to handle firearms. They serve in the military, vote, and drive half a ton of metal at speed, but they do all this with the emotional maturity of a baby goat. At this developmental plateau in my life, I had already done, and for some four years more would continue to do, plenty of "what-the-hell-were-you-thinking?" things. Many were relatively harmless lack-of-judgment calls, such as questionable choices in clothing and accessories. Others could have had dire consequences.

In Australia, on the cattle station, there had been moments of world-class stupidity. One such example was seeing if I could set the world land-speed record for pulling an unstable, ten-ton, steel molasses trailer with a tractor, on a dirt road, at a speed that caused it to start fishtailing.[30] On the verge of jack-knifing, I would be happily smiling away, oblivious to the attendant inevitability of catastrophic injury, loss of limb(s), destruction of equipment, and death in a mangled pile of steel, dust, molasses and wallabies. Nevertheless, it had all seemed like an entirely fun idea at the time – several times, actually. Endowed with these spectacularly impaired decision-making skills, I spent several years seeking out risk-taking opportunities and making impulsive choices in the relentless pursuit of instant

---

30 This is highly undesirable, unless you are trying to commit suicide.

gratification, without the slightest inkling of the consequences even crossing my mind. The only thought I ever had was "Woo-hoo!". But it really wasn't all my fault. There is a biological reason for this behaviour – evolution screwed up. The all-important frontal lobe, responsible for decision making, impulse control, sensation seeking, emotional responses and consequential thinking, only works in the male of the species at about ten percent of capacity until our early to mid-twenties. In layman's terms, the frontal-lobe develops at a very much slower rate than our ability to think up and execute general mayhem. For example:

Me: "Oh look, a sleeping polar bear."

Frontal Lobe: "Wow, cool!"

Me: "I wonder what would happen if I gave it a poke with this stick?"

Frontal Lobe: "Not sure that stick's long enough, man."

Me: "Well, it's the only one around on this ice shelf, so it will have to do."

Frontal Lobe: "OK, man. Hey, do you know how fast a polar bear can run?"

Me: "Nope."

Frontal Lobe: "Me neither."

Me: "This'll be fun! You ready?"

Frontal Lobe: "Locked and loaded! You 'da man!"

* * *

Frontal lobe and I paced around, eyeing the baggage locker keenly, but nothing happened, and no one looked even remotely interested in anything other than getting a Mai Tai in front of them as quickly as possible. So eventually my curiosity, which unlike frontal-lobe was always fully functional, got the better of me. I decided to take the joint outside and smoke it… and then I would hop in a cab to Waikiki.

RWS shortly after leaving Australia, September 1978

I settled down on a suitably remote bench away from the entrance to the terminal. There were some rather fetching hibiscus bushes nearby, long stamens reaching up to the sunlight from cream and red flowers, towered over by distantly tall palm trees that rustled nicely in the warm Pacific breeze. Hummingbirds whizzed about busily, traffic was light, and there were no authority figures in sight. I pulled out the joint, rolling it between my fingers as I checked it out. It was the smallest I had ever seen – about two inches long and as thin as a matchstick. Unimpressed, I lit it up anyway. It was rolled loose and burned fast, so I barely sucked on it twice before it scorched my fingers and was gone. Feeling a bit cross with myself for making such a fuss about nothing, I made my way back to the arrivals terminal cab rank, where American tourists were chattering excitedly about how many Mai Tai's they were going to order, practicing saying "Mahalo" and laughing loudly at each other's terrible jokes. After about five minutes, I noticed that the hibiscus flowers on the shirt of the man in front of me had become significantly brighter; sounds seemed louder, and hummingbirds markedly whizzier. The humidity began to envelop me, and by the time the family in front of me were getting into their cab, I realized I was more stoned than I had ever been before.

In a rare combination of both poor decision making and paranoia,[31] I decided that there was A) some very interesting stuff going on right here at the airport, and B) if I went to Waikiki, something might go terribly wrong; I might get delayed by women in bikinis and bartenders pouring Mai Tai's, get arrested by Steve McGarrett[32] and miss my connecting flight. Giving up on my mission to Waikiki, I cut out of the line, returned to the terminal and collected my bags. Finding a place to sit, I just settled down to people watch with a silly grin on my face. I don't think I have ever been so stoned or, indeed, so stupid, as my senses were assaulted by sights and sounds I had never encountered before. This was no normal airport, this was Honolulu! The people were brighter and happier, intoxicated by either the prospect of their imminent vacation, or the recent memories of the great times they had had. This was one happy airport! Surrounded by laughter and chatter, I tuned-in-and-out of conversations as if turning the dial of an analogue radio.

It went something like this:

"...and d'ya wanna see the size of my Wahoo?"

"Honey!!!!"

"... biggest damn fish I ever caught!"

---

31 Your amygdala helps regulate your response to fear and related emotions, like anxiety, stress and paranoia. When you use cannabis that's rich in THC, research suggests this may overstimulate the amygdala, making you feel fear and anxiety.

32 Hawaii 5-0 starred Jack Lord as Detective Captain Stephen "Steve" McGarrett, the head of a special state police task force in Hawaii. It was based on an actual unit that existed on the islands under martial law, after World War II. McGarrett's now-iconic catchphrase was "Book 'em, Danno!"

"Hush now honey an' stop braggin', ya know poor Grover didn't catch a darn thing."

"American Airlines flight 27 to Los Angeles, now boardin' at Gate 5."

"Mommy, I wanna candy coconut like Sally, pleeeeeeease…"

"… an' Jilly-Anne told me later that Glynnis had waaaay too many Mai Tai's and fell right in the swimmin' pool, an' it's a holy miracle she didn't drown…" (hysterical laughter).

"Last call for United flight 35 to Chicago."

"Travis, please don't strum on that ukulele anymore 'cos I'm just about fit to be tied. Just put it away now until we get home."

"Will Mr. Peter Whackenschnauser pick up a white courtesy phone for a message. Peter Whackenschnauser to the white courtesy phone."

The view from my bench at Honolulu International Airport, September 1978

Wow! This was the soundtrack to a Technicolor feature film of Americans on vacation, with their flower leis around their necks, Hawaiian shirts, big hats and bags of souvenir Macadamia Nut chocolate.

Movement was accentuated, sound was enhanced, and the colours were shifting and intense. I smiled and giggled happily to myself for hours, munching on several hot dogs to assuage my suddenly rampant appetite.

However, despite the superficially good time I was having, I had blown it. Frontal Lobe had allowed me to be derailed by the instant gratification of a small joint, and my fantastic opportunity to see Waikiki had gone up in a puff of Maui-Wowee. It would be another 13 years before I came back to Hawaii, and almost 30 before I eventually set foot on Waikiki Beach. So, I learned to carpe diem, and never accept joints from random strangers.

Leaving Hawaii behind, onwards I went to Vancouver, having needlessly sat in an airport for six hours while a mere three miles away lay Paradise, lost to me, on Waikiki beach. Ancient Hawaiian culture continued its inexorable march through time without me. Hawaii did not care one jot. I was insignificant. Maybe in another few hundred thousand years, Humankind's frontal lobe will catch up. Neither evolution, nor teenagers, are without their flaws, but one thing is true: since my drug-induced paranoia that day, I have never missed a flight in my life.

THE MALDIVES
Running out of Air

"You're fired!" These were not words I ever wanted to hear, but in hindsight they were not entirely unexpected. I was 23 years old and I knew my performance recently had been sub-standard. London and it's alluring nightlife had got the better of me – I was practically a vampire - my priorities were all wrong, and recession, striking miners and riots had created a challenging business environment in the UK. Sales, for which I found myself unexpectedly responsible in the small corporate communications company I worked for, were dismal. I had taken the job six months earlier in the position of producer. However as business declined there was a bit of a bait-and-switch, and I found myself being held accountable for sales. I really should have risen to the challenge, but my performance was poor, to say the least, and I blamed only myself. However, it was a moment that was to begin an unimaginable cascade of changes in my life, all for the better.

A few days later, Kirsten and I were sitting in the Guinea Grill, a small, old, dimly-lit and illustrious grill house off Berkeley Square in central London. It was early April 1982, the Falklands War had just begun and unemployment was at record levels. We had only been together as a couple for about six months, although we had known each other for as many years. Kirsten's divorce had just been finalised and her house sold. She had been married briefly to my first cousin, and although her divorce was not precipitated by me, our relationship was viewed askance by my family. We reflected on our life in general.

"We need to get out of England," Kirsten suddenly announced. "Let's go to India." Never afraid of bold moves, even those that would make lesser mortals mildly hysterical, when she makes up her mind she is unwavering in her determination; I had already learned to recognise the steely look in her eyes, and think twice before questioning her.

"OK," I replied, having nothing to lose. "When shall we leave?"

We had absolutely no idea that this lunch was a seminal moment for us, one we would look back on with the realization that it had changed our lives forever. As you will discover, we would not return to live in England for more than six years, and even then, very briefly. We ended up in California, where we have remained for more than 32 years. So important a moment was it, that many decades later, when we found the receipt from that fateful lunch, we framed it.

The lunch that changed my life

The Management, cradling an Arriflex 16mm camera,
somewhere on a glacier in New Zealand.

As this is the first time you will meet her, and she features often
and prominently in these stories, I should let you know that I often
affectionately refer to my wife Kirsten as "The Management". At
the time of writing, we have been married for 36 years. Many of the
adventures documented in these pages are ones we have shared, and
they would not have been the same, or in many cases even possible,
without her. She is a tireless researcher, fearless traveller, and lover
of people, conversation, culture, architecture, music, food, history,
dancing, art and smoked salmon sandwiches. An accomplished film
director, she is insatiably curious, more widely travelled than even
me, and has visited some of the most remote places on the planet.
Highly capable, she can turn her hand to pretty much anything she
chooses, except stacking a dishwasher. She will happily pull some G's
while hanging out of a doorless helicopter, secured only by a canvas
strap and flown by a Kiwi with a reckless contempt for the principles
of level flight. She is as cool as a frozen daiquiri in a crisis, has been

tossed by massive seas in an America's Cup yacht off New Zealand, and suffered severe hypoxia in the Himalaya. When held up at gunpoint by Zapatista rebels in the jungles of Chiapas, she promptly invited them to lunch, by the end of which they had agreed to guard her instead of holding her hostage. Her standards are high, and she does not suffer fools, but she is quick to make friends, and her sense of adventure is matched only by her sense of humour. She has been the best travel companion I could ever have wished for, and our journeys have been full of laughter, good food, fond memories and fun.

* * *

And so it was that about three weeks later, we found ourselves looking down on the breathtakingly beautiful Maldives, like so many scattered emeralds, set in gold, and floating in a turquoise sea. The Maldives sit astride the equator, south of India and west of Sri Lanka. They are a collection of 1,200 small coral atolls, stretching across 500 miles of the Indian Ocean, the visible coral-tipped vestige of a volcanic mountain range. The archipelago, which in its entirety comprises just 115 square miles of dry land, is blessed with some of the world's most beautiful beaches, clear turquoise lagoons, and extraordinary sea life. But in 1982, very few people knew about the Maldives, and their name was seldom, if ever, overheard in dinner party chit-chat. I had once seen an image in a National Geographic, and it was etched in my mind. Maldivian tourism was in its infancy; other than a handful of intrepid travellers (mostly Germans) the Maldives were barely on the map of international tourism.

We flew in from London, via Columbo, and landed on the newly built, runway-shaped island next to the capital city of Mahé. With time to kill before a boat arrived to pick us up, we wandered on the beach next to the tiny terminal building. This was not the palm fringed beach now synonymous with the Maldives, because the airport was built on landfill and the beach was there only because the land had to join the sea at some point. Thus, ignored by the people hurrying to and from the airport it was rarely visited, and we were amazed to find it covered in an abundant selection of beautiful sea-shells, many of which we had never laid eyes on before.

Ibrahim Nasir served as Prime Minister of the Maldives from 1957 to 1968 and then as the first President of the Second Republic from 1968 to 1978. Nasir is credited with many things, among them opening up the Maldives to tourism, building the international airport and transforming education. In 1972, he used his presidential leverage in a way that would probably have got him locked up anywhere else. Nasir and his partners formed a company called the Crescent Tourist Agency, and set about developing the islands Bandos, Furanafushi, Farukol-hufushi, Villingli and Baros for tourism. Although this was a trans-formative move that would dramatically improve the prosperity of the Maldives for generations, it was the equivalent of Boris Johnson, while Prime Minister, taking over the Isle of Wight for private development, and marketing it with his own tourism company. The first tourists to ever grace the Maldives, in 1973, were a group of Italians on a special trip arranged by a visionary travel agent named George Corbin.

So, less than ten years after the initial party, our pockets bulging with jewel-like shells[33], we found ourselves bobbing along in a small, converted fishing boat as we left the airport dock and headed for the island of Bandos.

Less than 400 metres in diameter, Bandos was then considerably more modest in terms of both accommodation and facilities than it is today. We arrived at the jetty and disembarked next to a small manmade tide-pool containing an abundance of lobsters. The pool was built of rough-hewn coral rock, its walls full of nooks and cran-nies that provided a theoretically ideal sanctuary for lobsters. All one could see was a waving antenna sticking out here and there. Sanctuary may be something of a misnomer because a sea turtle, recognizing that the constant supply of food on-hand made this an excellent place to hang out, was swimming lazily around the

---

33 This is now illegal.

perimeter, casually biting off any lobster extremities it encountered. The turtle had a look of exquisite pleasure on its face, rather like a very stoned teenager slowly eating a Haagen-Dazs. This explained the abundance of mono-antennae lobsters in the pool.

Once ashore, a small cluster of palm-roofed, open-sided buildings formed the centre of the hotel, most of them with sand floors. The kitchen-cum-dining room, cafeteria like, was the only fully enclosed building with a hard floor. A short distance away, on the edge of an impossibly white beach, were about 16 thatched huts, each separated from one another by a respectable distance. The small, round rooms and en-suite bathroom were simply furnished and offered a ceiling fan by way of air conditioning, but the view from each instantly made one feel like a castaway. Collapsing on to the bed, we both fell into a deep siesta.

The view from our little hut on Bandos Island.

On waking sometime later, the Management pointed out that my shirtless back had become a feeding ground for 275 mosquitos, and now sported as many bumps as a non-slip bathmat. Having leapt enthusiastically about the room, wreaking revenge with a rolled-up towel, we left the walls looking like a blood transfusion had gone horribly wrong and set off to explore the island. Turning left, we walked away from the pier. This was the desert island of my dreams. The brilliant white sand was lapped by warm, turquoise water and fringed with swooping palm trees, some almost horizontal and all heavy with coconuts. There was not another soul in sight. I climbed a low-angled palm and sat on its trunk, dangling my legs over the white sand. This was paradise.

The outer reef, marked by a thin line of white water, formed a distant perimeter, within which an abundance of sea life went about its daily business. Turtles, rays, crabs, and endless fish flitted, flapped, sprinted and undulated across golden sands of the shallow seabed, broken here and there with lumps of corals. Sea anemones waved their arms like a stadium crowd, as little fish darted in between them, crowd-surfing for any morsels of goodness they could find.

A Robinson Crusoe moment in the Maldives

It took just 15 minutes to walk the entire circumference of Bandos. The facilities were certainly governmental by today's standards, but the island was gorgeous, so it really didn't matter. The modest, open-sided, thatched bar, its sandy floor set about with a few bamboo chairs and tables, served beer and a small selection of Indian brand spirits. These were extremely dodgy and most likely brewed up in the back room of a taxi company in Bombay, using ingredients pilfered from an embalmer. There was, however, nothing rough about the prices they charged, as we would discover on checking out. Being a Sharia state, alcohol consumption was only permitted for tourists, and the resorts imposed a massive mark-up on the roughest-of-rough hooch. We quickly discovered that the best way to consume embalming fluid was in a cocktail, so we ordered eight and found that after a couple, everything went numb and they tasted just fine.

Remarkably, when compared to today, there were only four other people staying on the island with us: Brian and his wife Jane, also from England, and John and Lizanne from Johannesburg. With the help of multiple cocktails, we all rapidly got to know each other and by the end of the evening, were new desert island best friends. We agreed that this was like being Robinson Crusoe, but with cocktails, and staggered happily off to bed.

There was absolutely nothing at all to do on the island, except drink, eat, lie around...

...And dive.

* * *

I had grown up on Jacques Cousteau documentaries, and one of my life's dreams was to explore the underwater world at the first opportunity. Hello, Bandos! Ready to facilitate this dream, was the Barrakuda Dive School, run by a ridiculously tanned German named Gunter, who lived in a pair of Speedos that were clearly two sizes too small for him. Gunter explained to me that he offered a five-day diving course, culminating in a license. The diving in the Maldives was then, as it remains now, the greatest diving in the world. It is so good that, in 2009, the cabinet ministers of the Maldives held an underwater meeting on global warming, making the Maldives the first country in the world to hold a government meeting beneath the sea. As sea levels rise globally, the Maldives are at risk of disappearing altogether. An entire nation could quite possibly vanish.

I was like an excited golden retriever at the prospect of learning to dive, but The Management made it clear she would rather be goosed by an orangutan, so evidently I would be doing it alone. The diving equipment back then was rudimentary, to say the least. A weight belt, regulator, and bare-bones tank with a little pull-chain, to activate the reserve, was accompanied by an oxygen gauge that looked as though it had been salvaged from a U-boat. There was no life vest. The joy of being on an island with only four other guests was that I often had one-on-one tuition. Occasionally there would be a small handful of guests ferried over from another nearby tourist island. After some cursory instruction, which involved splashing about in the shallows, we went and sat on the sand about six feet down, and Gunter showed me how to clear my mask, equalise pressure, buddy breathe, and a few other essentials. That was it. "*Sehr gut!* Off *ve go zen!*" he said. I followed him onto the dive boat, and we bobbed out to the edge of the reef. For the next week, twice a day, along with a few fellow divers from other islands, I learned to master my buoyancy, breathing, dive tables and hand signals. The rest of the time I was absorbed in a wonderland of colour, agog at the incredible underwater world that surrounded me. I had snorkelled extensively in the Mediterranean, but this was in an entirely different league. The myriad of shells scattered on the ocean floor were types I recognised only from books. Everywhere you looked there were tiny neon clownfish, wrasse, spectacular red lionfish, massive groupers and rays cruising around in a multi-coloured architectural universe of corals, anemones, grasses and sponge.

Of course, any environment as fascinating and visually exciting as this will contain several things that will murder you in cold blood. Lionfishes belong to the Scorpionfish family. Equipped with a large, striped pectoral and dorsal fins, they are noted for their venomous spines, which can produce painful holes in humans. They are very pretty indeed, and as one knows, pretty things can often be poisonous. Speaking of poisonous, Stonefish are the most venomous fish in the world and, like us, they enjoy hanging out in the Maldives. They are about the size and weight of one of those irritating small dogs that people carry around in their handbags or stuff under the seat next to you on an aircraft. Unlike those dogs, they are a master of camouflage, blending in so perfectly with their surroundings that they are all but invisible, ideal for ambushing prey – and happy, wading tourists. The dorsal fin of a stonefish has 13 spines, weaponised with venom that induces severe pain, paralysis, tissue necrosis and heart failure. Anti-venom may save you, but it would be wise not to count on it when on a beach in a remote archipelago in the middle of the Indian ocean. Amazingly, a stonefish can survive for as long as 24 hours outside the water. Quite why they would need this ability is a mystery, although it could come in handy if one were to be left high and dry by the outgoing tide. The Maldivian tourist board recommends that you "Do not touch or sit on them" – very sensible advice.

Despite being tiny and absolutely Pixar adorable, the Blue Ringed Octopus is world's most venomous marine animal. No bigger than a tennis ball, the Blue Ringed Octopus is found in tide pools and coral reefs in the Indian ocean and, as one might expect, when threatened, bright blue rings appear all over its body. It's venom – 1,000 times more powerful than cyanide – packs enough punch to kill 26 humans within minutes. This makes the effects of its bite catastrophic, but also causes one to wonder why on earth a tiny animal that primarily feeds on crabs, shrimp and small fish needs a venom quite as apocalyptically deadly as Tetrodotoxin? It just goes to show that evolution doesn't always get it right.[34]

So, what happens if one is bitten by a Blue Ringed Octopus? If you ever find yourself in the Maldives... you need to know.

First, the venom blocks nerve signals throughout the body, causing muscle numbness. Following symptoms would probably include

---

34 See "Paradise Lost".

nausea, blindness, loss of senses and loss of motor skills. Ultimately, it will cause muscle paralysis – including the muscles needed for humans to breathe, leading to respiratory arrest. Just to add a neat little zinger to all this – no, there is no known antidote, and throughout this entire process, you will probably be fully conscious.

Every dive was different. On my penultimate day, Gunter announced, "Today, ve are dyving mit ze sharks! Sehr gut, jah?" This sounded rather thrilling to me, but the Management muttered that having to identify my remains would cast an unacceptable pall over her holiday. Gunter briefed our small group on the etiquette of shark diving:

"Bitte, no sudden moofs, stay sehr calm, und still. We vill all sit in ze circle on ze bottom at about sirty feet. I vill zen chum[35] ze vater a bit to get ze sharks interested, and ve vill stay veeery still, und vatch. It vill be fun, ja!"

If a shark were to get slightly too interested in one of us, he assured us that we should just "bop him on ze nose". Gunter paused. "… qvite firmly," he added for emphasis, and gave a little demonstration.

The Bandos Dive School, preparing for a dive. Gunter in
the striped shirt, RWS in the striped shorts.

---

35 Chum: Cut up bits of fish, such as heads, tails and guts.

Armed with this reassuring information, we set off, and 45 minutes later found ourselves sitting in a circle on the sand as several black-tipped reef sharks patrolled in the distance. Gunter, in the centre of the circle, and about 12 feet above us, began releasing chum. This had roughly the same effect as standing in Piccadilly Circus and blasting £100 bills out of an air-cannon while shouting "Free Money!"

Not surprisingly, things escalated with astonishing speed. Within 20 seconds we had six or more sharks darting around Gunter, as he opened his bag and tipped all the chum out.

A red cloud erupted around him, and instantly, out of nowhere, another ten sharks arrived. At this point all hell broke loose. There were sharks everywhere, twisting, turning, snapping and darting about to seize the morsels of chum. As the heavier pieces sank downwards, they tumbled wider, thrown by the eddies created by the shark's powerful tails agitating the water. Sitting on the sand, our eyes on stalks, we realized that the chunks were coming rather close to us. Sharks were now darting between and around us, close enough to reach out and touch. At this point it was becoming rather hard to determine at which point we should *"Bop ze nose"*. Besides, being in a sort of shark blender makes one instantly forget almost everything except the fact that one might at any moment be lunch. Thankfully, they seemed able to distinguish between floating fish-meat and floating tourist. Then suddenly, as if the head shark had just made a secret signal to signify the end of the meal, the sharks all slowed and began to move away, receding into the now rose-tinted cloudy water around us.

As if that were not enough excitement for one day, that afternoon I went for my second dive – just Gunter and I alone this time. We had been pottering about at around 60 feet for some time and had come across a large Grouper. Handing me his bulky camera, Gunter indicated I should take a photo of him floating above the Grouper to give a sense of the size of this huge, docile fish. I did so, and he then signalled that I should do the same. Handing over the camera, I positioned myself directly above the Grouper. As I looked towards the camera and breathed out, I experienced the moment all diver's dread. As I went to breathe in again, there was nothing. For all 23 years of my life, I had done this breathing thing, and it had worked just fine. Now, suddenly, bugger all.

My tank had run out of air, and this was the correct but rudimentary early warning system. Instantly, I grabbed for the pull-chain and tugged on it to release the small amount of reserve oxygen. This would give me another five minutes of air with which to return to the surface. Nothing happened. I tugged again, frantically trying to release the essential gas. I looked at Gunter, he could see there was something wrong, and chopped my hand against my throat in the signal for "no air". He immediately came next to me, taking the regulator out of his own mouth and handing it to me, pointing upwards to indicate that we should buddy-breathe to the surface. This is absolutely standard procedure for divers in the event one runs out of air. You share one regulator, each taking a turn to breathe and passing the regulator back and forth as you slowly float to the surface. I had practiced it with Gunter on day one. The reality, however, is entirely different. Having gasped for air once, and felt the surge of panic, as soon as you have that regulator in your mouth every fibre of your being tells you not to let go of it. I breathed. It felt good. Gunter tugged gently on the regulator, indicating he needed me to let him take a breath. I shot him a glance that made it clear he would have to kill me first if he wanted it back. He tugged on it a little more forcibly. I just looked at him, breathing in again, as if to make the point. Finally, starting to feel hypoxia setting in, he yanked it away from me and stuck it in his mouth, breathing deeply. The next time he passed it to me, he was careful to hold on to it. So, we settled into a rhythm of sharing and breathing as we slowly rose upwards, until we finally reached the surface and broke water.

Finding myself some way from shore, it was evident we would have to swim in. "Vell, zat vas exciting, vasn't it!" said Gunter, with a big smile. "Ve must have a teensy problem vis zat tank. I vill fix!"

"That... huuuuuuuh... would be... huuuuuuuh... an excellent idea Gunter... huuuuuuuh..." I panted, sucking in the sweet air.

"OK, gut, vell, I vill see you later, ja? Ciao!" he replied and, much to my astonishment, disappeared beneath the surface again.

If you have ever tried to swim on the surface of the water wearing a lot of heavy equipment, and weights that are designed to help you stay beneath it, you will have discovered that it is exceedingly difficult. What allows you to swim effortlessly below, behaves like a murderous giant squid on the surface, trying to drag you down to the depths. I struggled to swim, putting more effort into staying afloat than into forward motion and, as I reached the shallows, also had to try and avoid an encounter with a Blue Ringed Octopus or Stonefish. It was some considerable time before I reached the shore, hauling myself, exhausted, out of the water and up onto the golden sands of the palm fringed beach. This was another Robinson Crusoe moment, I thought, as I lay on the beach, gasping.

"What *are* you doing?" came a voice from above me. Apparently, I had coincidentally chosen to beach myself like a floundering fish, on the sand directly in front of our cabin. The Management, having casually observed a scuba diver hauling himself out of the water on his belly, had entirely failed to recognise that this was in any way unusual, or that said diver could possibly be in need of help, or that he might in fact be her partner. Eventually, on making the connection between my swimming trunks and me, she was prompted to come down and see what I was up to, quite oblivious to my near-death experience. My muttering something about oxygen, buddy-breathing and almost drowning, did little to enlighten her.

"Well, take all that silly stuff off and come and have a shower, it's nearly time for cocktails," was all the sympathy I got.

A few days later, on checking out, I proudly received my certification from Gunter, and a bar bill that could easily have been mistaken for a mortgage payment. The barman, seeing my pain, immediately mixed me a quick sharpener, on the house.

Having since dived in Tahiti, Hawaii, the Bahamas and Mexico, I look back at my time in the Maldives with the realization that I had been thoroughly spoilt. None of them came even close to the extraordinary tropical island diving experience offered by this once-lost gem in the Indian Ocean.

So, was our week there worth it? Absolutely. We were incredibly fortunate to be able to experience the Maldives when it was still one of the last great, unspoiled tropical archipelagos in the world. It was a once in a lifetime experience, utterly brilliant, unforgettable, and probably the best value for money holiday I have had in my life. If I could go back in time, I would do it again in a heartbeat, but not now.

Since those days, the Maldives has changed beyond recognition. Widely considered the most exclusive holiday destination on the planet for honeymooners, sun worshippers, high-net-worth travellers, divers and the inevitable celebrities, the Maldives are the ultimate luxury getaway. Eighty islands now host private resorts. Overwater decks, personal plunge pools, retractable star-gazer roofs, private islands, airport transfers by private yacht, treehouses, over-water bars where you can gaze at marine life through a hole in the bar floor, and private underwater spa treatment rooms are just some of the luxuries on offer. Over-the-top luxury tends to attract the sort of Instagram influencers and superficial jetsetters I don't much care for, and offers a level of pampering I certainly don't need, at a price I would rather not pay.

I discovered on that trip that luxury isn't everything. Give me a beautiful island, some lobsters, a dodgy dive tank and embalming fluid on-tap, and I'm happy.

I'm just a Robinson Crusoe sort of guy.

INDIA

Knickerless on the
Night Train to Madras

You realise I have no knickers, don't you?" said the Management. Having mislaid several pairs in the Maldives, she was in the middle of a knicker crisis. From the Maldives, we had flown to Trivandrum, one of the southernmost cities in India, and were heading for Madras on our first train journey. She suspected the laundry ladies on Bandos Island might have taken a fancy to them, as every time she sent them to be washed, fewer reappeared. She was down to two pairs, and now found herself to be knickerless on the night train to Madras. She had, out of desperation, taken to sharing my abundant supply of boxer shorts. However, due to their design, she would emit a distressed squeak several times a day, when they ventured into places she would rather they didn't. She was looking forward to getting to a proper department store in Madras to restock with something more feminine and anatomically appropriate.

* * *

A milling mass of humanity had greeted us in the ticket hall of Trivandrum Station for the one daily train that would take us the 495 miles to Madras. It was a complete flustercluck, to put it mildly. The line for the ticket window was not so much a line as a mob, with people waiting, gesticulating, shouting, sitting, standing on one leg, cooking, praying, breast feeding, meditating, eating, arguing, spitting, sleeping, begging, stealing, hawking and smoking, to mention a few. The cacophony was punctuated by announcements over an ancient PA system that were entirely unintelligible. An elegant, sari-ed lady nearby repeatedly asked her husband, "What are they saying?"

"I am not knowing!" he replied each time, his head wobbling from side to side with exasperation.

It became increasingly clear we would probably die of old age before we got to the ticket window. I could see the Management was becoming agitated. Seeing our confusion and concern, a kindly gentleman tapped me on the shoulder.

"Please be excusing me, sir, but you can be going to the window for tourist. See, over there?"

"A window for tourists?"

"Yes please," he responded, his head dancing from left to right. "You are not needing to be waiting in this unruly crowd. Please be going there and they will be seeing to your ticketing most promptly." Indians can be so incredibly kind and thoughtful.

He turned to our porter, scolding him thoroughly for being a complete idiot.

With little to lose, we slowly elbowed our way through the crowd to a small ticket window at the end of the row. It was closed. There was no one standing in line, or behind it, nor did it look as if anyone had done so since the Partition of India. It did indeed have a small sign, in several languages, that read, "Tourist Servicings" in English. The Management cast me a quizzical look when a voice suddenly appeared out of thin air. "Greetings! Please be telling me how I may be helping you, sir?"

A tall, turbaned and unnervingly thin man with a huge smile had magically materialised behind the window. His beard must have been getting somewhat out of control, as it was clearly trying to escape from the upside-down hairnet in which he had attempted to contain it. He looked absolutely thrilled to see us and, Trivandrum not being a popular tourist destination at that time, had quite possibly been waiting for most of his career for this opportunity to serve a living, breathing tourist.

"We would like to buy two first class tickets for the Madras train, please," I asked, as he brushed some dust away and rearranged several official looking rubber stamps.

"Aha! Yes, that is very good indeed, but she is ticketing to be at most maximum capacity." His face dropped and a look of deep gloom momentarily swept his face. "But please not to be concerning yourself," he said, a beaming smile returning, "you must be seeing Station Master, Sahib. He will be servicing you personally. Please be coming with me!"

"I am just trying to digest the possible implications of being serviced by the Station Master," said the Management, wide-eyed. Seconds later, a man popped out of a side door, gesticulating wildly.

"Please be following me, Sahib!"

We fell in behind him, his arms windmilling like a rogue minesweeper as he charged through the mob, shouting at people to get out of his way. The crowds, faced with imminent assault, parted obligingly and we made unexpectedly rapid progress across the ticket hall. Ushering us through quite a grand doorway on the other side, a torrent of Tamil was directed at a secretary, who activated a switch on an antiquated intercom system to announce our arrival. The answer was incoherent to us, but apparently affirmative, as Sikh Fawlty ushered us through an ornate teak door, adorned with a sign that read Station Master in an unnecessarily elaborate font.

The Station Master was a small, rather portly man in a very smart uniform, who obviously took his job seriously. He sprang to his feet and held out his hand to greet us as if we were visiting royalty. Felicitations were exchanged and introductions made. "Please be seated, I am most honoured to be welcoming you at my station. Would you be enjoying me with a cup of tea?" We agreed. The secretary was called for and tea was ordered.

Getting down to business after some small talk, he established where we wanted to travel, explaining that on every train a few first class seats were reserved until the last minute for tourists or dignitaries. Most people made train reservations months in advance in India, so all trains were usually fully booked.

"Next time, please be going straight away to the Station Master and he will be accommodating you."

This was all suddenly extremely civilized, and I could hardly believe that minutes before we had been in the middle of a crowd that looked as if a jolly good tear-gassing was imminent. Here we now were, having risen to the lofty status of dignitary, sipping tea as guests of the Station Master. India is full of surprises like this. He continued chatting away as he filled out forms, juggled carbon paper, and stamped things aggressively, as if exterminating a dangerous spider.

After some more chat about where we were headed over the next few weeks, he finally handed us triplicate tickets.

"Please be coming with me, so I can be escorting you to the first class seatings." We followed him through a side door, directly onto the platform, where the long train stood, a grand old steam engine gently hissing at its front. A heaving throng of humanity was busy trying to get everything and the kitchen sink on board for the 20-something hour journey to Madras. He took us to the first class carriages, of which there were two, and right to our compartment, which he presented with a flourish.

"Here are your seatings! Please be having a most comfortable and enjoyable journey!"

We thanked him profusely and bade him goodbye, leaving him to issue instructions to the conductor as to our proper treatment. The Management stood and surveyed the compartment. Whatever proper treatment the Station Master had in mind, there were some immediate clues that the conductor and his imaginary staff were going to have some considerable difficulty delivering. We had wistfully imagined a colonial-era level of comfort, tastefully decorated with dhurries and elegant throw-cushions. But what lay before us was disappointing in the extreme. There were two long benches, covered in dark green vinyl. Above them were two more, secured flat against the wall, which would presumably drop down to form two upper bunk beds. On the ceiling were four ancient, crud-encrusted black desk fans, arranged upside down. This constituted the air conditioning. Protruding from the wall under the window, there was a small surface that valiantly attempted to be a table, but failed dismally. If this was first class, I shuddered to imagine third. The expression on her face suggested the Management was mentally calculating the effects of sitting, knickerless, on hot vinyl in 100-degree heat for eighteen hours. The steward explained, in a way that was designed to make you think for a moment that it was entirely satisfactory, that there was no dining car, but that food was available in the form of a thali[36] that could be pre-ordered from him before departure and would be picked up en route and delivered to us. We ordered one each and returned to our seats, wishing we had prepared ourselves better for this insanely long train journey.[37]

On the platform, the presence of a couple of Westerners on the train had been noted and a dozen excitable people ranging from age 6 to 108, noisily attempted to sell us a wide range of highly question-able food and unidentifiable liquids at vastly inflated prices. Some-time after our scheduled departure, the engine driver hung heavily on the whistle and, with a lot of mournful hooting, we slowly began to move. Our mobile grocery emporium frantically tried to keep pace along the platform, ever optimistic we would have a last-minute change of heart and buy a jackfruit. Eventually, the last determined contender teetered at the end of the platform, and we chuffed, rocked, and hooted away from the station.

The reason we had chosen to travel by train was because it afforded a spectacular look at this extraordinary country and sure enough, outside the window, India began to unveil itself in all its gritty, dirty, gorgeous, colourful magnificence. If you want to learn the secrets of a country – look out of the window when travelling by bus, taxi, or train. It is a habit I have developed over 40 years of travelling. One minute we were seeing the roads, traffic, and facades of buildings old and new; the next we were "behind the scenes", passing slums, riverbanks and belching factories. Men and women squatted to heed nature's call wherever they happened to be, even on busy streets. Sacred cows wandered where they pleased. Rubbish and fetid piles of stinking garbage were everywhere, jostling for space with industrial detritus and construction debris. The rambling suburbs gave way to countryside and workers toiling in the fields with hardly a tractor in

36 A thali is a round metal plate with a selection of different curries and rice. The only choice one has is whether it be vegetarian or meat.

37 With a smoked salmon sandwich, for instance. However, smoked salmon was not readily in India at the time.

sight. Buffalos harnessed to ploughs were the machinery of choice. I opened the window and soot-laden smoke blasted into in my face.

It was dusk as we pulled into the station at Madurai, the night just beginning to throw its cloak over the city. The arrival of any train in any station signalled the start of a frenzy of activity. In addition to the station staff and railway employees, an entire ecosystem of several hundred people – more in the larger stations – depended on the arrival of a train to eke out a meagre living. The wheels had barely stopped turning before a small crowd of vendors attached themselves to every window, offering fruits, drinks, parathas, uthappam, poori and the ever popular and highly portable samosa. Smartly turbaned Sikh porters waited keenly for the first class carriages to come to a halt, so they could offer their services to the better-heeled travellers. Several leprous beggars made their way down beside the train, tapping on the window and pointing out their particular combo of missing limbs, as if presenting their credentials. Embarking and disembarking passengers jostled their way around each other, the guard shouting instructions and ineffectively shoo-ing away the beggars. We wondered if we would acquire some traveling companions in our compartment, but the only thing that materialized was our thali. The Management regarded it with deep suspicion, prodding a fork into this and that, as if expecting to uncover something unpleasant. I was hungry enough to eat a badger, and tucked into mine with gusto, finding it perfectly palatable. There was some sort of meat curry (probably goat), rice, baingan bharta and okra, along with naan bread and raita. I wolfed mine down. The Management pushed hers over to me, saying that if I wanted to get a bad case of Delhi-belly, an Indian Railway thali was a good place to start. Besides, she wanted to avoid having to use the loo unless her very life depended on it. What's wrong with it? I asked.

"Plenty, I would imagine," she replied, "and I don't intend to find out."

After dinner we attempted to read our books, but it had been a long day and we quickly became sleepy. There followed a succession of stations through the night, every two hours or so. The activity was the same at each, so they blended into a routine that punctuated our fractured sleep like the clickety-clack of the wheels. In between, each overhead fan made a different dysfunctional noise to help ensure our sleep was further disrupted. One emitted a rhythmic *grrt-grrt-grrt-grrt* on each rotation of its blades. Another, once it had achieved a certain climactic velocity and frequency, shook violently every couple of minutes. The motor of the third buzzed angrily, as if it were about to explode and the last one did not work at all. Several times I got up and attempted to pry, twist, bend, smack and verbally abuse them into proper working order, all to no avail. Without them the air became so stiflingly hot that to have them on was marginally the lesser of two evils. What air they did move around was sooty and hot, with notes of burnt carbon-brush, so they afforded minimum comfort at maximum decibels.

The sprawling, rusty, dusty Indian Rail network, then one of the largest employers on the planet, is a defining legacy of British rule in India. On February 23, 1982, the year in which we travelled, Shri P. C. Sethi, Minister for Railways, had given a speech in the Indian Parliament introducing the budget for 1982-83. Among the key points he made was that during the year "600 coaches, 18,250 wagons and 550 locomotives are likely to be condemned." Interesting choice of words. Then, in a staggering contradiction of strategy, he stated: "It cannot be denied that increase in the number of passenger trains has not kept pace with the growth of passenger traffic."

Given the aforementioned condemnation of rolling stock, this came as no surprise to many in the audience. On the subject of punctuality, or lack thereof, he went on to say:

"Unauthorised stoppage of trains by alarm-chain pulling, failure of rolling stock and other equipment, either because of their being in poor fettle or on account of poor maintenance and accidents are some of the major factors affecting punctuality of passenger trains."

Yes, well those would definitely be major factors. To emphasize quite how upset he was about the astonishing mess over which he was presiding, he finished by declaring "I am quite exercised about it."

The next 12 hours were spent trying to pass the time as best we could. The Management shifted uncomfortably on the hot vinyl. There was, at least, an ever-changing panorama of Indian life outside the window. Sometimes it was interesting: the crops and farming methodology, irrigation techniques and ever-changing landscapes —sometimes spectacular: beautiful temples and grand views frequently revealing themselves before being lost again — occasionally sad: small children, dressed in little more than rags, playing in filthy rivers. Never was it dull. Another thali came and went. The Management again refused it, opting instead for a packet of biscuits purchased through the window of the train at one of the stations.

The loo was avoided until it became absolutely necessary for me to go. It was simply a hole in the floor, through which one could see the railway sleepers passing in a blur below. The amount of bodily fluids and excrement that had not found its way through the sizable hole — either by design, sudden movement of the train or sheer incompetence – was quite extraordinary. In fact, there were deposits in places that caused me to wonder how on earth they could possibly have been placed, catapulted, sprayed, or ejected there. The Management, who had wisely managed to limit her intake to almost nothing, shot me an "I told you so" look.

* * *

By the time we finally pulled into Madras station, some 18 hours after we had set off from Trivandrum, we were tired, dirty, amazed, and rather overwhelmed. Built in 1873, it is the busiest railway station in south India. But we hardly took a moment to marvel at the intricate cast-iron work with which the magnificent red and white station was constructed. For the first time in our lives, we were experiencing culture shock. The realisation that 729 million[38] people lived mostly in a way that we found quite shockingly basic, was proving surprisingly hard to become accustomed to. That most of them seemed to think this was perfectly fine, was more astonishing still. Dazed, we selected a porter and elbowed our way through the crowds, taking precautions to watch our pockets. In the milling throng outside, we somehow managed to locate a taxi and set off to our hotel. On the way, we stopped at a traffic light and a beggar with no legs scooted up beside us and tapped eagerly on the window. He had bravely built himself a rudimentary skateboard and, positioned on top of it, deftly carved his way in between the cars, tuk-tuks, sacred cows and other traffic, at constant risk to life and remaining limb.

One of the colonial-era rural stations at which we stopped.

There are theories that beggars are maimed at birth by their parents, to ensure them an income for life, or that children are deliberately

38 Population of India in 1982. By 2021 it had doubled, to hit 1.4 billion.

maimed by criminal gangs, who will then exploit the beggar for their income. While there is a likely a grain of truth in this belief, the vast majority of beggars are there because they have genuinely had the misfortune to lose limbs through accidents or disease. There are simply so many millions of people in India who find themselves hideously disadvantaged by caste, lack of education, industrial accident, family, home, shelter or job, that begging is the only option for them. Thousands arrive in cities like Bombay and Madras every day, and any lucrative begging location is beset by dozens of them. There is even a village called Kapadia Basti, in Kanpur, where the entire population of 4,000 have been surviving on alms for centuries and are unwilling to switch occupations. They pose as holy men in saffron robes and travel far and wide to lurk outside temples, earning enough, rupee by rupee, to have a comfortable life – by poor rural village standards.

Our plan was to travel by train but stay in a comfortable hotel at each destination. At that time in India, there were five-star hotels and then there were the rest, which mostly had no idea there was a connection between hotels and stars at all. There was pretty much nothing in between, and if there was, they were impossible to find in the absence of the Internet. The five-star hotels were inexpensive by western standards, and we felt the need for good clean conditions, laundry, and decent food in between the long, dirty, tiring train journeys. And so we arrived at the Taj Coromandel. The glass doors slid open, and we stepped from stifling humidity into the delicious frisson of air conditioning for the first time in two weeks. We spent the remains of the day soaking away the soot and sweat in a bubble bath and luxuriating in the coolness of our room.

The hotel concierge, always our go-to problem solver in any situation far from home, shuffled awkwardly from foot to foot as The Management button-holed him about her knicker crisis. Being male and Indian in 1982, he was ill prepared for questions related to ladies' undergarments, but the gist of his reply was:

A) There was no "department store" in Madras

B) No, he could not readily suggest a suitable place to buy ladies underwear

C) Could we please, please, oh please, keep our voices down?

Every time the word knickers was mentioned he convulsed as if he had been lightly electrocuted. After some sweat-inducing interrogation by The Management, it was obvious he would rather climb onto a funeral pyre and set alight to it himself, than ask such an intimate question of his female colleagues. His body language suggested that his day would be enormously improved if we were both instantaneously and permanently abducted by aliens. Seeing we were getting nowhere, the Management took matters into her own hands.

"We must go to the embassy immediately!" she announced.

"Why on earth would we do that?" I asked, somewhat taken aback by the sudden change of subject.

"Well," she explained, "they will know where I can buy knickers."

"They will?" I asked, incredulously.

"And anyway," she continued, "we should drop in, introduce ourselves to the Ambassador, have a cup of tea and let them know we are here, in India."

"Why?" I asked.

"In case we die."

Never one to be told things twice, despite remaining sceptical that we would be offered anything more than a handshake by a junior clerk, I hailed a tuk-tuk and we set off for the British High Commission, nursing the hope of a quick resolution to the knicker crisis. On the way, I reflected that there were indeed various unfortunate fates that could befall us, as we wandered off into the Indian sub-continent. Mugging, robbery, traffic accidents, incidents with elephants or tigers, hospitalisation or death sprang to mind. The Management was right – it was a sound idea to let the Embassy know we were here, although I wasn't sure they would care much.

In case you do not know, as I did not, embassies are diplomatic missions in non-Commonwealth countries. The head of the mission at an embassy is an Ambassador, but in major cities other than the capital there may be a consulate, headed by a consul-general, consul, vice-consul, or consular agent. High commissions are diplomatic missions in Commonwealth countries. The head of the mission at a high commission, is a high commissioner, and in major cities other than the capital there would be a deputy high commissioner. As well as referring to diplomatic missions, the terms "embassy" and "high commission" refer to the actual buildings themselves. So, in Madras, it turned out we would actually need to go to the deputy high commission (building) to see the deputy high commissioner (person). So now you know.

After 45 minutes, to my complete amazement, we were sitting on the veranda of the deputy high commission, having tea with the deputy high commissioner and his wife. It turned out that British citizens traveling to or through Madras rarely bothered to stop by the deputy high commission and introduce themselves. The fact that we had made the effort, and that there were no major diplomatic incidents in progress at the time, earned us a warm welcome, the best cup of tea of my life and a ginger biscuit. The gardens were lush, tropical, and immaculately tended; it was hard to imagine there was an insanely busy metropolis outside. The DHC and I discussed the Falklands conflict, my grandfather's diplomatic career and our onward travel plans. The Management grilled his wife on the local availability of ladies' underwear. She explained that in India, lady's underwear was known as "unmentionables", so the purchase of them was not as straightforward as we had come to expect in the west. The local selection, she warned, would be extremely limited – she had brought all hers from the UK. She suggested a couple of possible shops and we departed soon after, hopeful the knicker nonsense would soon be resolved.

Never one to put off until tomorrow what can be done today – especially when it comes to underwear – the Management flagged down a tuk-tuk and we quickly found ourselves at the foremost purveyor of lady's undergarments in Madras. In a large room, there were several rows of tables, upon which were dozens of large, shallow boxes, each containing different types and sizes of undergarment.

Numerous Indian ladies scuffled hopefully in the boxes looking for what pleased and fitted them, casting me ferocious glances that made it clear I was not even slightly welcome. The Management joined in with gusto, busying herself optimistically. Every time I tried to leave and wait outside, there was a flurry of gesticulation, indicating I should stay right there. So, I stood by the door, the only man in the room, as she occasionally held something up for me to see. The expression on her face became increasingly desperate, and the other shoppers looked increasingly apoplectic at my presence. It appeared that Indian ladies were more used to granny pants than the trendy knickers of the west. They were large, drab in colour, unflattering and Victorian, designed to cover, conceal and render the lady parts as inaccessible as Fort Knox to all except the wearer.

"I think these knickers are an abomination. I could never possibly wear them."

"No, they really aren't your style at all."

"They are unsuitable, unattractive and, frankly, bloody unhealthy in all this heat and humidity."

"Maybe you should just go commando for the rest of the trip," I said, hopefully.

"Don't be ridiculous; if I can't buy them, I will just have to have some made."

"Made?"

"Well, of course. If you can have shirts or a jacket made in 24 hours, there must be some lovely ladies somewhere who can knock off a dozen pairs of lookalike Marks & Sparks[39] knickers."

I had to agree that made perfect sense, and resigned myself to the fact that I would soon know everything there was to know about the design, materials, and optional features of bespoke ladies' lingerie in India. For The Management, getting knickers made in Madras would likely be a breeze. She would almost certainly start by asking the concierge.

---

39 Slang for Marks & Spencer's, a British department store.

INDIA

A Maharajah, a Dog, a Rat and a Tiger

A cacophony of screaming and barking suddenly erupted, drowning out all cocktail conversation. Leaping to my feet, I ran down the corridor as fast as I could, immediately assuming the Management was being attacked by the dog called Binty. I arrived to find her standing outside the loo, tucking her shirt into her skirt in a manner that suggested *lavatoria interruptus*. The screaming had stopped, but the barking continued with renewed vigour, from inside the loo.

"There's a bloody rat on top of the cistern!" she panted, pointing to the loo, as Binty barked apoplectically.

* * *

Let's digress a little…

It was 1982, and, having travelled by train from Madras to Bangalore, Mysore, Goa, through Rajasthan to Jaipur and Udaipur, we had arrived in New Delhi. The night before departing to the Kashmiri capital, Srinagar, we had been invited for dinner by the Maharajah of Jind, to whom we had been introduced by a friend. Since she was now equipped with an abundant supply of bespoke knickers, made by a seamstress in Madras, the Management could accept such invitations with confidence.

In 1911, the British Government of India, in its infinite wisdom, decided that Calcutta was a bit of a mess, and so they moved the country's administrative capital from Calcutta to Delhi. Since the construction of a new city is quite a large, prestigious job, one would imagine it would be awarded to either the most famous architect of the day, or some high-ranking official's brother-in-law. In the event, the job was handed to a man called Edwin Lutyens, a largely unknown, self-taught genius who had built a few houses around southern England, albeit jolly nice ones.

It turned out to be an excellent choice. The foundation stone of the city was laid by Emperor George V during the Delhi Durbar of 1911 and, after 30,000 workers had toiled for 20 years a beautiful city emerged. The new capital was inaugurated on February 13, 1931, by Viceroy and Governor General of India, Lord Irwin. Built on a radial plan, similar to Paris and Washington D.C., New Delhi was graced with grand avenues, elegant monuments, cool fountains and tree-lined residential areas. It was a magnificent celebration of British colonialism, which delighted the majority but annoyed a few, most notably Nehru, who thought it "a visible symbol of British power, with all its ostentation and wasteful extravagance". Nevertheless, much of India thought it was a great improvement on Calcutta and wanted to live there.

During the twentieth century, in England, a bungalow described a very modest abode. Designed to have only one level and usually smaller and less expensive to build, they were largely occupied by those who were elderly or on lower incomes. Originally, the word bungalow described a type of thatched hut, lived in by Bengali farmers in India and sometimes surrounded by a wide veranda. But under Lutyens and the British, there came a notable change to the concept of the bungalow. They altered the style dramatically and built what they called bungalows all over British India. The grand residential area of New Delhi, designed by Lutyens as part of his vision of the city, became known as the Lutyens Bungalow Zone, or LBZ. It was a 2,800-hectare area designed to house government officials and their administrative offices. But the bungalows of the LBZ were very different to the British version. A typical street in the LBZ was Kasturba Gandhi Marg, lined with expansive lots featuring white, double storey, bow-fronted houses with tall pillars, porticoes, and colonnades, surrounded by well-tended lawns. These "bungalows" exuded colonial grandeur.

In the years since the glory days of the Maharajahs, Indian society had undergone monumental changes, and this particular Maharajah now went by the name of Robin Jind and had a day job as a presenter on local television news. A charming and generous man of impeccable lineage, his family's fortunes had taken a precipitous dive after the Partition of India. He and his wife were apparently separated, possibly even divorced, but they lived with their children on different sides of the same enormous two-storey bungalow, so it was hard to tell. This rather eccentric arrangement was required by financial circumstance, but they all seemed perfectly happy with it.

Their bungalow, like most on the street, was in a state of some disrepair and needed considerably more than a lick of paint. An American would have called it a "fixer-upper. This is only one notch above "a tear-down", which involves bulldozers. Indeed, in the coming years, many of these grand colonial townhouses would be mercilessly bulldozed to make way for high-rises and office buildings. For now, they sat, paint peeling and mildewed, looking rather sad and neglected.

None of this seemed to be getting Robin down or, if it did, he didn't show it. We arrived and were warmly welcomed into a large drawing room, filled with what appeared to be the contents of several palaces, and patrolled by a hyperactive dachshund named Binty. Large sofas were flanked by ornate end-tables laden with silver urns,[40] marble cigarette boxes inlaid with semi-precious stones, and a plethora of things in need of a vigorous polish. Old black and white family photographs in silver frames stared out from every surface, an enduring record of tiger hunts, durbahs, weddings, processions, and other memorable events from decades long past, competing for attention with elaborate statuary and vases. The walls, congested with portraits of formally dressed and turbaned male ancestors, were also home to several medieval weapons of intimidating ferocity and pointy-ness. At one and of the room hung a massive tapestry depicting a glorious victory in battle, which seemed to involve a lot of people suffering a violent death by either elephant or the aforementioned pointy things. At the other end, a massive tiger pelt was spread-eagled on the wall, its head almost up at the ceiling, jaws agape as though leaping skyward to catch its prey.

Robin took us into the perfectly 1950s blue Formica kitchen to serve drinks. In startling contrast to the rest of the house and

---

40 Possibly containing the remains of family members or pets.

contents, it was in mint condition and looked as if it had never been used. The reason quickly became clear, as Robin opened the door to the central courtyard and began talking to someone outside. As we moved closer, we saw there were several people out there, working over and around an open fire in what looked like a camp kitchen, lit with hurricane lamps.

"What are they doing Robin?" I asked.

"They are cooking dinner," he replied. Anticipating my next question, he added, "they never particularly liked the kitchen and have always preferred to cook outside. It's just the way they do things in India." Thus, the kitchen had remained largely unused.

We returned to the drawing room and sat, surrounded by all this erstwhile opulence, and chatted over drinks about life, politics, the Falklands crisis and his family.

In 1947, the princely states of India had comprised 40% of India and 23% of its population, as vassal states under a regional ruler, in an alliance with the British Raj. Unsurprisingly, the arrangement had been designed by the British to benefit themselves the most, allowing them to poke about in the internal affairs of individual states and issue annoying proclamations when necessary.[41]

At the time of the British withdrawal, there were 565 princely states, the most important of which were Hyderabad, Mysore and Travancore in the south followed by Jammu and Kashmir in the north, Sikkim in the Himalaya, and Indore in Central India. The rulers of the most important ones had been entitled to a twenty-one-gun salute on ceremonial occasions. The less important ones had been allowed fewer guns. There is something rather obscene about one's importance being measured by the number of guns fired in your salute. How ridiculous would it be if this continued today?

The era of the princely states came to a screeching halt with Indian independence in 1947, when they were summarily integrated with

---

41 The Indian Motor Vehicles Act 1914 required all vehicle inspectors to have freshly brushed teeth.

India. Things went downhill from there: in 1949 their powers to rule were removed and the Maharajahs were given a Privy Purse by way of a pension. The Privy Purse was then abolished in 1971 and, after a two-year legal skirmish which the Maharajahs predictably lost, all privileges and allowances from the Government had ceased to exist by 1973. The last remaining vestige of their once lofty status and wealth was that, according to the hereditary convention of succession, the eldest son of the successive generations continued to claim the title of Maharajah.

* * *

Although undaunted by pretty much anything life throws at her, and despite having enjoyed a couple of gin and tonics, The Management has a very short fuse when it comes to rodents of any kind. To have one invading her space at such a private moment was certain to cause considerable distress. I calmed her down and we left Binty to take care of the rat. On returning to the drawing room, flushed with adrenalin, she related the intrusion to Robin. Apparently, hearing some scuffling above her, she had looked up to see a small, pointy, be-whiskered, brown face and a couple of beady eyes looking back down at her. Robin chuckled, replying that such an incident was quite normal. The rats, he explained, came and went pretty much as houseguests do, and it was not considered especially alarming. I could tell The Management found this cavalier approach to the local *Rattus-rattus* population quite shocking, but she bit her lip and smiled sweetly at him in a way that satisfied politesse but left her real opinion obvious.

A few more minutes passed, and conversation had begun to return to normal, when there was another outbreak of barking. To our complete amazement, the rat (or quite possibly a different rat) streaked into the drawing room, pursued by a snarling Binty, his eyes ablaze and little feet a blur. The rat headed straight under the coffee table, became airborne as it emerged, and landed on the tail of the tiger pelt which hung about three feet off the ground. In a move that seemed quite well practiced, it scuttled up the tail as if it were a rope and disappeared up and under the pelt. Binty tried unsuccessfully to emulate this feat. A slight undulating bulge gave away the position of the rodent as it moved rapidly up the pelt towards the head as the dog, apoplectic with equal amounts of excitement, rage, and bloodlust, made futile run-ups at the tiger in an attempt at continued pursuit.

We sat, open mouthed with astonishment. Robin found this highly amusing. "Oh, very good indeed Binty! What a very good fellow you are!" he said, grasping Binty's collar and pulling him onto his knee to calm him as if he had just retrieved a ball. He then turned to us, continuing the conversation where he had left off, as if nothing untoward had just taken place, and with no apparent further concern for either the rat now lurking within the tiger, or the incandescently barking dog on his knee. The Management did not share his relaxed attitude to the uninvited dinner guest, looking between me and the tiger with a wild-eyed expression that implied I should do something immediately to resolve the situation. I shrugged in reply, careful to employ a complex brow-semaphore and eyeball-rotation technique which roughly translated meant: "If you think I am about to climb up under that tiger and somehow deal with the rat you are mistaken. And, if I did, it would most likely come sailing right out of said tiger, straight up your skirt, so let's just move on and pretend it isn't there."

Dinner went ahead. punctuated by outbreaks of enthusiastic barking, occasional strategic movements by the rat, and a lot of flinching from the Management. By that point, she thought she was seeing rats everywhere and had a very hard time getting through her chicken jalfrezi. It must be said that I rather enjoyed this unusual evening, and it remains one of the highlights of our trip, a shining example of old-world Indian eccentricity, hospitality and a carefree attitude to the ever-present rodents of New Delhi.

Somewhere in India, 1982.

Today, the few remaining Lutyens Bungalows command eye-watering prices. *The New York Times* called them "real estate Rolexes", and, among New Delhi's social elite, they are the ultimate status symbol. Most are government owned, as almost every privately owned Lutyens bungalow was demolished between 1980 and 2000. The Central Public Works Division has now decided that the bungalows have "gone beyond their lifespan", "are unsafe" and "should be demolished". The idea is to replace them with modern high-rises, and the developers are lining up to get a share of the lucrative contracts. When this inevitably happens, a true gem of Delhi's colonial era will have been lost forever, along with a lot of rats.

INDIA

Himalaya, Hiking
and Hashish

Someone had told us that the best way to get from New Delhi to Srinagar, in Kashmir, was by bus. I had serious doubts about this information. Almost every day in India there is a bus crash somewhere. In the state of Bangalore alone, approximately 120 buses are involved in fatal collisions each year. The Management and I used to call it "the bus crash of the day," and it was usually reported in a small area on the front page of the *Times of India*, detailing the number of injuries or deaths, the approximate location and, occasionally, the cause. "Falling into a river", "intoxication" and "running in poor condition" were popular ones. Almost every day the last line was the same, saying "…and the driver was absconding". Having read so many horror stories about the accidents, the buses themselves, the mountain roads, the passengers, the drivers, and the sort of journeys that made one's blood run cold, we decided that we would rather have our ears nibbled by a hyena than take the bus. Therefore, on leaving New Delhi and heading north, the best way for us to get to the foothills of the Himalaya, was clearly by plane.

* * *

Between 1846 and 1849, the British fought two campaigns against the Sikhs and won them both, demanding considerable spoils. There probably ensued a frank and meaningful conversation:

British General: "We have won fair and square, and as such we demand considerable spoils, so cough up."
Sikh General: "Spoils? Hmmm… exactly what sort of spoils did you have in mind?"
British General: "Well, we thought money would be nice, and rather a lot of it please."
Sikh General: "Aha, I see. Well hang on a moment while I have a quick chat with Ranbir over here, the Chancellor of the Sikh Exchequer." (*Whispering aside*)
Sikh General: "Hey, Ranbir, how are we for cash at the moment?

Ranbir: "Well, it's all pretty grim to be frank, these campaigns were pricey in more ways than one. There was the food, the weapons we bought from that dodgy Turkish arms dealer, and then the…"

Sikh General: "OK, I get the picture, so how much have we got?

Ranbir: "Well, I could probably rustle-up a couple of hundred quid. Would that do?"

Sikh General: "I strongly doubt it. What else have we got?

Ranbir: "Well, there's Kashmir, which costs us an arm and a leg to run – and that place is going to be nothing but trouble, mark my words – so how about we offload it to the Brits?

Sikh General: "Brilliant, Ranbir! They can never resist an opportunity to plant another damn flag! Also, they will love the lake and all those mountains because it's too bloody damn hot for them in the lowlands, where they burn like babies in a Tandoor.

Ranbir: "Indeed, General, and it will also annoy the hell out of that bloody Hindu Raja of Ladakh and Jammu next door. He is a right pain in the arse.

Sikh General (to British General): "Well, General, I have had a word with Ranbir, and we can offer you the entire State of Kashmir, with its cool lake and picturesque mountains, where you can spend the hot summers in great and opulent comfort without the need for Punkah-wallahs.[42] How about that?

British General: "Terrific, we'll take it! Carruthers, get another flag ready, there's a good chap."

The British (who as we all know, didn't play well with others in colonial matters) accepted, knowing full well that the Hindu Raja who ruled neighbouring Ladakh and Jammu was itching to add Kashmir to his real estate portfolio. They promptly flipped it to him for a paltry £80,000, in a move clearly designed to annoy the hell out of the Sikhs. The Raja, on the other hand, could hardly believe his luck,

---

42 *Punkah-Wallah* (India/Pakistan) A punkah was a manual fan, sometimes ceiling mounted. The Wallah was the servant whose job it was to work it.

and welcomed the British with open arms, setting aside a couple of shady gardens near Srinagar for them to camp in while escaping the hot summer months on the plains. Before long, as is the British way, someone said, "I say, chaps, I think it would be a very fine thing if we built a club for ourselves."

And, so, a British club was built, and a British library, a British bank (in comforting mock Tudor style), and a very grand house for the British Resident, who was appointed by the British to generally keep an eye on things and pull the reins in the background.

It was, one must remember, rather difficult to pop back home to "Blighty" for a holiday at the time.[43] After it was opened in 1859, the Suez Canal played an important role in trade between India and Great Britain, reducing the travel time from more than six months via the Cape of Good Hope, to roughly nine weeks. Even so, going there and back with enough time to spend a few weekends in the country, visit your tailor in Savile Row, attend your cousin's wedding and pick up a supply of fruit cakes and knickers, would necessarily take the best part of six months. Thus, whatever the reason for your visit, it was unlikely to be a short stay.

So, the British came in droves to Kashmir, which was renowned for its hunting, shooting, fishing and cool weather, and before long it became increasingly tricky to find somewhere suitable to stay. In fact, so popular did Kashmir become with the British, that the Raja's government felt it necessary to impose some rules, one of which forbade them from buying land.

As a result, the first houseboat was built around 1885 by a Kashmiri shop-owner named Narain Das. He had suffered a fire in his shop, forcing him to temporarily move it onto a boat, which he moored in

---

43 The word Blighty is an affectionate nickname for England. Rupert Graves, the British poet and classicist, claimed that it was derived from the Hindustani word *blitey*, meaning home. It emerged during the Victorian rule of India and was first used in the Boer War in Africa, before becoming a permanent part of the vernacular in the muddy trenches of Western Europe during the First World War.

a convenient spot. With some improvements, including living quarters, his floating shop became the first "houseboat". Das specialized in supplying the British tourists with food from their motherland, such as ham, soda water, Patum Peperium,[44] capers, tea, beer, gin, biscuits and more. His customers were loyal, and very fond of these treats from home, so business continued uninterrupted. Little did Narain know that he was the inventor of the first of thousands of "British shops" that can now be found in cities all over the world, catering for the marmalade, Marmite, Jaffa-Cake, baked-bean and commemorative Royal baby chinaware needs of ex-pats. It turned out that wasn't to be his only claim to fame.

Along came a hunter called M.T. Kennard, who wanted to spend the winter in Kashmir. It was too cold to camp, and he had trouble finding a suitable house to rent, so on seeing Narain Das's floating shop he was inspired to create his own, much more luxurious houseboat. He employed the best local craftsmen to convert a boat to a much higher level of comfort and spiffiness than the locals had previously found necessary, and the British community were duly impressed. Narain Das cleverly saw the potential of Kennard's idea. He turned to the Hanji community of Srinagar, who lived on and built small boats, and started commissioning them to build spiffy houseboats for the English visitors. By 1906 there were hundreds of houseboats on Dal and Nageen Lakes. They became the fashionable place to stay and were given a range of inspiring names like *Savoy* and *Buckingham Palace*, to remind their guests of home and convey a sense of expansive luxury they would certainly not deliver; one must admire their marketing expertise.

There were parties, a lot of gin, some canoodling, croquet, quite a bit of philandering, and inevitably a sprinkling of scandal here and there. The British ladies would promenade, as they were wont to do,

---

44 An anchovy paste also known as Gentleman's Relish that the British are very fond of, created in 1828. It has a strong, salty and slightly fishy taste. The secret recipe is known by only one employee at Elsenham Quality Foods, who manufacture it.

and discuss all of the above at length, especially the philandering. In 1904, writer Margaret Morrison described an evening in Srinagar, under the trees by the club:

> "People stood in groups chatting, while the glow died away westward in the sky; small boats crowded the steps, waiting to take home their owners, people called to their servants to carry the books they had chosen from the library, the dogs got in everyone's way... Then each stepped into his canoe, goodnights were called, and, to the splash of paddles, each one was speeded to his boat or bungalow.'

* * *

The short flight to Srinagar afforded us spectacular views of the Himalaya, without the high risk of death associated with bus travel, and we were glued to our window for most of the last part of the flight. In 1982, due to the continuing umbrage between India and Pakistan, Srinagar airport was, as it still is, a large military base and airfield, at which some commercial flights are allowed to land. This is all rather intimidating as there are many more guns than smiles. Outside the airport the usual flash-mob of taxi and tuk-tuk drivers loudly and aggressively competed for the attention of arriving passengers with all the charm of a swarm of hornets. The Management, now quite used to this assault, skilfully navigated the throng, until she found someone who met with her approval. Issuing some instructions, we piled in and made our escape. These moments of arrival or departure at Indian airports and train stations always made me feel as if I was being slowly squeezed by a boa constrictor. You never quite knew what was or wasn't going to happen, if you were going to be relieved of some of your belongings, or indeed quite where you were going to end up; that apprehension was ever present.

Hooting and swerving our way to the waterside, we arrived to find rows of pointy-nosed shikaras waiting for their guests. Shikaras are the workhorse of Dal Lake and as synonymous with Srinagar as gondolas are with Venice. They are used as taxis, goods transport, floating shops, and a vehicle for every sort of water-borne service or commodity you could ever need. If you want to buy flowers or a banana, pick up some Tide, have your rubbish disposed of, your laundry done, a dead body removed, or your fortune told – there's a shikara for that. One could think of them as the "Apps" of Dal Lake. The single wooden oar used to propel them is, for some extraordinary reason, made in Indiana, USA, but no one seems to know why this is. Each shikara now lined up at the dock was about 15 feet long, and was bedecked with ornate carving, enthusiastically tasselled shade-curtains, vibrantly colourful cushions, and a sign proudly displaying the name of the houseboat with which it was affiliated. It rather looked as if each had been decorated with the assistance of some fine Kashmiri hashish.

We had been given the name of a particular houseboat, the *Sukoon*, which means "peace of mind" and, on finding its namesake shikara, there was an explosion of earnest welcoming activity. This seemed to be fuelled by the belief that if everything was done in the manner of an emergency evacuation, but with more congeniality, it would instil confidence in the guests that they had sensibly put their trust in a very fine establishment indeed. Our bags transferred, the driver tipped, and all introductions and pleasantries completed, we cast off into another world, my boa-constrictor vanishing as rapidly as it had arrived some hours before. Drifting along at a serene, calming pace, the tightness and apprehension of our travel evaporated with every splosh of the oar, as we gazed in wonder at this spectacular lake, peacefully embraced by the silently rising majesty of the snow-capped Himalaya.

The houseboats named *Savoy* and *Buckingham Palace* were still there, at least in name, moored among the water lilies and lotus. As hotels are rated with stars, so Dal Lake houseboats are also rated, but on a scale that starts with "deluxe", and then plummets through grades A to D in the same way an out-of-control lift might, and with much the same amount of screaming. In 1982, deluxe roughly equated to "OK, in a funky sort of way". A genuine attempt had been made to create all the comfort, opulence and service one might expect at Blenheim Palace; but the reality fell somewhat short of the intended mark. Despite the abundance of tassels, velveteen, and intricately carved wood, the layout of the sitting room felt overly formal. The greeting was warm and friendly, with a lot of bowing and smiling to reflect the genuinely sincere pleasure that you had graced the host family with your presence, but the electric socket in the bedroom had been installed with no regards to building codes whatsoever, if indeed any existed. The fear of electrocution was enhanced by the noticeable proximity to water and the slightly damp, musty smell in the air. The tomato soup we were served as a first course for dinner was definitely tinned, but with the unmistakable aftertaste of soap. The curry was of course delicious, and it was served with grace and efficiency, with the whole family pitching in.

Houseboats on Dal Lake, Kashmir.

The next couple of days were spent relaxing and exploring the lake in a Shikara. Drifting among the water lilies, we visited the floating market, which sold everything you would expect in an Indian market, except from a Shikara. There were dozens of boats, bobbing about together in a predetermined spot, as the owners chatted with friends and waited for a customer to drift up. One might be laden with tomatoes and onions, another with okra, cucumber, and eggplant. There were colourful spice boats, household goods boats, and an even a goat boat, with attendant flies, that made me momentarily wonder about becoming a vegetarian. Away from this floating hustle and bustle, there was peace and calm in abundance. I love being on water, in any form or fashion; it immediately imbues me with peace and the sense of separation from the land, freeing me from all the stress and worry of daily life. Occasionally this peace would be disturbed by another shikara arriving alongside uninvited, trying to persuade you to have your photo taken, sell you hashish or tell your fortune. We could only admire their limitless spirit of enterprise.

* * *

Before long, the mountains beckoned to us from the veranda on the Sukoon, and we were assured that a trip up to the mountain ski resort of Gulmarg would be an excellent way to spend a couple of days. We said goodbye to our hosts and drove along mostly straight roads, lined with an avenue of tall trees that went on for miles. Gulmarg means "meadow of flowers" and the small hill resort about thirty miles southwest of Srinagar is exactly as the name suggests, especially in spring. Known as the Switzerland of India, at about 9,000 feet, it is India's best known ski resort, and also the highest golf course in the world. Now I am not a golfer, but apparently the ball flies at least 10% farther at high altitudes, which my rudimentary physics suggests would be the case because the air is less dense, so there is less friction to slow the ball's forward motion. I gather this adds a level of complexity to the game that even experts find quite confounding, as if the game itself wasn't confounding enough already. The greens had several people on them, all of whom looked as if they were fairly cross. The ski-lifts stood stark and silent against the green valley and towering mountains of the Pir Panjal Range of the western Himalaya that embrace it. The meadow was a riot of bluebells, daisies and buttercups as we wound up the road to a promontory jutting into its centre. Here sat the Highlands Park Hotel, surrounded by eight acres of gardens and with the most breath-taking view of the Himalaya one could imagine.

Presidents, prime ministers, royalty and Bollywood stars have all enjoyed the hospitality and charm of this small and unique hotel. One modest central building contains the main reception, lounge and restaurant, surrounded by eight separate cottages that house an assortment of rooms and suites. The hotel walls are adorned with golfing paraphernalia, animal skins and traditional Kashmiri hangings. Rooms are heated using traditional wood-fired Bukharis instead of a central heating system and the ceilings are of pressed metal. The family run hotel was built in 1965 for Indira Gandhi's trips to Kashmir. I find this a novel way for a head of state to travel.

"Mr. Bannerjee."

"Yes, Prime Minister?"

"I wish to be visiting Kashmir this year, please arrange for the building of a hotel in a suitably magnificent location in which I might stay... and possibly meditate. That will be all."

"Certainly, right away, Prime Minister."

The hotel's claim to fame is that a number of Rishi Kapoor movies were filmed there, including one called *Bobby*, the premise of which involves Bobby making astoundingly inappropriate advances to a schoolgirl in a short skirt, while singing constantly. In the highly improbable event an Indian friend ever mentions the film in conversation, you can say "Ha! Of course! Do you remember the lengthy but popular song, 'Hum Tum Ek Kamre Mein Band Ho?'" You may add, for considerable impact, "Did you know the film was shot in and around the Highlands Park hotel in Gulmarg in 1973". Your friend will be rendered speechless by your extraordinary knowledge of Indian cinema. The title "Hum Tum Ek Kamre Mein Band Ho?" means "If you and I were locked in a room" and the song involves Bobby and the schoolgirl circling suggestively around a bedroom, leaving the audience in little doubt as to what they would really like to be doing to each other, were the Indian film censors not watching. Transitioning outside, the chase continues on horseback, before the seasons suddenly and inexplicably change from summer to deepest winter and they roll suggestively in the snow before returning to the bedroom. Give it a Google. It's fascinating.

Alpather Lake, known locally as Frozen Lake, is located deep in the back-country high above Gulmarg, and remains completely frozen until mid-June. The lake lies at about 12,000 feet, at the foot of the twin Apharwat peaks. We discovered it was possible to take the one-day 13km trip on horseback, leaving at dawn and returning early evening. In fact, there was no other way to get there. We met our guides at dawn and set off up a rough track, on two long-suffering but sure-footed ponies, led on foot by our guides. As we climbed steadily upwards, the track wound alternately across stunning flower meadows, alive with bees, and through fragrant pine woods. Gradually the trees began to thin and eventually disappear as we passed through the tree line. After that, there was only grassy meadow for a few hundred vertical feet, before the grass gave way to rocks and low, scrubby bushes, and the path became only barely visible. Our guides' choice of footwear was extraordinary; each wore nothing more than a pair of flip-flops. Despite this, they never once stubbed their toe or missed a step and were as sure-footed as the horses themselves.

Our guide and pony, with flip-flops as chosen hiking gear.

At the snowline, beside the trail, we came across a small open-fronted shelter and a couple of horses grazing nearby. Made of a few sticks and a tarpaulin, held down with rocks and pieces of muddy grass, it appeared to have been set up entirely for our benefit. Two men squatted inside, cooking as they chatted over an open fire. We were introduced to Amit and Kasan, who beamed toothlessly at us, and there ensued a lot of animated greetings between them and our guides. It had become clear that we were the only people on the trail today. No others had set out with us, nor could we see any behind us. I assumed our guide had called his cousin the night before and said "Tourists tomorrow, Amit! At 9 o'clock, fire up shack number two – we're in business!" The horses grazed on the scrubby grass and snorted at each other as we squatted in the shack and, for a few rupees, ate a quite passable breakfast of omelette and Lavasa bread with hot black tea. As we ate, we gazed out, down a scree-covered slope, over the forests and meadows far below to Gulmarg and the mountains in the near distance behind. A pair of Griffon vultures circled on massive wings in the distance. It was spectacular, in its utterly silent, soaring majesty and we felt incredibly lucky to be able to see it this way.

Stopping for breakfast, on the way up to the Frozen Lake, 1982.

Remounting the protesting horses with our stomachs full, we continued upwards for some time through patchy snow and rocky scree, before reaching the peak. We paused to take in the view; there before us lay the Frozen Lake, shimmering sapphire blue and surrounded by virgin snow. Small flecks of ice floated in the water, making it glisten like a blue translucent Slushy. Leaving the guides, we scrambled over boulders, down to the shoreline and, cupping our hands, we scooped up handfuls of pristine, icy water. We sipped, our hands numb; it was probably the cleanest water I would ever drink, free from the pollution far below. We sat for a while, entirely alone, soaking up the beauty of this remote and beautiful place, the clarity of the water and the majesty of the mountains all about us.

That evening, back in the bar of the Highlands Hotel, I was enjoying a scotch and admiring the view while I waited for the Management to join me, having made herself sufficiently presentable for dinner together in an almost empty hotel. It turns out that this takes some considerable time, as it is almost the same level of preparedness as required for dinner at the White House. The bar had been empty for some time when I heard the sounds of people entering the other end, and drinks being ordered. They sounded British, so I glanced over in their direction. The man's face, which I only partially saw, seemed familiar. I turned away, processing the image in my mind and trying to compare it with all the people I knew, but couldn't quite make a match. I shifted on my chair to afford myself a slightly better view. He turned momentarily to look down the bar and, suddenly, I had it. It was John, someone who was not in my immediate circle, but who I knew by acquaintance reasonably well. I got up and walked over. We were both astonished to find ourselves here, in the same small hotel in one of the most remote places on the Indian sub-continent.

It turned out that he and his bride were on their honeymoon, and had just arrived here from Jaipur, where she had had a close call with an unsavoury mob who had surrounded her when she had wandered a short distance away from John to take a photograph. As in any country, they are many wonderful, kind and gentle people in India, but there are also some sketchy ones. Incidents like this remind us all to always to be on the lookout when traveling because there are people out there who will part us from our money, belongings and dignity in less time than it takes a crocodile to snap its jaws shut, and with about the same lack of emotion.

We had a wonderful dinner, both amazed at what a small world it is, and afterwards sat outside smoking a little hashish while watching the sun set on the Himalaya. As is the way with hashish, we got into a conversation about the etymology of Himalayas versus Himalaya that involved a lot of giggling and only a small amount of logic. As Arpanet[45] would not adopt TCP/IP[46] for another eight months, and the concept of the World Wide Web was not even a twinkle in Tim Berners Lee's eye, we needed the assistance of an encyclopaedia. We found one in the bar. Back in the day, all good bars made an encyclopaedia available to their patrons, because it lessened the need for irritating bar brawls and noisy pistol duels caused by disagreements over the date of the Battle of Waterloo. It turned out "Himalayas" is an anglicized version of the word "Himalaya". In his book *Life in The Himalaya*, Maharaj K. Pandit[47] wrote:

> "Let me begin by pointing out the use of Himalaya in singular form throughout the book as opposed to the pluralised version widely used in literature. The latter is, put simply, a colonial legacy. Himalaya is a Sanskrit name (Him = snow, Alaya = home). Like the Alps and the Andes, the Himalaya cannot be pluralized. I have generally used the term Himalaya to mean the entire mountain range."

It comes as no surprise that the British, in addition to all the other dodgy things that they did as the colonial power, would engage in the random pluralisation of perfectly good words that had been around for a very long time indeed without asking to be pluralised. "I say, Carruthers, I think those Sanskrit chappies must have got it wrong, because the plural of Himalaya simply has to be Himalayas, what?"

---

45 The Advanced Research Projects Agency Network (ARPANET) was the precursor of the Internet.

46 TCP/IP (Transmission Control Protocol/Internet Protocol) The communications protocols that allow digital computers to communicate.

47 Dean of the Faculty of Science and Professor of Environmental Studies at the University of Delhi, and a Radcliffe Fellow at Harvard University.

Drinking from the frozen lake.

The next day we left John and his new wife and set off on the last leg of our journey, via New Delhi to Bombay. As a parting gift, he gave me a very small amount of hashish, about the size of a couple of peas, to make the journey more interesting. Hashish, as you almost certainly know, is a cannabis concentrate made from the resin of the cannabis plant (Cannabis sativa or Cannabis indica). If you do not know this, you have probably been living underneath a penguin in Antarctica, and really should try and get about more. The cannabis plant grows rampantly throughout Northern India along the Himalaya (its putative origin) and is still an important cash crop for the locals. Hashish has been used across the Indian subcontinent for medicinal and religious purposes for thousands of years and was even sold in government shops (along with opium) during the British Raj, and for a long time afterwards. It is still popular among young professionals, tourists, and Indian Sādhus.

A Sādhu is a holy person in Hinduism and Jainism who has renounced familial, societal, and earthly connections. This, apparently, is made much easier to do by smoking an enormous quantity of hashish and spending your life completely parrot-faced. Sādhus often wear simple white or saffron coloured clothing, and sport dreadlocks that look exactly as if they have been made by someone who has smoked an enormous amount of hashish and given up halfway through to go and get a Mars bar. Some wear nothing at all, which is called being "sky-clad", because it better symbolises their renunciation of worldly things – and besides, it's too hot in India and they are much too stoned to do the scrubby-slappy-laundry-thing anyway. There are as many as five million Sādhus in India today.

Not looking anything like a Sādhu, but with a little bit of hashish tucked away in my money belt, we left Kashmir behind and took a plane to back to New Delhi, where we were to make our final arrangements to leave India. In many ways, Kashmir was the highlight of our three-month trip. We had travelled the entire length of India, from south to north, and the Himalaya were every bit as spectacular as I had imagined they might be. Srinagar's Dal Lake, with its bobbing houseboats and shikaras was utterly restful, and our ride from Gulmarg up to the Frozen Lake, a unique and memorable experience. Kashmir was a magical place, surrounded by mountains, beloved by the British, fought over by India and Pakistan, and covered in wildflowers and cannabis.

As you will discover in the next story, the little gift of hashish from John, though intended to make our journey more interesting, would soon prove to be an awful lot more trouble than it was worth.

* * *

Today, the Himalaya is the climate crisis we haven't quite heard of; even if emissions are cut significantly, by 2100, 36% of the glaciers in the

Hindu Kush and Himalaya range will have disappeared. If emissions are not cut, the loss rises to 75%. Massive rivers, with their source in the Himalaya, pour into India, Pakistan, China and other nations providing water to 1.65 billion people. The impact of climate change in the Himalaya is unthinkable, and yet, seemingly, inevitable.

Gulmarg is now a trendy ski resort of the Indian middle classes, with multiple lifts and zooty hotels. The Highlands Park Hotel is still there and probably has not changed a whole lot from the 1980s. The track we took to Frozen Lake is now well worn and, if you wish, you can ride the gondola most of the way there.

On Dal Lake, the number of houseboats has dropped from about 3,000 when we were there, to about 600 today. There is now a new generation of houseboats with updated, but sometimes questionably aspirational names, such as Rolex, New York, Holiday Inn and Serious Moonlight. But these famous houseboats, the face of Kashmir tourism for nearly a century, are fast disappearing, because the state government has banned the repairs and reconstruction of houseboats. The government blames them for polluting the lake, which they undeniably do. The houseboat owners say their solution is a tiny fraction of what pours into the lake every day from land, which is undoubtedly true. One third of the remaining houseboats are in urgent need of repairs and it may not be long before the Dal Lake houseboats disappear forever.

INDIA
The Honey Badgers

There is a huge transient tourist population in India, most of whom are constantly on the move. They come from all over the world. Some are true tourists, like us, keen to see the sights and soak up the culture and history. Others fall into the "hippy/bohemian" category, in India to find enlightenment, inner peace, meditate, live on pennies a day and smoke a vast quantity of hashish. They are usually friendly, in much the same way a horse is, if it knows you might have a carrot, but lose interest and wander off as soon as they realise you don't. They are harmless, mostly travel by bus and often carry a musical instrument, which they are prone to playing, loudly and rather badly, from time to time.

Then there are the western white tourists we called the Honey Badgers. Professional junkies, they aren't remotely interested in playing an instrument, unless it has a needle on one end. They are as mean as hell, can be highly aggressive when cornered and give zero fucks about anything except sniffing out drugs – preferably heroin; or the money to buy them – preferably someone else's. One of them is usually quite articulate, the other mostly monosyllabic. Often highly intelligent, they came to India to find an inexhaustible supply of cheap drugs, and in this quest they were invariably successful. After a while, they ran out of money and could not afford to leave, so they sold their passports and cruised from place to place, constantly on the hunt for drugs to feed their insatiable habit. Fearless and highly motivated, they scam their way around, opportunistically thieving, causing trouble and generally making themselves about as desirable as, well… a honey badger in one's train compartment.

* * *

Surrounded by a seething mass of humanity, the Bombay Rajdhani Express train sat at New Delhi station, its giant diesel engine gargling away to itself. We found our compartment in "first" class and settled in for the agonisingly long, 20-hour, 860-mile journey. It was the final leg of our trip through India, and from Bombay we would fly to Ethiopia. No one else had joined us by the time the train hooted and chuffed its way out of the station, and we congratulated each other on the peace and privacy that we would be afforded. It was not to last long.

Some hours into the journey, when we had spread ourselves out quite comfortably, the door opened and there stood two very dodgy looking characters indeed. Unhealthily thin, not recently in close proximity to a bar of soap and with poor skin, grey pallor, lank hair and rather scruffy clothing, they stood momentarily at the door, assessing us on a number of levels. Their rheumy, beady little eyes flitted over us. Were we hostile, friendly, manageable, members of the armed forces or possible targets to be taken advantage of? The conductor shifted uneasily from foot to foot behind them, with eyes down and guilt written all over his face. Knowing we were young, unlikely to make a fuss and had plenty of room in our carriage, he had clearly accepted a bribe to upgrade them to First Class, where they knew they might find easy pickings. We had come across their ilk a few times on the trip, skulking on the outer edge of markets or happening alongside us in a tuk-tuk. It was our worst nightmare. We had just been joined in our tiny space by Mr. and Mrs. Honey Badger.

"What the fuck!" ventriloquized The Management.

"We've just been gazumped!" I mumbled back.

They stumbled in, backpacks flapping, and we reluctantly tried to consolidate our belongings onto one side and free up space for them, while trying to convey through breathing technique what an outrageous fucking imposition it was.

"Where've you come from?" Mr. Honey Badger asked.

"Srinagar," I replied.

"Cool, man. Where are you headed?"

"Bombay."

"Monsoon's hit there, so I hear."

"Yes, that's right."

We watched Mr. and Mrs. Honey Badger store their belongings and settle down, the small talk quickly fizzling out. They spoke to each other under their breath, in a sort of mumbled code that was the equivalent of whispering and rather unnerving to us. Mrs. Honey Badger asked to borrow my *Time* magazine and proceeded to read it upside down for half an hour, turning the pages every now and again. After a couple of hours, whatever they were tanked-up with was beginning to wear off, and there was an increasing amount of squirming and mumbling. Mrs. HB got up and said she was going to the loo. In her absence, Mr. HB flipped into articulate conversation mode and tried to chat us up. We responded cautiously, instinctively knowing that he was trying to loosen us up and make us relaxed. His companion returned and scuffled about a bit; more mumbling ensued. Then Mr, Honey Badger opened his mouth.

"I wonder if you would mind if we took some of our drugs? You see the lav is pretty unhygienic, and we really need to, so we've no option but to..." he shrugged, "...do it here."

He pointed to where, effectively, we were sitting.

Taken aback by their sudden switcheroo, we both looked very uncomfortable.

"It won't take a moment, really," he added, as if that would make it all completely fine.

The Management and I looked at each other, realizing that although it was about six light-years from fine, we had no choice and certainly weren't about to leave them alone with our belongings. So, we acquiesced, in the awkward way the British do when they are strong-armed into something they would rather eat roadkill than agree to.

"Er, yes, well, I suppose, erm... well, if you have to, and it's very quick, then er, well... OK... yes, fine, right, yes, go ahead... if you must."

Without waiting for us to change our minds there was an immediate flurry of activity and unexpected coordination, driven by the unseen force of addiction. Paraphernalia was produced, small envelopes of heroin, syringes and spoons in which to dissolve it were laid out, prepared, heated, stirred, filtered, filled and injected in less time than it takes to make a gin and tonic, right there in front of us. We could not help but watch, amazed and enthralled, as one might watch a cow having an enormous, steaming, liquid shit without being able to tear one's eyes away. Suddenly it was all over and packed away. Mr. and Mrs. Honey Badger slumped in a blissful high.

If you've never seen two junkies prepare, inject and disengage on heroin, don't worry, it's nothing exciting. We felt sorry for them, and held each other a little bit tighter.

* * *

Corruption was, and still is, a vibrant business sector in India, providing an excellent cost-of-living supplement for millions of government and institutional employees. Part and parcel of daily life, bribery is particularly widespread at a local level. A recent survey covering twenty of India's 28 states estimated that 50% of the population had paid bribes at least once in the previous year. If you want to register your house, get your driving license, have your water connected, or even get a birth or death certificate, a bribe is usually required to make it happen. Small businesses must pay off a crowd of people each month just to stay in business: health, safety and hygiene inspections, and a permit to stay open late all require a bribe. If you don't pay it, you are out of business. Of those surveyed, 20% said most bribes were paid to local police, who expect a bribe for every small infraction, with the threat of arrest and jail-time providing effective leverage. You don't even have to do something wrong. Police just randomly stop cars and make up something to extract a bribe, earning about $2 a pop. We didn't know it yet, but the conductor, who had already extracted a bribe from the Honey Badgers in return for a First-Class seat, was now looking to earn a few more rupees from them. The night passed uneventfully, albeit in incredible discomfort, while the honey badgers remained passed out from their hit, so there was no attempt at any shenanigans.

We pulled into a station sometime shortly after dawn the next morning and had been there no more than five minutes when…

…the door to our seating section opened and in walked…

…two policemen.

Faster than a chameleon's tongue snaps a grasshopper off a leaf, I saw Mr. Honey Badger bolt up and expertly palm something off to his companion, who made it disappear into her nether regions as if sucked into a black hole. As policeman number one stepped through the door, the eyes of the lead policeman had first settled momentarily on the Management and me, due to the angle through which he entered, allowing the Honey Badgers the 2.4 nanoseconds they needed to execute what was obviously a well-practiced transfer of goods. The policeman now immediately tuned into them, realising that they were potentially the more profitable targets. Passports were aggressively demanded, produced, inspected and retained, but you could tell it was a cursory move. Sure enough, the police asked if they had any drugs and started doing a thorough and none too gentle pat-down of Mr. Honey Badger, while Mrs. HB stood with her arms crossed and a smug look on her face. Finding nothing on him, they turned to her, asking the same question again.

"No," she said, "nothing", and just stood there. I suddenly understood what everyone except us knew perfectly well: that a policeman could not possibly search a woman, and that there was unlikely to be a policewoman available within 800 miles. Realising that they had been effectively foiled by the Honey Badgers, they turned to us in the hope that we might produce some revenue. I was searched, whereupon they instantly found my money belt.

Oh shit, I suddenly thought.

Rummaging around inside it, they discovered two things that immediately brightened their day: two pea-sized pieces of hashish and the cash equivalent of two years' police salary.

Ker-ching!

As I mentioned, travelling in the 80s required cash or traveller's cheques. Credit cards were uncommon and generally only accepted in major cities. Cash was king. On this, the last leg of our trip, I had strapped the cash with which to buy our two air tickets home when we got to Bombay around my navel. The total amount was about £600. The average policeman earned about £300 a year. So, at this point, I was seriously shitting myself. Imagining how this might go down, I saw a few bleak options; the most terrifying of which was that I would be arrested, thrown in an Indian jail to await trial on drugs charges, while all our money was stolen, and I died of dysentery. I would rather have had both my legs chewed off, slowly, by a goat than suffer this fate. Of course, the alternative was that they could just take all our money and leave us penniless, which would definitely be preferable.

What happened next, however, took us by complete surprise.

Holding the hashish in the palm of his hand, policeman number one became more friendly. He started to scold me in a fatherly way.

"You have hashish, yes?" he said.

"Yes," I said.

"You go jail in India long time for this, you know!"

"I know," I responded gloomily.

"But… I am friend… maybe we can make arrangement?"

"OK," I said, not cottoning on at all to the direction the conversation was taking and thinking that the whole friend thing was a bit far-fetched. I stood there wide-eyed, a complete newbie at this, waiting for more, until a pregnant pause enveloped us. The Honey Badger, an old hand at this, stage-whispered:

"He wants money."

"Ah! Right! Of course… wh…"

"If it wasn't for you, they wouldn't bloody be in here," snapped The Management at Mrs. Honey Badger.

"What is the fine… I… I can pay now, er, if you like" I stammered at the policemen, hoping desperately I was not digging myself into an even deeper hole. The policeman shrugged, cleverly not committing to anything that could specifically be called bribery but knowing he had me by the balls. I dug into my money belt, pointlessly trying to shield with my hand the wad of bills he had already seen. How many hundreds should I give him, I wondered, having never bribed anyone in my life. Having no idea, I began to pull out a small bundle of notes to hand them over.

"That's far too much!" hissed Mr. Honey Badger. "The going rate is only one thousand rupees, tops!"

I paused, terrified of getting it wrong. The Management made an encouraging face at me, as if to say, "It's OK, we need to do this." So, bowing to Mr. HB's superior knowledge and obviously extensive experience, I gingerly handed over one thousand Rupees[48], in the same delicate way that one might hand-feed a piece of steak to a tiger. Without saying a word, policeman number one took, folded, and pocketed the money in one fluid, practiced move. Then, to my complete and utter astonishment, he made to hand me back the two tiny pieces of hashish. I backed off as if he had just pulled his gun on me.

"No, no, thank you, no," said The Management, shooing animatedly with her hands in the international recognized gesture for please take your goat/leprosy/hashish away from me.

"You have it! It's for you…" I said. "Keep it!"

Having become familiarized with this particular bribery protocol faster than the vertical acceleration of an ejector seat, I was now fully aware that if I accepted it back, he would simply call his mates at the next station and tell them where to come and get their daily allowance and so on down the line. He shrugged, turned and was gone, probably to give the conductor his share of the back-hander – and two small pieces of hash.

The Honey Badgers breathed a sigh of relief when the police had left.

"Phew, that was a close one." Mr. HB said. "Good thing they didn't find our smack!" [49]

The Honey Badgers laughed and tried to start multiple conversations with us, but The Management – fearless traveller, lover of

---

48 About £50.
49 Heroin.

people, conversation, culture, architecture, music, food, history, dancing, art, and smoked salmon sandwiches was not – it has to be said – in her happy place.

Glowering at them she said, "What station are you getting off at?"

"The next one is our stop. We change for Nagpur," came the response.

"Excellent. I can hardly wait" she snapped back.

Before long, they grunted and shuffled out of the compartment, and we were finally left in peace.

The monsoon, which we had steadfastly managed to avoid during our trip, was indeed waiting for us in Bombay, giving us an intense drenching with pea-sized raindrops.

We left India with many happy memories of extraordinary experiences, generous, interesting, kind people, and fascinating places. But India is all about opposites and balance, the yin and the yang. You don't get all the enriching experiences without the beggars, the leprosy, poverty, overcrowding, smell, bribery, thieving, food poisoning and incredible heat; yet another – albeit extreme – lesson in how one must take the rough with the smooth to get the best. India, a country that can eat you up and spit you out, made a permanent impression on us, and it taught me so much about travel, and people, and life. I had arrived in India a naïve traveller. But items in my own overhead baggage compartment had shifted during our extended trip. On leaving, I no longer considered myself a tourist – I had become a traveller.

KENYA
One Night in Nairobi

The Management and I had been out of touch with the world for some days when we arrived in Addis Ababa, in August of 1982. As we descended to land, we looked down on a kaleidoscopic quilt of farmland below. Verdant squares of green jostled against rich browns of fallow and terracotta reds of plough, laid like a patchwork blanket on rolling hills. There was nothing to concern us as we waited for our onward flight to Nairobi, except possibly the age and provenance of both the chicken sandwich we ate, and the aircraft we were about to board.

A few hours later, on our final approach to Nairobi, the announcement from the flight deck came as some surprise.

"Ladies and Gentlemen, we will shortly begin our descent into Jomo Kenyatta International Airport. Please do not be concerned to see Army soldiers surrounding the plane on our arrival. We are the first flight in after the *coop* and this is a standard procedure. Have a nice day and thank you for flying with Ethiopian Airlines."

"What does he mean, the *coop*?" asked the Management, thinking it must be something to do with the brightly coloured lady three rows back who had boarded with a rooster in a crate.

"I think he means coup," I said. "As in coup d'état".

We looked at each other, amazed that this seemingly vital piece of information was not only being mispronounced but only communicated to us on final approach. I looked around the plane, expecting to see scattered outbreaks of mild hysteria, but no one seemed in the least bit phased by this pronouncement. To be fair, most of our fellow passengers looked like they had lived through a few. Some could well have been personally responsible for several sub-Saharan despotic substitutions. We were just going to be stopping for one night in Kenya, on our way to Johannesburg, so hopefully this wouldn't thwart our plans.

Sure enough, on landing, the aircraft was met by an Army vehicle with a dramatic yellow "Follow Me" sign on it. The captain obeyed, and as soon as we came to a halt the plane was quickly surrounded by soldiers.

As our first experience of Africa, this was quite intimidating, but we disembarked without incident and filed into the customs hall. There, it seemed to be very much business as usual. Our passports were stamped by a smiley customs official who assured us that everything was now fine; the coup had failed and all those responsible had been briskly rounded up and thrown into jail. If they were lucky, I thought.

The usual motley selection of taxi drivers who waited outside to accost fresh tourists seemed particularly eager to please, perhaps because the failed coup had deprived them of revenue for several days. The Management selected the one she deemed to be the least offensive, based on a complicated algorithm she had perfected over many years. All I knew was that it involved rating factors such as use of English, charisma, number of wheels on the vehicle, cleanliness of hair and clothing, body odour, evidence of smoking, and her own mood on that particular day. The fortunate winner piled our bags into an ancient Peugeot, which appeared to be largely held together with duct-tape, and we set off. In a moment of great optimism his mother had christened him "Professor", and he was a friendly, eager chap, although his driving skills left much to be desired.

At that time, the A104 Mombasa road was the only bit of dual carriageway in Kenya and the main route into the city from the airport. Turning onto it, we immediately found ourselves at a roadblock. Passports were duly produced, a few perfunctory questions asked to establish our credentials as tourists, and we were sent on our way. No sooner had Professor driven half a mile when we came upon another roadblock. This struck us as rather amusing because there had been no way of joining or leaving the motorway since the previous checkpoint, rendering the check entirely redundant. Nevertheless, the troops manning it were keen as mustard, in the unlikely event there had been some nefarious parachuting or tunnelling activity in between the two exits. As we produced our passports once again, the guard noticed a portable boom box cassette player that I cradled on my lap and instantly became suspicious.

"Radio?" he asked.

"No," I responded cautiously, immediately sensing that he meant the sort of radio that would be useful in a coup, rather than of the type required for relaxing on a beach to the dulcet tones of Bryan Ferry.

"Radio," he repeated as the barrel of an AK-47 swung toward me and in one swift movement, a long arm extracted the boom box through the window in much the same way an elephant might have. An officer was called over, and it was examined with deep suspicion from all angles. It was one of the latest versions, purchased recently in London and doubtless never before seen in Nairobi. It was silver and had a great number of switches, dials, buttons, and largely pointless LEDs. I quickly realized this could be a problem. There was a lot of discussion about the buttons, and our passports, as Professor animatedly interjected to try and explain to them that we were just innocent tourists. They unceremoniously told him to shut up, or they would shoot him, which he sensibly did.

"What tape do you have in there?" the Management whispered.

"What? I really think we have more important things to worry about," I whispered back, testily.

"Just tell me, what's in it!"

"Shit! I don't know! *Kaya*, I think. Why?"

"Reach over, press play, and turn the volume up."

"What? Why?"

"Stop asking why, and just *do* it!" she said, through gritted teeth.

Indicating that I wanted to show them something, I hit the play button, spun the volume, and Bob Marley's "Easy Skanking" erupted forth with most impressive volume and satisfactory bass notes. They looked amazed for a moment, before erupting into smiles, laughter and some spontaneous dance moves. Reluctantly, they handed the boom box back, smiling and joking and shaking their heads in disbelief that they could possibly have been so silly as to think that I, a Bob Marley fan, could ever have been a threat to national security. Professor ground the gears and took off at considerable speed, relieved that a major diplomatic incident had been averted through the cunning use of reggae.

* * *

The storied Norfolk Hotel has been around since early colonial days. It opened for business on December 25, 1904, offering 40 guest rooms, a billiard room, and a restaurant with a French chef. After some years it became popular with the increasingly notorious Happy Valley set, consisting mostly of hedonistic British and Anglo-Irish aristocrats and adventurers with the most wonderful names. Members included Bror von Blixen-Fineke and his wife, Karen Blixen, Lord Delamere, Denys Finch Hatton, Sir Jock Delves Broughton and his wife Diana, Lord Erroll and Lady Idina Sackville. According to Ulf Aschan, Bror Blixen's godson and biographer: "Witty, attractive, well bred, and well read, Happy Valleyites were relentless in their pursuit to be amused, more often attaining this through drink, drugs, and sex."

It was not uncommon for weekend house guests to be expected to exchange spouses. Drugs were commonplace; champagne ubiquitous. Their behaviour scandalized polite society and was a rich source of titillating gossip, well documented in James Fox's bestselling novel *White Mischief,* (turned into the Hollywood film, starring Greta Scacchi). "Are you married, or do you live in Kenya?" ran a popular joke.

At a time when most of Africa was under colonial rule, discipline was dispensed with an iron hand, and there was a ruthless focus among white colonials on profiting from their occupation at the expense of the people. The ruling invaders were often cruel and arrogant, riding roughshod over the tribal ways and traditions of their unwilling subjects. But Lord Delamere was cut from a different cloth. Prior to settling in Kenya, he had been severely mauled by a lion while on safari. Facing certain death, his Somali gunbearer, Abdullah Ashur, had jumped onto the lion, giving Delamere precious seconds to retrieve his rifle and save them both. Due to the injuries he sustained, he limped for the rest of his life, but maintained a deep and enduring respect for Somalis; and, one assumes, lions.

Delamere was a contradictory character. He had a number of African friends, and particularly enjoyed the company of the Maasai, becoming one of the only white men at the time who took the trouble to learn their language. Despite his evident respect and friendship, they were nevertheless inclined to help themselves to his cattle in order to supplement their own herds. He seemed to think this a perfectly reasonable quid pro quo.

Over the course of his life Delamere strove tirelessly to develop a working agricultural economy in Kenya. Experimenting with different seeds and livestock, he endured numerous costly failures in his attempts to introduce new crops and breeds that could withstand the unforgiving equatorial climate. He poured his personal fortune into the land, and despite his comfortable lifestyle, lived most of his life on the verge of bankruptcy.

Known to his friends as "D", in his leisure time he was a legendary badass. On more than one occasion, for the general amusement of himself and others, he rode his horse into the bar of the Norfolk hotel and, in full evening dress, attempted to jump clear over a table without disturbing the place-settings. He was also fond of shooting bottles off the bar, which he then politely asked to be added to his tab. One particular evening a new manager, unfamiliar with his antics, suggested that maybe he had had enough to shoot, and should go home. Delamere promptly threw him in among the carcasses in the meat-safe for the night, to reconsider his rank insolence.

Delamere's love for Kenya and the Maasai caused him to disagree strongly with the British government regarding its policy in the colony. He died, in 1931, £500,000 in debt, a massive amount back then. But for all his faults, and those of his fellow white colonialists, he left the country a priceless gift. His legacy was his lifetime of research and experimentation, that would become the foundation of an agricultural economy that allowed Kenya to grow into one of the most stable economies in Africa.

As a reminder of the frequent battles he fought against the British government on behalf of his beloved Kenya, and his invaluable contribution to the prosperity of the fledgling country, a statue was erected in his honour and a road named after him. But in 1963, on the occasion of Kenya's independence, Delamere was immediately and unceremoniously discredited, along with other figures from the colonial past. and his statue was removed.

A lesser known, but no less remarkable woman in the Happy Valley set was Karen Blixen's friend, Beryl Clutterbuck Markham. Much admired for her great beauty and adventurous spirit, she was extraordinarily talented at anything to which she turned her hand. As a young girl, growing up motherless in Africa, she learned Swahili and was taught to hunt boar, barefoot and armed with a spear, by the Nandi tribe. At 16, she married a much older local farmer and by 18 had established herself as a racehorse trainer, setting up at the Ngong racetrack where she enjoyed considerable success. Distracted by the glamour of flying, she was the first woman in Kenya to receive a commercial pilot's license, becoming an expert and fearless bush-pilot. Beryl honed her considerable skills on rough unprepared landing strips, running supplies and spotting game for safari operators like Blixen and Finch Hatton. She often flew at night, with no radio and only a compass to guide her. Extraordinarily beautiful, entirely uninhibited, and relentlessly promiscuous, by her early twenties she was divorced and remarried, but nothing seemed to slow her down. Her list of lovers was a seemingly unending rollcall of the rich, the famous and even the royal; unsurprisingly she was no stranger to scandal and publicity.

Since Charles Lindbergh's 1927 west to east crossing of the Atlantic, no pilot had successfully made a westward flight, against the wind, from England.[50] Those who had tried had never been heard from again. On September 4, 1936, Beryl took off from RAF Abing-

---

50 Jim Mollison was the first pilot to perform an east to west solo trans-Atlantic flight from Portmarnock in Ireland to Pennfield, New Brunswick, Canada, in 1932.

don, southern England. Twenty gruelling hours later, her engine failing, she crash-landed on Cape Breton Island, Nova Scotia, becoming
the first person to cross from England to North America non-stop.
One cannot underestimate the difficulty of such a crossing, battling
strong headwinds, in extreme cold, with only the freezing waters of
the Atlantic beneath her, death was a far more likely outcome than
success. Her instant celebrity was well deserved. Moving to California to work as aviation advisor to Paramount Pictures, she wrote
about her adventures in her excellent memoir, *West with the Night*.
Although well reviewed, it sold poorly due to the distractions of war.
In 1952 she returned to Kenya, and continued her successful career in
racehorse training, being responsible for no less than eight winners
of the Kenya Derby.

* * *

Surrounded by the ghosts of the Happy Valley set, we checked in
to the Norfolk Hotel. The desk clerk enthusiastically explained that
de coop had failed miserably in its attempt to overthrow President
Daniel Arap Moi. At midnight the previous Sunday, a group of soldiers from the Kenya Air Force had taken over the radio station and
announced that they had overthrown the government. The group
had tried to force several Air Force fighter pilots to bomb the State
House, but they had only pretended to follow the orders. Once airborne, they had instead dropped their bombs on the slopes of Mount
Kenya, severely traumatizing a herd of wildebeest and some meerkats.
Loyalist forces led by the Army quickly suppressed the coup, but not
without some civilian casualties.

The clerk finished the paperwork and handed us our keys. "Due to
de coop, there is currently a curfew between 9:00pm and 4:30am," he
announced in the cheerful tone of voice usually reserved for telling
guests they have an upgrade to a nicer room. "Please don't go out
as we cannot be holding the responsibility if you are getting shot.
Breakfast is being served from seven. Please be having a lovely stay."

When The Management finds a cab driver she likes, she tends to stick with them, and in this case, she had warmed to Professor, questioning him relentlessly about his family, his work, and all the possible things he could drive her to see while she was in Nairobi. He had told us there was an excellent wildlife park just seven kilometres from the centre of Nairobi; and so it was arranged that he would pick us up after lunch and take us there.

Opened in 1946, The National Park of Nairobi was the first national park in Kenya, and although it covered a modest 28,000 acres it was indeed exceptionally well stocked with an impressive variety of wildlife. Initially, due to its proximity to the city there had been some confusion between animals and local residents about who was going to eat whom. This was sorted out when the animals demonstrated that they were significantly more adept at killing amateur urban poachers than the poachers were at killing animals. So, separated by nothing more than a fence it has since worked very smoothly, with no further misunderstandings.

For us, the day had become overcast, the animals were all somewhere out of sight, and the Management had started to feel slightly queasy. Jet lag, the soft bumping around of the car, and Professor's helpful but lengthy explanations of things he thought we would find interesting conspired to put us both to sleep. We awoke half an hour later to find that nothing had changed, so we decided to beat a retreat and head back to the Norfolk.

At 9:00pm that evening, the curfew went into effect. Precisely five minutes later, the Management went into the bathroom, announcing through the door that she would likely not be coming out for several days. She had left Ethiopia, but apparently Ethiopia had not left her: a nasty dose of e-Coli had hitched a ride in the form of the chicken sandwich. It wasn't long before instructions were issued through the door: I should go and procure doctors and medication in whatever order they could most rapidly be found – ideally packaged in a well-equipped medevac Lear Jet, fuelled-up and with a flight plan filed for the London Clinic. I reminded her of the not insignificant matter of the curfew, but her reply made it abundantly clear that me getting shot at was shockingly low on her list of priorities compared to Lomotil[51] and Lear Jets.

So, I headed out to the front desk to make a plan. No, it was highly likely I would be shot if I left the hotel; no, they would not be responsible for my safety when I went back to my room with that information; no, they could not call a doctor – curfews applied to doctors too, apparently; no, there were no doctors that they were aware of staying as guests; and yes, they thought it unwise to go waking everyone up to ask; no, they didn't have any Lomotil, nor a Lear Jet.

Requesting the hotel have a cab, engine running, waiting outside for me at precisely 4:30am, I returned to our room. The noises coming from the bathroom indicated that, if anything, The Management was getting worse. It was a long night, the details of which I will spare you; suffice to say that it was as twice as bad as you can imagine, and then some.

Little did we know that long night in 1982, that Beryl Markham, the pioneering aviatrix and author, was just seven miles away from us. At 80 years of age, she was living in poverty near the Ngong racetrack, where she still trained thoroughbreds. At that time, she would have been quite unaware that her past was unexpectedly catching up with her and was about to change what remained of her life. On the other side of the world, a California restaurateur by the name of George Gutekunst[52] was reading a collection of Ernest Hemingway's letters. Among them was one in which Hemingway waxed lyrical about Markham's writing:

"Did you read Beryl Markham's book, *West with the Night*? I knew her fairly well in Africa and never would have suspected she could and

---

51 Industrial alternative to Imodium.

52 Gutekunst was the charismatic co-owner of Ondine, a well-known French restaurant in Sausalito, and friend of Hemingway's son, Jack.

would put pen to paper, except to write in her flyers' logbook. As it is, she has written so well, and marvellously well, that I was completely ashamed of myself as a writer. I felt that I was simply a carpenter with words, picking up whatever was furnished on the job and nailing them together and sometimes making an okay pig pen. But this girl... can write rings around all of us who consider ourselves as writers... it really is a bloody wonderful book."

West with the Night was about to get a second chance.

I shot out of the hotel at 4:30am, and much to the credit of the night staff there was indeed a cab waiting outside. Nairobi was eerily quiet, its dusty streets lit by the occasional streetlamp, like empty spotlights waiting for a lone performer. I asked the driver to step on it. The Nairobi Hospital was curfew quiet, and there was no one on reception. Knowing that any delay was unacceptable, I charged about the empty corridors and eventually found a nurse. I explained that my wife had some hideously virulent form of stomach bug camped out in her intestines, and that it was more than my life was worth not to return immediately with large quantities of drugs. Thankfully she was sympathetic and led me to the utterly charming doctor on duty. He patiently listened while I described a range of symptoms that sounded increasingly like Ebola. Loading me up with a pharmacy of things that he assured me would make the Management feel much better, he sent me on my way insisting no payment was necessary.

A mere 20 minutes later, I was back in the room, administering medications and deflecting questions about what had taken me so long. In pretty short order things began to improve, and at noon the Management suggested perhaps I should call for Professor. Always curious, and a tireless researcher, she had read that the Hominid Skull Room at the Nairobi National Museum was the single most important collection of early human fossils in the world, and well worth a visit. We might just have time to pop in before our flight to Johannesburg. The Management was on the mend.

We picked up a British Airways flight to Johannesburg later that afternoon. Although its reputation waxes and wanes with the notoriously variable quality of its service and attitude, the British have an inordinate pride in their national flag carrier, and it sent a tingle down my spine to see that massive 747 parked on the apron at Kenyatta Airport. We had flown on all manner of airlines in the last three months, from Air Lanka and Air India to Ethiopian Airlines, so the welcoming smile and a very British "good afternoon, sir, and welcome aboard," was especially comforting. There was even tea and scones on the menu.

The relatively short flight down to Johannesburg was uneventful, but on arrival Kenya had one last surprise for us. Much of the modest little collection of jewellery we had bought in India during our trip was missing, having been skilfully removed by the baggage handlers in Nairobi. Nevertheless, this was to be a memorable flight and a turning point in our lives; South Africa was about to deliver us the biggest surprise of all.

Although we were only intending to stay for two weeks, little did we know that we would actually stay for more than five years. Between 1982 and 1987 in Johannesburg, we would both be offered jobs, start proper careers, get married, honeymoon, have our first child, become sensible, buy our first house, and even start our first business[53]. When travel, fate and serendipity all converge, extraordinary life-shifting events happen.

* * *

George Gutekunst successfully republished West With the Night, *and it is still ranked by National Geographic as among the best adventure books to read today. Beryl Clutterbuck Markham, who hunted wild boar barefoot with a spear and flew solo across the Atlantic, died in 1986, after complications resulting from a fall while petting her dog.*

---

53 Frontal lobe had finally caught up with my life.

SOUTH AFRICA
Into the Storm

Charles, our pilot, surveyed the large pile of luggage we had stacked beside his small Beechcraft Bonanza. "You must be certifiably insane!" he exclaimed. "You can't possibly take all that with you. The laws of aerodynamics dictate that we will simply not become airborne with all that on board." We all looked at each other. I wondered if it would be a good moment to mention bumble-bees, but decided against it.

"I told you to travel light and bring only a little bit of luggage. That is not luggage!" said Charles, waving his hand in the general direction of the large pile of booze, "that is a pub."

It was a sunny summer's Friday morning at Lanseria airport, just north of Johannesburg, South Africa. Charles's sister had kindly invited the Management, myself, and a friend of ours named Anthony, all in our early twenties, to join her for the weekend at the family's game lodge near Tuli, just across the border in Botswana. Many families we knew in Johannesburg owned a small game lodge; it was the African equivalent of a cottage in the country, where they would go for a weekend of game viewing. Back then, most were modest, bungalow-type structures of basic construction – the logistics of building anything more complex in the middle of nowhere saw to that. There is also a robust general aviation community in South Africa, encouraged by generally excellent flying weather, long distances and an abundance of dirt airstrips. Many people had small private planes.

Situated at the confluence of the Limpopo and Shashe Rivers in the far eastern corner of Botswana, this area is known as the Tuli Block and it is here where Botswana, South Africa and Zimbabwe converge. It was home to the largest elephant population anywhere in Africa, and we were excited to have the opportunity to get up close and personal with these magnificent animals for a couple of days. Tuli was very remote, which meant either a hideously long drive to get there, or a 90-minute flight. Charles had earned his wings a couple of years earlier and was, by all accounts, an excellent pilot, if disconcertingly young. He had kindly agreed to fly us, although, had he been familiar with our standard weekend kit, he might not have.

What Charles had said was true. Now we looked at it next to the baggage compartment of the Bonanza, there did seem to be rather more luggage than would fit, and quite a lot of it was indeed recently on the shelves of Solly Kramers.[54] Three cases of beer, four five-litre boxes of wine, a bottle of whiskey, two bottles of gin, four six-packs of tonic, and some Angostura bitters sat stacked on the apron. Beside this were two coolers packed with food (mostly lemons and sausages, if I recall), and four small overnight bags. This all seemed pretty essential to us at that stage of our lives, but not getting airborne would put a serious damper on our weekend plans. But, as the pilot-in-command we accepted that he had the final say, and agreed to try and cut down the weight, albeit with a bit of good-natured muttering about pilots not understanding the historical relevance of gin on a safari.

After much discussion we agreed that, at a push, we could lose some lemons. Charles said more needed to go, so we sadly jettisoned a case of beer, half the tonic water and the Angostura bitters. At this point, Charles made us all stand on a scale, weighed everything, including us, did some calculations and declared that we were not even close.

"Either one of you stays here, or you lose the booze; and it has to be at least 40 pounds more or we are not getting airborne."

So, while Charles muttered about, checking the engine oil and fuel, we had a stroky-beard meeting and all agreed that we would rather spend a weekend in a Sudanese jail than leave more alcohol behind. Then, quite suddenly, it dawned on us we had overlooked an easy source of non-essential weight loss. Hooray!

We opened our overnight bags, and each removed a toothbrush, toothpaste, a spare t-shirt and a pair of shorts. We then threw three, almost full bags full of clothes, back in the car and packed our

---

54 A well-known chain of South African bottle stores.

"essential overnight items" in one bag. The weather was warm, we would be in the bush, we could wash a t-shirt and it would dry in a flash. What more could we need? Having got our priorities right, we proudly presented our innovative weight-loss solution to Charles, who weighed everything again and declared that we had hit our target. We loaded all the booze onto the plane, Charles arranged it all to his satisfaction, and we piled in. Take-off involved using about the same amount of runway as a fully laden 747, but we staggered into the air and climbed out on a northerly heading for Botswana.

* * *

Johannesburg is the largest city in South Africa and one of the 50 largest urban areas in the world. Located at an elevation of 5,751 feet, it is on the eastern plateau of South Africa known as the Highveld.[55]

The Management and I had been living and working in Johannesburg for a couple of years, and guests would often arrive to stay with us, quite unaware of the altitude to which they had unexpectedly ascended. They were surprised to find that instead of jet lag, they had a headache, the runs, and couldn't sleep. "Altitude sickness," we would tell them dismissively, "you'll get over it in a day or two". When one descended to sea level, it was always pleasantly surprising that one's car acquired noticeably more acceleration, and you could drink an astonishing amount of alcohol without any apparent ill effects.

Meteorologists know that the Highveld has a "subtropical highland climate". What this means to the rest of us is that every afternoon in the heat of summer (between November and February), clouds billow 20,000 feet high, conjuring up dramatic lightning, thunder, and brief but absolutely torrential downpours that cool the air beautifully and freak out about 20,000 dogs. Occasionally, the weather decides to screw with everyone, and drops several hundred

---

55 Johannesburg airport was used to test Concorde during the 1970s, for take-off and landings at high elevations ('hot and high' testing).

million hailstones the size of golf balls on everything left outside, including cars, crops and sleeping sunbathers.

Hailstones are pretty interesting. Simply put, they are formed by small ice particles being tumbled around inside the gigantic structure of towering cumulonimbus clouds. As the internal winds fling them thousands of feet up, and down, and up again, they gather more water on them at the bottom, which freezes as they go up, making them gradually larger and larger. Eventually, when they get too heavy for the internal updrafts to support, they simply drop out of the cloud from about 25,000-feet. Research has found that a hailstone's terminal velocity is roughly proportional to the square root of something or other, but no-one gives a damn about that. The nub of it is that hailstones can reach a speed of up to 100 miles per hour, tear off the siding from houses, smash windows, destroy crops, cause severe injury or death to people and animals, and make your car look like it has been used in an action sequence in a Michael Bay movie. In the strongest supercells, which produce some of the largest hail, one might expect to see two-to-four-inch diameter stone's that will fall at around 70 miles per hour. However, the largest hailstone ever recovered fell in Argentina in 2018. Called "Victoria's hailstone", it was one of three hailstones recorded during a storm over Villa Carlos Paz and measured around 9.3 inches. That one probably was traveling at well over 100 miles an hour when it slammed into the ground.

In the Transvaal, South Africa, in 1936, hail the size of coconuts – yes, coconuts – killed as many as 26 people, and a herd of rather surprised cows. Fifteen inches of rain fell in fifteen minutes, which is the same as the entire annual rainfall in Eritrea. Pea-sized hail in Great Britain is always fun to see; everyone points and says, "Ooooo look! Hail!". It is a sobering thought that in other parts of the world hail can – and will – kill a cow.

After about an hour in the air, it was exactly these nasty afternoon thunderheads we were now trying to avoid as we flew towards Botswana. Our flight plan took us to small dirt airstrip just over the

Botswana border, near Pont Drift, but it became increasingly obvious that the towering thunderheads were moving to block our path. It was possible they might even box us in. We flew around the base of one, then dodged left behind another. I was in the co-pilot's seat, so had a grandstand view of nature, gathering herself up for a serious tantrum. Great heaps of white cloud were lit up with bright sunlight; others were dark and threatening. It was spectacular, in a really disconcerting way. Charles was trying to reach the customs post on the radio as we flew between these giant canyons of roiling cloud.

"Where we are going is just down there," he said over the intercom, pointing to a wall of cloud. "If we can't find a way through soon, we may have to spend the night in Louis Trichardt." There would have to be a pretty serious situation for one to voluntarily spend a night in Louis Trichardt, a small, unremarkable town in the Northern Transvaal. We could sense things were getting a bit dicey. Again, we banked left, then right, as a towering cloud blocked out the sun.

Suddenly, Charles said. "OK, I see a hole. I think we can just drop down through it." He quickly pushed the yoke forward with one hand, talking to the customs post on the radio in the other, as we descended steep and fast, towards a small gap in the cloud. Suddenly there was rather a lot going on. Charles was employing a technique called a forward slip, which is used when you need to lose altitude quickly, and it makes anyone unused to it feel as if the wings have just fallen off the aircraft. As we plummeted downwards, much as a bucket of lead might, we could see a spot of ground through the gap. This was not as comforting as you might imagine, because it was coming up at us very much faster than we wanted; In the back, Harriet, Anthony, and the Management had suddenly gone rather quiet. The giant thunderheads loomed high above us, casting a dark shadow over our tiny airplane. There was no going back now. Down and down we dropped, until finally we whizzed through the hole and quickly levelled out under the cloud cover. Banking sharply right, we continued to descend towards a dirt runway that had appeared immediately ahead. We did a low-level pass over it to check for any itinerant wildebeest, as was common practice, before looping up and around to return for smooth-as-dirt landing. It was all very exciting. I felt glad to be alive when we landed.

The air was steamy hot, and although the thunderheads billowed above and around us, they were illuminated by dramatic sunshine, and we remained dry as they began to move away to the west. The airstrip was close enough to the Pont Drift border crossing to have been designated as a customs and immigration point for cross border general aviation traffic. Charles simply called customs on the radio, and they confirmed they would send out an officer in a Land Rover to meet us at the airstrip and do the immigration procedure. A novel arrangement. We would then take off and continue for another ten minutes to the landing strip at the game lodge.

Charles pulled off the runway onto a patch of dirt and shut down the engine. "OK, we wait here until customs arrive. Sometimes they can take their time, so go stretch your legs, but don't go far – there are animals," he said vaguely, and with massive understatement.

To the best of our knowledge, there had been no known incidents of lions attacking Beechcraft Bonanzas, so we decided it would be best to sit right down under the wing and have a much-needed cigarette and a beer. Almost immediately – which in Africa means about 45 minutes – we heard an engine and a battered white Land Rover appeared bumping towards us through the bush. It pulled up a little way from the plane, and out lumbered a stout Botswanan man in khaki trousers and a voluminous blue denim shirt. We all got up and walked over. Charles introduced himself, to which the man responded "Hello, arm-pit."

We thought this was a bit strange. Was it an insult?

"Well, hello, Pete, thank you for coming out!" said Charles, at which point we realized that he had in fact said, 'I am Pete". Two sidekicks busied themselves removing and setting up an orange folding table and two chairs from the back of the Land Rover. Armpit took a battered brown briefcase from the front seat, and took the official hat of a Botswana Customs Officer from it. Perching the hat on his head in a token acknowledgment of his status, he sat heavily down on the flimsy chair, which flexed dangerously in surprise. He carefully took out a book and an official Botswana Immigration stamp from the case, arranging them neatly on the table in front of him.

Bush customs arrive to admit us to Botswana with appropriate formality.

"OK, first person, please!" he beamed at us.

So, in no time at all, an official customs post of the Botswana Government had been set up, just for us, on an orange plastic table, in the middle of the bush, surrounded by scrubby trees, and probably several hyenas and a leopard chewing on a kill. The only thing that made this look vaguely less surreal was the airplane parked 20 feet away (well, no... actually it didn't). Armpit took his job very seriously, examining every page of each passport, commenting with interest on the far-off places we had visited, exclaiming "Aaaiiii! Heh, you have bin to so *many* places!"

We would have made an attractive lunch for a lion.

With passports officially stamped, photographs taken, and goodbyes said, Armpit and his assistants packed up the portable border post and withdrew to the edge of the runway to watch us take off. Once again, we needed to use every inch of the runway to get airborne, but soon we were skimming low across the bush on the final ten-minute hop to the airstrip near the lodge. We saw three separate herds of elephants in just that short journey.

Elephants are lovely. But, apart from being big, trumpety and generally magnificent, they are problematic in more ways than people imagine. The problem we all know about is that across vast areas of Africa they have long been poached, and their numbers continue to fall. Huge efforts have been made in the war on poachers, but as long as the bat-eating, rhino-horn snorting fuckwits out there want ivory, poaching will be extremely hard to eradicate. In Southern Africa, where elephant conservation has been a victim of its own success, they have an entirely different problem – too many elephants. Given plenty of food, room to roam and good security, it turns out that elephants breed like rabbits – great big, grey, farty rabbits that each hoover up about a quarter of a ton of vegetation a day.

They are extremely destructive, and over time will eat so much that the trees disappear, and the bush turns into grassy savannah. This deeply upsets the giraffes, who suddenly find themselves with nothing to eat. The birds bugger off somewhere else, because they can, and the residents of a leafy suburb of Pretoria are suddenly wondering why they have an infestation of toucans. Conversely, the lions think it is terrific, and get fat and happy, because there is nowhere for anything to hide. On it goes, along the chain, affecting different species in different ways, many of them adversely. You can understand how a delicate ecosystem can quickly go pear-shaped. Botswana can ideally support about 50,000 elephants, but the population is now about 130,000. If you have too many of any one animal in an ecosystem, you can usually dart, capture and move them to an underpopulated area with relative ease. But elephants weigh between three and seven tons each and can get quite cross and uncooperative when you try to boss them about, so relocating a herd of them is insanely difficult and expensive. Moving tens of thousands? Completely out of the question.

The evening was spent on the veranda talking and laughing comfortably, as friends do. Just beyond the perimeter of light thrown by the house was a hive of unseen activity, the grunty-rustlings of the African night a constant reminder of where we were. Occasionally, a lion would roar somewhere in the distance, a sound that invariably halted conversation while we all pricked up our ears. Was that roar closer than the previous one? Satisfied it was not, we continued our banter. I must admit that more than any other animal, including lions, hippopotami scare the living daylights out of me – with good reason – they kill more people each year in Africa than any other animal. Not bad for a vegetarian. Moreover, they are sneaky and keep disappearing, so you don't know where they are.

After a good night's sleep, we rose at dawn for the first game drive. The Land Rover was more rickety than the rather smarter vehicles one usually found in the commercial safari camps, but perfectly adequate.

We drove for about half an hour in the dawn twilight, before stopping near a pool at a watering hole. We had barely been there for ten minutes when a large bull elephant appeared silently from the bush and came down to the water. Then, one after another, an entire herd followed – including mothers and their calves. The most extraordinary thing was that they moved with barely a sound, just a gentle rustling of their ears and the occasional snap of a twig. Had we not been paying attention, these enormous mammals could have snuck up on us completely unawares. I would have made much more noise myself than a bull elephant weighing several tons. We watched in awe as they drank greedily from the water.

Even though we did not make a sound, it was clear they knew we were there. The older elephants would occasionally raise their trunks in the air, sniffing in our direction. For whatever reason, they decided we presented no danger and were not worth interrupting their morning routine for. Having sated their thirst, they began sucking up water and spraying it on themselves, until their wide grey backs were darkened and glistening. Several of the smaller teenagers rolled in the mud, while the babies splashed about excitedly, as children do. Still there was no noise but the sound of the water being sloshed about by feet and trunks. After they had thoroughly wet themselves, there began a process of scooping up dust with their trunks and throwing it on their heads and backs. An elephant's skin is more sensitive than one might imagine, and they do this to protect themselves from the sun, and from annoying insects. As the dust and dirt was tossed in a great arc through the air, particles were caught in the rays of the early morning sun and lit golden, making for the most beautiful sight.

All of this went on for about 20 minutes until suddenly, as if on some unheard cue, they all turned and headed silently back into the bush again. In less than a minute, they had vanished as quietly as they had arrived. We were thrilled to have witnessed this extraordinary scene and chattered excitedly as we climbed back into the Land Rover.

Throughout the morning we saw more elephants, as well as the lion we had heard the night before. We came across them under a tree, lazing about in very relaxed fashion. There were four females and one male, all lying down, occasionally flicking their tails to swat away flies.

It was clear they had recently been on a kill as the fur around their mouths was still stained pink with blood. Last night had been a good night. They also were uninterested in us, their stomachs too full to care.

Returning to the house for breakfast, we had the luxury of a morning siesta, then a lazy day, like the lions. At 4:00pm we set off again and spent three hours spotting warthogs and some giraffe, and enjoying the vast array of bird life, including gorgeous Lilac Crested Rollers and hideous Marabou Storks.

If you haven't been on safari, I cannot recommend it highly enough. It is something everyone should do at least once in their lives. I understand that getting up at four in the morning to go for a five-hour game drive in the blistering sun is not everyone's idea of a vacation, but you must temper that with the fact that you can have two siestas, if you wish, before going out again for the sunset drive. There is absolutely nothing even remotely like the experience of standing in back of a Land Rover, watching the sun rise over the African bush, a herd of zebra and a giraffe silhouetted against the rising orange disc. It cuts to the very core of one's being; at that moment you are acutely conscious of the fact that you are standing in the cradle of civilization itself. It is a unique, unforgettable and life-changing experience.

Everyone agreed it was an excellent weekend. We saw a wide variety of game, especially elephants. A lot of sausages were consumed around the fire, and we made quick work of the liquor – except for the bottle of Angostura Bitters, there was some of that left, – and on the return journey, having lost a lot of weight, we took off almost vertically. We got the alcohol out of our system soon enough, but the trip to Botswana stayed with us forever.

* * *

The dirt airstrip we flew into is now owned by Mashatu Game Reserve. It has been renamed Limpopo Valley Airport and upgraded to a 5,000-foot paved runway, and commercial flights from Lanseria arrive and depart twice a week. Plus ça change!

BOTSWANA
Escape from Gaborone

"**R**ichard, it's Mark," said the voice down the phone at half past nine, one September morning in 1983.

"Mark, how good to hear from you! How's things in Botswana?" I said in as jolly a tone as I could muster for the time of day.

"Fine," said Mark. "Well, not really very fine... actually... not bloody fine at all. I am in a spot of trouble. I don't have much time, so you have to listen. I've been arrested and I'm in jail, in Gaborone. I could use some help, if you're not too busy. Can you get up here?"

"What? Jesus, yes. OK. Right," I stammered, scrambling for words.

"That's very good of you, thank you. I am in the Central Prison. Just come as fast as you can. Oh bugger, they are telling me I have to hang up already."

The line went dead.

My old schoolmate Tim Lanigan O'Keefe and I had just been beginning to stagger around the kitchen of our small rental house in Johannesburg, and get a handle on a blistering Saturday morning hangover, when Mark called. We sat nursing a coffee at the kitchen table and discussed the call, Mark's predicament, and our response. Our plans for this particular sunny Saturday in Johannesburg in 1983 had involved a bit of grass skiing,[56] not driving to Gaborone to rescue a friend from jail. And if I was to do anything at all, I needed to get rid of the angry troll in my head, which was wandering around kicking things vindictively.

Tim, who was always pro-active and positive, immediately started formulating a plan with a slightly military air.

"Right, what time is it now? About ten, OK, well we need to wear suits and ties –got to look like we mean business," he began. "If we leave in an hour, it shouldn't take more than about five hours to get to Gabs, then the first thing to do is try and see the poor man, so we can find out what the hell happened. We can be at the jail by about teatime, then do a quick recce[57] to find our way around..."

---

56 An incredibly silly and insanely dangerous sport which involves spending an inordinate amount of time in a plaster cast afterwards.

57 British slang for reconnaissance, or scout.

"You mean sixteen-hundred hours?" I interrupted, teasing him. He raised an eyebrow at me.

"OK," I said. "To Gabs we go! I'll organise a hotel, don't forget your passport. We'll leave in half an hour. Have you got any bloody paracetamol?" Without any warning at all, a regular *Boy's Own* adventure had just kicked off.

Leaving Jo'burg, we headed northwards towards Gaborone. Once away from the city, the road was the same for nearly 400kilometres; mostly straight, with wide grass verges to allow for a lot of swerving, and scrubby bush and low trees as far as you could see either side. We were always alert for pedestrians who, in the countryside, considered the road as much a public sidewalk as a road. They had a shocking disregard for the laws of physics and, in particular the potential effect of kinetic energy on human bodies. Slowly swaying ladies with impressive bundles on their heads, men bearing firewood, children herding assorted livestock, livestock herding assorted children and more; all used the road as if cars had not been invented yet and seemed quite amazed when one appeared coming straight at them at close to 100 miles per hour. In addition, there were rural jalopies driven by the country-folk that had long exceeded their scrap-by date, but still ran by some strange confluence of duct-tape and witchcraft, mostly without any mechanical fluids present.

Large pieces of bodywork frequently became detached, lying where they fell, like metallic roadkill. Major critical malfunctions, such as the engine dropping out or wheels falling off were common, and the car, in this deconstructed state, was usually left in the road. Often the driver and passengers, bereft of mechanical know-how, would be gathered around it, trying to will it back into life again. I had once come home to find our gardener staring mournfully at a stationary, silent lawn mower that was all of six months old. On asking him what was wrong with it, he shook his head forlornly, saying, "Boss, she is condemned."

In addition to all these hazards, many South Africans love driving fast, usually as fast as possible, sometimes faster. South African

Police are, unsurprisingly, equally fond of speed traps. Back in the 80s they used a mind-buggeringly dangerous method of trapping, the likes of which I have never encountered before or since. Selecting a temptingly straight section of road, they would run two pressure-sensitive black cables across the road, about two feet apart, which were almost impossible to see. Then, using rudimentary equipment that measured the speed at which a vehicle crossed these lines, they would set themselves up some 500 yards further down the road, in a medium-sized bush. Drivers coming the opposite way, seeing the waiting cops, would then flash their headlights furiously at any oncoming vehicle, to warn them; it was unwritten law that you should do so. So, the police would sit in the bush for some considerable period of time as car after car cruised past them, just under the speed limit. Eventually, an inattentive driver on the opposite side would not see the trap and would fail to flash oncoming traffic. Shortly after this, an unsuspecting car would cross the lines, usually at something approaching three quarters the speed of sound, whereupon the officers would enthusiastically leap out into the road in front of them, waving their arms wildly. The ensuing evasive action produced a lot of swerving and clouds of rubber smoke, before the driver invariably steered off the road onto the grass verge to slow to a stop without getting rammed by the car traveling three feet behind his bumper. This left the policemen's route back to safety cut off by the out-of-control vehicle, so they had no option but to stay out in the road, and face any traffic traveling in its slipstream. As you can imagine, this was a recipe for disaster. At worst, there were multiple-car pileups, general mayhem and, occasionally, death. At the very least it resulted in a hyperventilating cop, with an adrenaline overdose and a gun, appearing at your window as angry as a frog in a sock. Never a dull moment in Africa. Tim and I drove fast, with our eyes peeled, and I was delighted to have a co-driver.

We reached the border at Klipfontein, close to Gaborone, without incident. Passing easily into Botswana, we reviewed our plan, which then almost immediately unravelled. As we drove the last few miles into the city, for some inexplicable reason, but probably due to a complete lack of any signage, I went around a roundabout the wrong way and we were promptly stopped by the police. "Oh fuck!" said Tim, as we pulled over. "What do you think is the best approach?"

"Thompson Twins?" I suggested.

"Brilliant! Let's do it!" he responded.

The Thompson Twins were two incompetent, bickering detectives in Hergé's comic series *The Adventures of Tintin*, and an imitation of them could often be usefully employed to confound and confuse officials to the point where they just want to get rid of you. We leapt out of the car, vociferously arguing with each other at the top of our voices in pidgin French.

"Nincompoop!" Tim yelled at me.

"*Tu es completement fou – votre chien n'est pas faim!*" ("You are completely mad. Your dog is not hungry"). I shouted back. In between accusations and insults to each other, we both alternately apologized profusely and grovelingly.

"*Nous sommes desolé, Monsieur le Gendarme!* ("We are sorry, Mr. Policeman") said Tim.

"*Oui, absolument desolé!*" ("Yes, absolutely sorry") I agreed, adding for emphasis "*Aiiiiy, caramba!*" in Spanish, and slapping the side of my head. This had the effect of immediately rendering the policeman's usual spiel completely unworkable. Turning to Tim, I yelled, "*La plume de ma tante est dans le jardin,* idiot!" ("My Aunt's pen is in the garden, you idiot").

"*C'est pas dans le jardin!*" he screamed back, "*c'est dans la pou-belle!*" (It is not in the garden; it is in the rubbish bin).

The policeman could barely get a word in edgeways. Tim pulled off the coup-de-grace by shouting, at the top of his voice, to an imaginary third person:

"*Zut Alors! Je suis en-retard!* ("Heck, I am late"). And then, very sweetly to the policeman: "*Garcon, l'addition, s'il vous plaît!*" ("Waiter, the bill if you please").

He then kicked the car as hard as he could, before hopping around on one leg as if in pain. The policeman had had enough, and with a brief admonishment that we must obey the Botswana Highway Code, summarily waved us on our way so he could continue his day in an altogether less surreal way. Tim, warming to the success of his role, signed off with a flourish, *"Merci monsieur le gendarme! Maintenant, nous allons immediatement au boulangerie!"* ("Thank you, Mr. Policeman! Now we are immediately going to the bakery!") he said triumphantly, throwing an apple at me, for good measure.

So, if you're ever in trouble with the police just remember the Thompson Twins, and try your luck.

* * *

Botswana Central Jail was my first experience of any jail, let alone an African one. We went to the visitors' gate and were signed in, searched, and shown to the waiting room. After some time, Mark was led in, wearing prison overalls. He was understandably on edge as he relayed the full story.

Some months before, he had taken a job with a South African security fencing company. They had won a contract for a job in Gaborone and sent Mark up there to run the crew. Since then, he had been living in a tent in the fencing camp, just outside Gabs. Late in the afternoon the day before, he had finished work and was making his way back to the camp along a dirt road on the outskirts of the city. Stuck behind a slow lorry, and seeing there was no traffic coming, he had pulled out to overtake. The lorry driver, failing to look in his mirror or indicate, had suddenly began to turn right, forcing Mark off the road. In the ensuing accident, a pedestrian had been badly injured. A crowd had quickly gathered, and Mark had only been saved from an angry, possibly violent, confrontation by the arrival of the police. He was not at fault, had not been drinking, nor had he been driving dangerously or fast. It was the type of unfortunate accident all too common on African roads. Both Mark and the truck driver had been arrested and thrown in jail, as was the way in Botswana. Mark was inconsolable. It didn't help that he was being held in a cramped cell with 15 other inmates, most of whom were openly hostile towards him.

Leaving the jail, we were downhearted. Seeing Mark so despondent had shaken us. Suddenly it wasn't a *Boy's Own* adventure anymore. Shit, as they say, had got real. We checked into the Gaborone Sun Hotel and started making calls, first to a friend who had lived in Gabs, for a recommendation of a lawyer, then the British High Commission, and then the lawyer. The High Commission emergency line was about as useful as a lead lifebelt. The lawyer, on the other hand, was very accommodating and promised he would go and see Mark first thing Sunday morning.

Botswana is an arid, scrubby country, about the size of France, much of which is given over to the Kalahari Desert. At first glance, it apparently has nothing much going for it, other than a thriving safari tourism industry for people who want to see a rhinoceros before we humans hack them all into extinction. What the hell is wrong with Viagra? I could easily digress but will resist this time. A former British Protectorate, the lesser-known golden goose of Botswana's success has been one commodity: ethical, conflict-free diamonds. More extraordinary is that the government has managed this immensely valuable natural resource very well indeed. That makes it pretty much unique on a continent where countries routinely squander their people's wealth, lock up political rivals, engage in pointless wars and are eaten away from the inside by corruption, rank stupidity, tribalism and general thievery. In many cases this was as a result of the legacy left by western imperialism.

Upon independence in 1966, Botswana was one of the world's poorest countries, with a total of 12 kilometres of paved roads, 22 university graduates, and 100 secondary school graduates. But by African standards Botswana was, even by 1983, a commendable model of good management, well on its way to becoming one of the least corrupt, most stable countries in Africa. There were new hospitals, excellent schools, free healthcare, and education for all. Today, the road network covers 7,000-kilometres, and with $8 billion in central bank reserves, the government's credit rating is the highest on the continent. Only South Korea and China boast such startling increases in national wealth. For the visitor, Botswana's capital, Gaborone, is a generally clean, safe and functioning city, with decent hotels and an infrastructure that works. But as a city preoccupied with the very serious financial business of diamonds, it's really pretty dull. You definitely wouldn't go there for a fun time.

With a lawyer set up to see Mark in the morning, the Embassy unresponsive and visiting hours over, there was little more we could do than go and discuss matters over a beer.

Twenty-seven beers and a burger later, having gone over everything again and again, our senses had become dulled to the circumstances in which Mark found himself. We began looking around for something else help pass the time.

"I have an idea!" said Tim, pointing unsteadily across the lobby. "Let's go gambling!"

Gambling is legal in Botswana, and it was surprising that neither of us had registered, on arrival, the fact that the airport was full of fruit machines. Normally, this would have been a dead giveaway. Focusing carefully towards where he was pointing, I could see a large doorway, framed with a bright flashing neon sign, chasing lights and all the garish decorative elements synonymous with casinos worldwide. All that was missing was Michael Keaton's Beetlejuice shouting "Roll up! Roll up!"

Neither Tim nor I were gamblers, but I had on occasion had some fun at the blackjack tables of South African casinos. I always set myself a modest budget and played until that budget was spent. Sometimes I would last 20 minutes, sometimes all night, but I never dipped into my pocket above my set limit.

"How much have you got to lose, Tim?" I asked. He looked at me, wobbling slightly.

"Nothing to lose, old chap... we might as well go for it."

"That's not what I meant. How much are you prepared to lose? Twenty, fifty? A hundred?"

"I'll tell you when I've lost it," he said, as he lurched off his chair, waving one hand in the air. "Let's go!"

Sunday morning began rather slowly and delicately, the memory of the night before slowly reassembling itself in our foggy brains. Although I preferred blackjack, as the outcome depended on at least some element of skill, Tim had insisted we play roulette. The alcohol had said, "Yeah! Go for it!" so we had thrown caution to the winds, pooled our resources to create a pot of fifty Rand[58] and headed for the tables.

Perhaps we had earned good karma for leaping to Mark's rescue, or perhaps the alcohol gave us just the right amount of bravado, but Lady Luck was smiling on us that evening. Slowly but surely the little pile of chips in front of us grew. The drinks kept flowing and the pile kept growing, and after some time we were joined by two quite provocatively dressed local ladies, who seemed very friendly indeed. They clapped appreciatively every time we won something and consoled us when we lost. There was much animated discussion between us as to the colour and number of our next pick. After a while, the women began to get a bit touchy feely and a bit of shoulder rubbing started. I leaned close to Tim and attempted to whisper in his ear.

"Who the hell are these two?" I asked, naively, indicating our two voluntary companions.

"Hookers," whispered Tim, as if it were perfectly normal, which I suppose it was.

"Oh! I thought they worked for the casino!"

"Don't be ridiculush," slurred Tim.

We played on, getting increasingly vocal about our gains and losses, until a change of croupier prompted us to quit while we were ahead. The ladies of the night took this as their cue to part us with as much of our money as possible and went into overdrive.

"Hey, handsome," said Lady A, putting her hands in all sorts of startling places. "Why don't you boys come back to our place and we can get jiggy?"

---

58 About £30.

"Yeah, we have nice place, and we give you good time!" said Lady B, trying to nibble Tim's ear.

Drunk as we were, neither Tim nor I were of a mind to head out into the African night, to an unknown destination, rich with spoils, to get jiggy with strange women. Apart from anything else, we were sufficiently attuned to Africa to know that this would have been, for a wide variety of reasons, a monumentally bad idea. As we walked across the lobby towards the elevator, we eventually managed to take our leave from them as politely and firmly as we could, much as one might disentangle oneself from a particularly sticky cobweb, into which one had unexpectedly stumbled. You know, the kind that immediately triggers a lot of wheeling arm rotations? It is fair to say they were not best pleased, and as the doors closed, hurled several derogatory comments at us belittling our manhood and sexuality.

Tim and I slumped in our room, having a totally unnecessary nightcap from the minibar.

"I shink-ish bedtime."

"Wha' time izzt?"

"Jesush, it's two in the morning!"

"How mush did we win?"

Tim put a handful of chips on the table and we counted them slowly and deliberately, like small children.

"850 rand![59] Bloody marvellous!"

"Brilliant! Lesh go to bed."

* * *

We rose late, nursing our second hangover in as many mornings, but chuffed by our win at the tables. We proceeded to fuel up with an enormous, carb-loaded breakfast. The lawyer was due to see Mark at eleven o'clock, so at noon we made our way over to Central Prison,

---

59 In 1983, about £500. At the time of writing, about £36, which is indicative for the precipitous decline in the value of the Rand.

bearing a Kit-Kat and nuts from the mini bar, and the grey pin-striped suit we had brought for him from Johannesburg. Sunday at the jail was busy, with many families visiting, and the car park was crowded with cars and mini-bus taxis, and church-fresh ladies with elaborate hats and cartwheeling with children in tow. As the only two white guys there, and dressed in suits, we stuck out like two white guys in an African prison. We waited our turn to be processed through security and finally found ourselves sitting in front of Mark.

"So, what did the lawyer say?" we asked. Mark looked despondent.

"Well, this sort of accident is apparently common in Botswana[60] and it is likely the judge will fine me and let me go. I wasn't drunk or driving dangerously. I have to be in court at nine tomorrow morning. Anyway, there is something else that is a bit of a problem."

"Oh, bloody hell, what?" said Tim.

"Well," began Mark, wringing his hands. "Before I left Jo'burg I needed some work clothes, so I went to one of those army surplus places and picked up several pairs of camo-trousers, a few t-shirts and a jacket."

I wondered where he was going with this and how his choice of wardrobe could possibly be a problem.

"They were dead cheap and perfect for the job. Anyway, it seems they have caused a bit of a rumpus. I got a visit from a couple of chaps yesterday afternoon – I think they must have been 'Secret Police' or something. They got word from the prison that a white chap wearing SADF[61] camouflage trousers had been arrested and they seemed to think I was some sort of South African spy. They weren't very friendly."

"Oh, shit!" said Tim and I in unison.

This was an "Oh, shit!" moment, because the 1980s were not exactly a high point in relations between Botswana and South Africa. With

---

60 In 2017, pedestrian deaths were around two per day in the greater Gaborone area alone. Statistics for 1982 are not available.

61 South African Defense Force.

the Botswana Government's tacit approval, the African National Congress (ANC) used Botswana as a refuge and had set up several guerrilla training bases in Gaborone. Under the guise of weekend tourists, ANC recruits would receive basic grenade training and be given a list of things to lob one at. In retaliation, the South African Defence Force (SADF) conducted occasional cross-border raids to shut these operations down. In 1981, the Botswana Government, with the not unreasonable excuse that it needed to better defend itself, did an arms deal with the Russians. This gave the SADF a complete sense of humour failure and, in April 1982, shots were exchanged across the Botswana-South African border.

"So, you were wearing this SADF camo gear when you had the accident?" I said. Mark nodded.

"Houston, we have a problem," said Tim, dramatically.

"Oh, God, I know!" said Mark, clearly in some anguish. "Look, I have even more of the bloody stuff out at my camp, and I think it might be a good idea if you went out there and got rid of it right now – burn it on the fire. At the same time, maybe you could grab all my gear, and my passport – there's not much, just throw it in my duffle bag."

Mark is one of the most delightful people you could ever hope to meet. Gentle, kind, quintessentially British, eye-wateringly funny, hard-working, accomplished dog-whisperer and lover of women, there is not a bad bone in his body. If someone had suggested to me that he might be charged with spying for South Africa, I would never have believed them.

"Oh, and speaking of passports, there's one more problem." said Mark, just when we were hoping there wasn't.

"*Another* one?" Tim and I said in unison, again.

"Yes, well, it's a small one really… small in the overall scheme of things. My Botswana visa has expired, so getting out of the country without problems with immigration could be a bit tricky."

By this time, Tim and I were feeling slightly overwhelmed, so we agreed to jump off that bridge when we came to it. Following

Mark's directions, we set off for the camp, our heads whirling with the implications of what he had just told us. On leaving the prison, his visit from the secret police was foremost in our mind.

"They will be following us," said Tim.

"Who?"

"The goons," said Tim, looking around conspiratorially. "The Secret Service. No doubt about it, we will have to be very careful. This could get nasty."

We had gone about half a mile, with Tim looking anxiously in the mirror every few seconds, before our fears were confirmed.

"There's a white car a little way back," said Tim. "Turn left at the next circle."[62] I duly turned left. "Bugger! They are following us; we'll have to try and lose them."

The next ten minutes were spent weaving left and right along the dirt roads of various Gaborone sub divisions, trying everything we could think of from years spent watching action thrillers about how to lose someone who was tailing you. I was somewhat dubious that we were in fact being followed, but Tim was convinced.

"Turn left here… accelerate! OK, right at this one… now left by that dog… watch out for that man, he looks drunk… they're still behind us, but further back…"

The fact that we were actually being pursued by the secret police of an African nation was starting to dawn on us with an increasing sense of gravity. It is never a good thing to hear the words "pursuit", "African" and "secret police" in the same sentence, especially when applied to oneself. The good news was that we were only being followed by a lone car, and that it was generally a slow speed affair. A desire to capture us was probably not on their agenda, as they had not been joined by other vehicles, sprouting guns, machetes, and attitude. More likely, they had just been assigned to keep an eye on us, not apprehend us – for the time being. Nevertheless, in true car chase tradition, we had a lucky encounter with a reversing lorry, managing

---

62 A roundabout in Southern Africa.

to scoot around it before it blocked the road, and so made good our escape. I felt as if several dozen hummingbirds were doing a Busby Berkeley[63] number in my stomach. Our pursuers were presumably shat on from a dizzy height by their superior for being so stupid as to have lost us.

Following Mark's directions, we arrived at the fencing camp in the bush, not far outside Gabs. There was a gate with a combination lock, and, inside, piles of fencing posts and high rolls of wire. At the back, several tents had been pitched but as it was Sunday, there was no one around. A campfire was smouldering, so someone had probably cooked breakfast. Emptying Mark's tent of gear, we found his passport, stuffed the few possessions he had into his duffle bag and threw the remaining camo clothing, papers and any other evidence of Mark's presence, onto the fire, where it blazed satisfactorily. We left as soon as we were sure everything had been destroyed, locking the gate behind us, and headed back into Gaborone. We drove cautiously, expecting at any moment to encounter a police roadblock, as if that would somehow attract less attention. Conversely, the sight of a car driving cautiously was extremely unusual and seemed to attract a great deal of attention.

A bystander might have remarked, "Oh, look, there's a car driving very strangely – it just stopped at that stop sign."

We managed to get back to the hotel without incident, parked the car and headed back to our rooms. Not wanting to be seen anywhere, we ordered room service and spent the evening emptying our minibars, in fear of hearing a rifle butt hammering on the door at any moment.

None came. The next morning, we donned our suits and ties and headed to the courthouse. It was a sweltering hot day in Gaborone, and we saw Mark briefly before we went in. He was very nervous, and very hot.

---

63 Busby Berkeley was famous for producing elaborate musical dance numbers in films during the 1920s to 1950s that often involved kaleidoscopic geometric patterns.

"What were you thinking?! You brought my winter suit! Look at me, I'm sweating like a farm animal! Wish me luck."

We did, while his lawyer quickly ushered him inside and Tim and I found a bench in the hallway to sit on. The proceedings ran long, as there were quite a few cases before Mark's, but eventually he reappeared, with a slightly amazed look on his face.

"What happened?"

"Well, he gave me a 500 Pula fine, and probation."

"This sort of accident is not uncommon in Botswana," said the lawyer. "And this fine is quite a lot of money for the average Botswanan."

"So, are you free to go?" I said.

"Yes," said the lawyer. "He is on probation, but he's a free man. I suggest you get him across the border as fast as you can."

We bundled Mark into the car and quickly back to the hotel for a shower and a change of clothes. I paid our mini bar bill while Tim took Mark up to the room. Three nights in an African jail, in 30-degree heat, had given him the bouquet of an incontinent goat. While Mark was washing off the goatiness, Tim and I cracked a beer and had a quick stroky-beard meeting to devise our escape from Botswana.

"If the secret police are genuinely interested in us, now is the time they are most likely to come and get us," Tim said. "Mark's out of the prison and we are all together."

I spread out our map. "There is an exit from the car park to the road behind the hotel, so we could walk out of one of the side doors into the car park, and hope that our Goons are only watching the front?" I suggested, tracing a route on the map with my finger. "Then we could go around all these back roads to see if we are being tailed, and head towards the border this way."

Tim thought for a moment. "They will be assuming we will take the closest way out. So, instead of going back over at Klipfontein," he said, continuing the line on the map, "how about we head down to Lobatse or Ramatlabama and cross there."

"That makes sense," said Mark, who was towelling his hair with one hand and drinking a beer with the other. "Ramatlabama is in the middle of nowhere. Not many people use it, and I might have a slightly better chance of being able to blag my way through the visa problem."

"OK, let's get out of here," I said, grabbing my bag.

We got out of Gaborone without anyone following us, as far as we could tell, so either they had lost interest, or our initial tail had not been replaced by a more competent team. One would have to think that even a slightly trained intelligence service goon would be able to keep an eye on us, three amateurs in a car with South African plates. We headed south at the speed limit and about two hours later came up to the border. Mark had remained silent throughout. There was no traffic on the Botswanan side and only one *bakkie*[64] coming through from South Africa. Being a low traffic border crossing, this was not a drive through facility, and we had to park, get out and walk up to a window. Our strategy was that we would all walk up together and present our passports in one stack of three, with Mark's at the bottom. We decided our best hope lay in overwhelming them with good-natured banter. There was only one window open. Behind it sat a pleasant looking Botswanan lady with a brightly coloured scarf around her head. Next to her, on the desk, was a large white cabbage. We all clustered around the window, Tim and I smiling and saying hello in an exaggeratedly jolly way.

"*Thupama e monate!*" ("Good afternoon!") boomed Mark, in Setswana. Mark, always incredibly engaging, with his big smile, turquoise eyes and exuding charm from every pore, could light people up in a way few can. Having not spoken a word since we left Gaborone, this came out of the blue; our plan to not attract attention was rapidly going pear-shaped.

"OK, *le kae?*" ("OK, how are you?") responded Mrs. Customs and Immigration immediately, with a huge smile. She began flicking

---

64 Pick-up truck.

through Tim's and my passports, checking the entry stamp, looking carefully at us, then stamping the exit stamp. She put Tim's passport down on the counter, next to mine and started to flick through Mark's. We held our breath. It looked as if Mark would surely be rumbled.

"*O mo botse!*" ("She is beautiful!") said Mark suddenly and loudly, just as she reached his visa page. Mrs. Customs and Immigration looked up, thinking this compliment was being paid to her, to see Mark pointing at her magnificent cabbage. Completely distracted, she burst into peals of laughter, slapping the desk as her shoulders heaved and her large bosom bounced up and down. Seeing he had struck pay dirt, Mark pressed home his advantage.

"*E ke bokae?*" ("How much is this?") "Please can I buy it?" he said in both Setswana and English.

Mrs. C&I exploded with laughter again. "Noooo, it is not for sale, it is for my dinner!" She turned to tell her friend the other side of the office what Mark had just said, and they both doubled up with laughter, as did we. Catching her breath and wiping a tear from the corner of her eye, she turned back to Mark and, without even a glance at his out-of-date visa, stamped his passport, closed it and pushed all three back under the glass towards us. I grabbed them as fast as I could, and we thanked her profusely.

"*Ke a leboga, mma!*" said Mark. "*Itumelele dojo!*" ("Thank you! Have a nice meal!")

"*Tsamaya sentle,*" ("Go well!") She called after him with a giggle.

"*Mokoro wa me o tletse ditlhapi!*" ("My hovercraft is full of eels")[65] shouted Mark back, waving cheerily. We pulled away, and could see she was still heaving with laughter. Instead of her ruining our day, we had made hers. We were free and clear, on the road back to Jo'burg, rescue complete, a chapter in Mark's life closed, and a major diplomatic incident averted.

I needed a beer though.

---

65 From the Monty Python's Flying Circus "Hungarian phrasebook sketch".

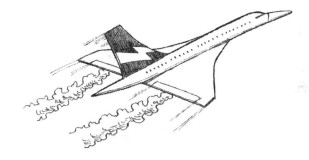

LUNCH
At the Speed of Sound

I felt a frisson of excitement as the engine thrust rose, although our brakes held us firmly in place. There were unfamiliar vibrations and a sense of pent-up energy, temporarily restrained by mere slivers of carbon. The brakes snapped open and, with unimaginable power suddenly unleashed, my adrenalin surged as Messrs. Rolls and Royce thrust us down the runway at 250 miles per hour.

It was April 1991, The Management and I were planning a business trip to London for a series of meetings. The year before had been a rough year for airlines, one of the most painful in history, and Pan Am had just gone bust. A standard return business class ticket from LA to London was $5,000. With sales dwindling, in desperation, Air France offered a brilliant promotion: if you bought a business class, return ticket from New York to Paris, they would fly you one way on Concorde at no additional cost. As our client covered business class tickets, this was a once in a lifetime opportunity to travel on Le Concorde, à Paris.

* * *

Earlier that morning, ground crew scuttled about Air France flight 001, fuelling, checking, loading, cleaning, and provisioning her with the contents of a small royal kitchen. Concorde had presence, like the Audrey Hepburn of aircraft – impossibly thin, impeccably turned out, with beautiful flowing lines, an air of grace, and an unusually attractive tail. When she arrived, everybody stopped and turned. Her needle-sharp nose stood out among the bulbous snouts of the other aircraft, leaving her slimline, supersonic, fighter-jet pedigree beyond doubt.

In the Concorde lounge, the Management returned to our seat with a little plate of nibbles and a smoked salmon sandwich. I was about to say I thought eight in the morning a bit early for a smoked salmon sandwich, when I remembered that in her opinion there is never a time when it was too early, or too late, for a smoked salmon sandwich. A waiter arrived with two glasses of the sort of champagne we would never buy for ourselves, and never drink at that hour of the morning, but would have been certifiably insane to refuse. It took barely a nanosecond for my "Madness not to" synapse to crisply slap my "Not right now, thank you" reflex. My suprachiasmatic nucleus (that's a group of about 20,000 nerve cells tucked away in the hypothalamus that is our master clock) instantly did an emergency reset to Parisian lunchtime, and my primary motor cortex instructed my arm to take the glass without further delay, before the opportunity wandered off and presented itself to Mr. Hedge Fund next door. All this took under two seconds. It was a useful variation on the Neanderthal reflex that enabled the instantaneous capture of a saber-toothed squirrel that had stuck its head out of its hole for a quick look around.[66] We knew we were poised for a once in a lifetime experience and the start of a high-speed, airborne *grande bouffe*, the likes of which few lucky souls experience. So, we both settled back in our seats with a glass of excellent fizz and a smoked salmon sandwich, confident in the knowledge that it was now entirely appropriate to consume both so early in the morning. Carpe Cristal!

On boarding the aircraft (tail number F-BTSD, but more on that later) we found two-plus-two seating stretched the length of the plane. Although only sixteen-feet shorter than a 747, Concorde was about the width of an average bus, so it was more like boarding a stretched executive jet, than a commercial airliner. The doorway was low, requiring a slight stoop, but this didn't seem to faze the four French models who undulated aboard ahead of us. They oozed sex appeal, in a way that makes one quite irrationally pull in one's stomach and straighten one's back, in the entirely mistaken belief this will make you irresistibly attractive and inspire them to give you their telephone number. Within seconds of being seated, we had another glass of vintage fantastic-ness, and some more scrumptious little nibbles pressed into our hands. As I had read, the windows

---

66 It is interesting, but completely irrelevant, to note that an illustration of the saber-toothed squirrel-like mammal known as Cronopio Dentiacutus reveals the creature's striking resemblance to Scrat in the film Ice Age.

were noticeably smaller than average, rather like Donald Trump's hands,[67] and I found I had to duck down slightly, craning my neck to see out. This was an observation, not a complaint, I explained to The Management, who had stealthily hoovered up my little *amuse bouche* while I wasn't looking. My *bouche* was not *amused.*

In most aircraft, the taxi-out is the most mundane part of the trip, often lengthy and best used as an opportunity to nod-off, or see how surreptitiously one can excavate one's nose. In Concorde, it was an entirely different experience. Looking out of the window, I noticed that almost everyone on the ground stopped what they were doing to watch as Concorde passed by. People never tired of her, knowing they were witnessing a unique aircraft of extraordinary beauty. Even the baggage handlers, bus drivers, fuel trucks, ground personnel, and construction workers, who probably saw her daily, all stopped, turned, and watched, imagining for a moment that they might one day be inside, looking out. Their daydream was fleeting. Concorde taxied fast, like a speed-walker in a crowd of dazed pedestrians. More surprisingly, she even jumped to the head of the queue, slipping rapidly past other waiting aircraft, and barging right into the number one take-off slot. One might think this would produce a torrent of snark from other aircraft:

"Excuuuuse me, Concorde! This is Delta four-zero-seven. Are you aware there is a *line* here … aaasssss-hole!"

But no, this queue-barging was officially due to prudence, not a privilege of rank. Concorde's massive Rolls Royce Olympus 593/610 turbojet engines, each equipped with afterburners,[68] were extremely inefficient on the ground, and when taxiing could burn as much as two tons of fuel. It was essential to get from ramp to runway as

---

67 Don't take my word for it. After Trump's state visit to Britain in 2019, I have it on rock-solid authority Queen Elizabeth II told her hairdresser that she immediately noticed Trump had "very small hands indeed". I am not kidding.

68 An afterburner is mostly used on military supersonic aircraft. Its purpose is to provide a temporary increase in thrust, and improve the profitability and excitement of movies like Top Gun..

fast as possible, to ensure a safe amount remained in reserve. This ensured the pilots didn't have an "oh fuck, Carruthers!" moment somewhere over Shannon, as all four engines suddenly went quiet. In fact, none of the other pilots resented her as she rolled past them and slid into position at the top of the queue. In the aviation world, everybody loved Concorde, and there was a good deal of deference involved – in the same way one might invite Maggie Smith to jump the queue at Starbucks without anyone else objecting in the slightest.

In the baking hot summer of 1976, one of the new Concordes was doing "touch-and-go's" for a week at RAF Brize Norton in Oxford-shire, about three miles from our family home. My best boyhood buddy, Tom, and I, hopped on our bikes and pedalled furiously over to Brize. The road ran right along the end of the runway and was controlled by traffic lights, which we could easily ignore. We threw down our bikes on the grass verge, right at the fence on the centre line of the runway, lit up a big spliff, and happily watched Concorde roar in 30 feet over our heads, touch down, light up its afterburners and thunder back up into the sky again. Round and round it went, for several hours each day. There was no more outrageous fun a teen-age boy could have had in 1976, short of being propositioned for a threesome by Goldie Hawn and Farrah Fawcett.

Fifteen years later, back at JFK, I was again having outrageous fun, but this time – astonishingly – on the inside looking out. Teenage me would have been delighted. The nose-wheel lifted, a giant invisible hand pressed us back hard in our seats, and with all four engines at full throttle and afterburners ablaze, we thundered steeply skywards. Yeeeeeehaaaaagh! Banking thrillingly to avoid irritating New Yorkers more than they are naturally, we completed a 180-degree turn and streaked out over the Atlantic. Thousands of people on the ground reluctantly turned their eyes back to what they had been doing, their day made momentarily less mundane.

Although gas guzzlers on the ground, in the air at Mach 2, Con-corde's engines were the most fuel efficient ever built. A large, digital speedometer mounted on the front bulkhead showed our speed as we accelerated through the sound barrier. Apart from the thrill of take-off, here was no sensation of travelling that fast; it was smooth as silk. Nor was there any unexpected noise. So, the perception of speed was entirely in one's head, and felt no different from a normal aircraft. What was different, in every way, was the level of in-flight service. Our flight time was estimated to be three hours and 20 minutes, and exactly 20 minutes after wheels-up, our tables were being laid for the most extravagant airborne meal one could imagine. There was no in-flight entertainment – none was needed – so that left just enough time for a long lunch while cruising faster than a rifle bullet. There was salad, medallions of fresh foie gras, caviar, boeuf-en-croute (perfectly cooked), lobster, crêpes suzette, petit-fours, and more. The wines included Taittinger Comtes de Champagnes, a Chablis Premier Cru, and a Lynch-Bages. In the time it took to pour a glass of any one of them, we had travelled 26 miles. We finished it off with a cup of delicious stratospheric coffee and a speed-of-sound Cognac. A lot has been written about the miserable quality of food aloft, and the airlines have led us to believe that the challenges of catering in the air make the achievement of a high standard extremely difficult. Concorde conclusively proved that it is possible to serve up quite excellent meals and did so successfully for many years.

As I had been told it would, the window felt warm to the touch. Due to friction at high speed, the outside of the aircraft gets extremely hot, and the entire plane expands 10 inches in length during flight. There was even a spot in the cockpit, by the navigator's desk, where a six-inch gap appeared between the panel and the back wall. On any other plane, this would be a good reason to run screaming for a parachute.

Craning my neck once again, I could see the spectacular curvature of the earth and the blackness of space above, even though it was broad daylight over the mid-Atlantic. I imagined its surface, 58,000 feet below, under a layer of puffy white clouds. With no other civil traffic operating at its lofty cruising altitude, Concorde had exclusive use of dedicated oceanic airways, or "tracks" independent of the lower routes used by the other portly aircraft lumbering across the Atlantic. Far above the weather and the transatlantic bus route below, these tracks never changed, so Concorde's course was always the same. John Hutchinson, Concorde Captain, once explained:

> "The only thing that tells you that you're moving is that occasionally when you're flying over the subsonic aircraft, you can see all these 747s 20,000 feet below you almost appearing to go backward, I mean you are going 800 miles an hour faster than they are. The aeroplane was an absolute delight to fly, it handled beautifully. And remember we are talking about an aeroplane that was being designed in the late 1950s – mid 1960s. I think it's absolutely amazing, and here we are, now in the twenty-first century, and it remains unique."

The last delicious crumbs of our lengthy, stratospheric Mach 2 lunch were cleared away. There was barely time to hand out certificates signed by the flight crew, authenticating our journey, altitude, heartburn, and speed, before we were descending to land at Paris Charles de Gaulle. Due to the extremely large surface area of its delta wing, Concorde comes in to land fast, and at a very high angle of attack (nose up). It feels rather like a chairlift at a ski resort that comes in quickly, then slows rapidly, tilting you backward, before dropping you onto a steep, badly grooved patch of snow that makes you immediately topple flat on your face, or crash into a small child. Once again, a fast taxi put us quickly at the gate, and we were bid farewell to in a chorus of "Au revoir!" by the flight crew.

The crash at Paris's Orly Airport in 2000 sealed the fate of Concorde. Expensive to operate, loaded with increasingly obsolete avionics, and fuel hungry engines, the British and French Concorde fleets were first grounded then, in 2003, decommissioned. British Airways retained ownership of all their Concordes, ostensibly to prevent Richard Branson from getting his hands on one and operating it in Virgin livery. This would have been their worst nightmare. Branson had publicly announced that Virgin was interested in purchasing the entire British Airways' Concorde fleet for £1. This was a symbolic offer, as it was the amount BA had paid the British Government for them in the first place. British Airways, who would rather have given their Concordes to the Army for target practice than let Branson get his hands on them, told him to go to hell. Keen to needle his arch-rival, Branson claimed that, when BA was privatised, a clause in the agreement required them to allow another British airline to operate Concorde, if BA ever ceased to do so. The British Government flatly denied that any such clause existed, pouring cold water on Branson's hopes. One day all will be revealed, but I happen to know that Richard keeps a scale model of a Virgin Atlantic Concorde on his desk as a permanent reminder of how close he came to owning them.

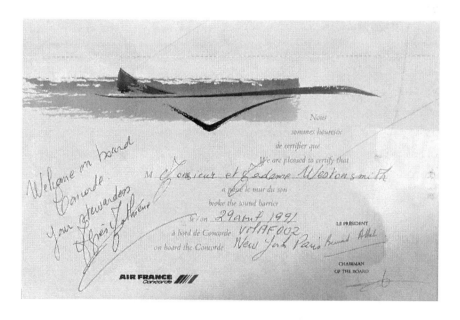

Every passenger received a Concorde Flight Certificate.

Little did we know that this particular aircraft, known as "Sierra Delta" (for the last two letters of its F-BTSD call sign), was for a couple of reasons going to turn out to be a very special Concorde. The following year, it would set the world records for the fastest flights around the world, in both directions, in 32 and 31 hours respectively. At the time of writing, it still holds them.

But there is something even more special about Sierra Delta that only a few people know. When the entire Air France Concorde fleet was decommissioned, along with all the other Concordes, there was one exception – Sierra Delta. On June 14th 2003, Air France handed over ownership of Sierra Delta to the Air and Space Museum at Le Bourget. A group of French Concorde engineers proposed that it be kept alive after its delivery to the museum. Since then, Sierra Delta has been on the aviation equivalent of life support, nursed by this dedicated team, the only remaining Concorde in the world that was never decommissioned.

Although she is not airworthy, the preservation of Sierra Delta is second to none. Once a week, ground power is switched on and her flight deck, interior and navigation lights burst into life. She is lovingly cared for by former Air France Concorde engineer Alexandra Jolivet, who heads the team that keeps the hydraulics systems, electrics, nose, visor and flight controls all in working order. In such a state, Sierra Delta is the great white hope of Concorde aficionados the world over, who believe that one day she might return to the skies. However, putting the giant Rolls Royce engines back in working order and restoring the airframe to an airworthy condition would be a gargantuan task of unknown duration, and with no hope of financial viability. So, despite the weekly efforts by the small group of dedicated engineers at Le Bourget to keep her alive, it is very unlikely she will ever fly again.

Deep in the darkest recesses of Charles de Gaulle, the baggage handlers were busy giving zero *merdes*[69] about our bags, as they stopped for a Gitanes[70] break. Unlike the blisteringly fast crossing we had just made, our luggage struggled to move 1,000 yards. In the time it

---

69 Shits.

70 Gitanes, meaning "Gypsy", is a brand of cigarettes synonymous with France. The first art-deco packet design was produced by Maurice Giot in 1927.

took for us to receive it, Concorde could have comfortably covered the distance from Paris to Istanbul. The baggage representative I explained this to shot me a withering look that clearly communicated his dislike of all things not French – especially me – accompanied by a Gallic shrug of indifference for additional emphasis. Nevertheless, some items definitely shifted in me on this flight, and Concorde remains the highlight of my life's airborne experiences. I am eternally thankful that I seized the moment and booked the ticket. Although one may never be able to fly on Concorde again, it will be interesting to see if the new generation of supersonic passenger aircraft, such as Boom, live up to her lofty standards.

Vive Le Concorde!

ST. THOMAS, VIRGIN ISLANDS
I am Taking Your Son

I was at St. Thomas airport in the U.S. Virgin Islands, with our eldest son, Xan, who was about twelve at the time. Xan was a bright boy, gregarious and fun. He was on his way to England to see his grandparents, and I was heading back to LA. We were going to part ways at New York. We were waiting in line to get my ticket changed for the new flight that my travel agent had already arranged with the airline but, back in those days, it actually needed to be applied to a piece of dead tree in order to work. There was someone ahead of me at the desk, so Xan and I waited patiently. After about 15 minutes, the man at the desk turned around.

"This is taking a very long time," the man said. "I am so sorry to be holding you up, but our ticket seems to be rather complicated."

It was Richard Branson.

"That's quite alright," I replied, smiling. "We still have some time before our flight".

"I hope it won't be much longer," he grimaced.

Turning back to Xan I whispered, "Do you know who that is?"

"No, who?"

"Richard Branson!"[71]

"Wow!! Coooool!

Several more minutes passed, and the desk agent was still holding on the phone to some distant office, so she beckoned me up, saying to Richard, "Do you mind if I see if I can help this gentleman while we are waiting?"

"No, no, of course, please do," he replied.

"How can I help you, sir," she asked.

I explained that I simply needed a new paper ticket as I had changed my flight, and she started working on both our tickets together. It turned out that Richard and I were on the same flight to JFK. He was going to on London, with this wife Joan, son Sam and daughter Holly, connecting to a Virgin flight at JFK. As the agent

---

71 Founder & CEO of the Virgin Group. Best known for founding Virgin Records and Virgin Atlantic Airlines, and now the billionaire head of the global Virgin Group.

worked, Richard and I started chatting. About 20 minutes went by, in which we covered a lot of ground and got on famously. It turned out he had a house just outside Oxford, close to my parents, where Xan was headed. Xan was chatting with Richard's son Sam, who was almost the same age, and they seemed to be having a good time.

As the agent finished issuing his ticket, Richard suddenly turned to me and said

"Look, rather than put Xan alone on that AA flight, why doesn't he just come back with me on Virgin from JFK? I am sure we will have a spare seat and I can easily have one of our cars drop him back to your parent's house?"

"My goodness, that's incredibly kind of you, Richard" I gushed. "but I am sure he will be fine on his flight. thank you though, very much!" Having barely known him half an hour I wasn't sure if he really meant it, and didn't want to take advantage. Despite being one of the most famous men in the world, he was still a stranger to me (it's a British thing).

So, with his ticket issued, we said our goodbyes and he headed off to board. What a delightful man, I thought.

"Papa! He just offered to take me on his plane!"

"Yes, darling, wasn't that sweet of him?"

"But you said no!" He looked astonished that I had declined the invitation, giving me that "WTF!" look that children give you before they are allowed to say WTF without being grounded for several years.

"Yes, darling, but often you can't just accept an invitation right away, because people sometimes offer things to be polite, but they don't really expect you to accept. It's just good manners."

"Well, that's stupid. Why would they offer if they don't mean it?" Xan said accurately, looking crestfallen.

Our tickets were quickly sorted, so Xan and I followed about five minutes later. We got to the plane just before they closed the doors. Richard and his family were in first class, and we waved on our way past to take the last two available seats at the back of the plane.

The flight was uneventful and relatively brief. At JFK it took quite some time to unload, and we were last off the plane, with the flight attendants and crew. Xan and I walked up the jetway, and out into the corridor. Standing there, much to my amazement, was Richard, with one of his smartly dressed Virgin Atlantic supervisors, holding a clipboard and a radio.

He had been waiting for us.

"Ah, there you are, Richard!" Richard said to me. "I just wanted to let you know that I checked, but apparently we are full up on the London flight, so I am really terribly sorry, but Xan won't be able to come with us."

"Richard, that's too kind of you! Honestly, there was no need to wait for me, really! Please, don't worry, I know Xan will be fine!" I could not believe that he had not only taken the trouble to ask on arrival, but to wait for me to come out to tell me it wasn't possible. What sort of person would do that? Xan shot me a see-he-did-mean-it! look. We chatted together all the way to the baggage carousel, said goodbye, and he went to one side to join his family and Xan and I waited for our bags on the other. I had deliberately left plenty of time before my flight to LA, but Xan's connection was in about an hour, so was a little on the tight side.

There was a long delay before the baggage carousel even started turning, and by the time the bags started dribbling out, I was becoming concerned that Xan might not make his connecting AA London flight. It was starting to look increasingly likely that we would both be staying the night at JFK and then flying the next day.

Just as I looked at my watch for the umpteenth time, I felt a hand on my shoulder and a voice. "It's all organised!"

It was Richard. Again.

"Look, I can see Xan is going to miss his flight because of this luggage delay," he said, indicating the departures board. "But I don't think my plane will leave without me," he smiled. "We've a seat that's opened up, so he's coming with us." There was no use protesting any further; as far as he was concerned it was a fait accompli. Xan looked as if he had just been offered a VIP tour of Wonka's chocolate factory, which in many ways he had.

"Write down your parents' address," said Richard. "I will have a car take him straight there. Also, give me their phone number. I will have someone call them early in the morning, while we are all still in the air, to make sure they don't leave for the airport."

"Richard," I said. "I can't thank you enough, but it feels pretty weird just handing Xan to you and walking away. Are you really sure this is OK with you?" Xan poked me in the ribs, to emphasise that traveling *first class to England with the Branson family* was really quite OK with him, and could I please not screw this up.

"Don't be silly, it's perfectly fine. They can play video games all the way[72]," he said, tousling Xan's hair. "You'll be OK, Xan, won't you?"

Xan nodded vigorously.

"I will personally make sure he gets safely to his grandparents," Richard said as Xan began walking off with Sam, already unbothered about me.

Richard and I chatted until our bags finally made an appearance. Shaking Richard's hand, I thanked him and Joan profusely, and turned Xan over to the Branson family. It felt odd to hand him over to people I had known for less than four hours, and yet it also felt completely right. I was not even slightly worried. Branson's offer was not made in a brash, boastful way. It was born out of a genuine generosity of spirit. He had no need or desire to impress me – he didn't even know me. I liked him for that. Richard's kindness got me to thinking: the strangest things happen when you travel, because you are putting yourself out there in front of fate and saying, "Do with me what you will!" It is pretty much a sure bet that if you had stayed at home, Richard Branson would not ring your doorbell and offer to take your son to London.

The next morning, the phone rang unusually early at my parent's

---

72 At the time, only Virgin offered Game Boy hand-held video games players in First Class. An unheard of perk for kids.

house. I can imagine my father grumbling, "Who the bloody hell is calling at this ungodly hour?"

Three hours later, Xan was delivered to them safely, as promised, in a gleaming black, chauffeur-driven Range Rover, having had the best flight of his young life, and an experience he would never forget. My father summed Richard up succinctly. "What an extraordinary, thoughtful and generous man." I couldn't agree more.

★ ★ ★

Some months later, after Xan had flown back to the US, unaccompanied, I noticed that he did not receive airmiles for his trip. When I asked a Virgin representative why this was, I was told that unaccompanied minors were not eligible for airmiles credit on flights. I protested that his ticket cost no less than an adult ticket, and that it was ridiculous that should be the rule. He agreed, but said that was all he could do. I wrote to Richard, pointing out that he had an opportunity to earn the loyalty of young travellers who could be customers for life. The letter I got in reply says it all.

Virgin Management Ltd

120 Campden Hill Road, London W8 7AR
Tel: 0171-229 1282 Fax: 0171-727 8200

22nd September 1995

Our ref: VACR/220995/ed

Mr Richard Weston-Smith
BRAINSTORM

Playa Del Rey
LOS ANGELES
California 90293
U S A

Dear Richard

I was delighted to receive your letter. We'll certainly look you up when next in L.A. - in the meantime, if Xan is free any week-end, tell him to ring　　　　and we'll send a car to pick him up.

You're right. There's no good reason to exclude an under-12 who is paying full price. I'll have the rule changed next week and either give the child credit or his parents. I'll also copy this letter to Liz Harlow at Virgin Freeway and make sure you get credit for Xan's last flight from L.A. as a "thank you" for pointing it out.

Best of luck to you all.

Kind regards

Richard Branson
Chairman
Virgin Group of Companies

cc:　Liz Harlow

SWITZERLAND
From Paris to
the Pectinarium

The Management and I pulled out of Paris on the TGV[73] precisely on time – a level of railway punctuality usually only achieved by the Swiss and Japanese. It has been claimed that Japanese trains run a combined total of less than one minute late in an entire year, including delays caused by natural disasters – an extraordinary feat, if true. Any delay elicits a torrent of grovelling apologies from the railway company. Rail officials have been known to hand out late notes to delayed commuters, so they can justify their slight tardiness to their employer and avoid a humiliating loss of face. British trains, by comparison, ran a total of 448 years late in 2018, clear evidence of the epic uselessness of British railways.

This journey was part of a multi-city business trip, and we were staying only one night in Geneva before returning to Paris. We were not on holiday; we had no expectations that this would be anything other than a purely functional trip. Go, get it done, and return.

We had purchased second class tickets, and I noted as we glided out of the Gare du Lyon that the compartment was more than adequately comfortable. It was a Monday, and our only fellow travellers were a group of Japanese tourists at the other end of the carriage. Tiring of watching the suburbs of Paris rumble past and hearing an announcement that the buffet car was open for business, the Management and I lurched to secure ourselves a croissant and coffee.

Ten minutes later, we were back in our seats with an assortment of food spread out in front of us that was born more out of curiosity than hunger. The natural yogurt we had bought only because of the darling little terracotta pot it came in, and the contents proved to be astonishingly good. I had a vague notion that the pot might be well suited for some subsequent use, but never came to any firm conclusion as to what that might be. A butter pot? Home to a small cactus? Neither of them appealed. I had ordered a croque monsieur, simply because I could, and because it reminded me of my childhood. My mother spent much of her young life in Paris and made them for us

---

73 TGV: *Train Grande Vitesse*, which means train of big speed.

as a treat, much to our delight. The croissant was obligatory, and the Management (as by now the reader might well expect) chose a smoked salmon sandwich. It was good, but she couldn't eat it all, so the remaining half languished on the table for the rest of the trip, as if silently admonishing us for being so extravagant.

Le train had by now accelerated to *grande vitesse*, and the French countryside was blasting past at bewildering speed. Bucolic villages, herds of Charolais, charming farmhouses, and the odd château were here and gone faster than you could say, "Oh, look a ———". There was the occasional bracing "THWACK… whoooooooooooosh… phhhhhhhHTT" as we passed another TGV at a closing speed of about 300 miles per hour – in stark contrast to the musical burbling of "Little Tokyo" somewhere at the back of the carriage. Pastoral fields gave way to rolling vineyards and finally the Alps, in all their tectonic majesty, hove into view. In no time at all, we were trundling into Geneva. That is the wonderful thing about Europe, you can just trundle into another country in time for lunch. I imagine the Barbarians may have found that rather appealing too, but from an invade-and-conquer perspective.

Monday
    Breakfast: Liechtenstein (light pillage).
    Trundle.
    Lunch: invade Switzerland.
    Trundle.
    Dinner: lay siege to Lyon.
    Bed.

The Noga Hilton Hotel on Lake Geneva was quite a remarkable example of "WTF?" hotel design. Every surface was chromed and mirrored to the point where it was hard to tell which way was up, and I quickly walked into three walls believing they were corridors. The interior decoration had been done by a graduate of the Vladivostok School of Brothel Design, and all the lobby shops sold an array of merchandise that would have made Liberace jump for joy. We were escorted to our room down a long corridor that bore an uncanny resemblance to the night-sleeper to Edinburgh (but much shinier) and eventually arrived at a spacious suite entirely decked out in royal blue Formica and white marble. What were they thinking?

We had planned to spend the afternoon working, before a meeting at 5:00pm, and normally I would have done just that. But something in me that day suggested we should throw of the shackles of routine and make the most of a glorious spring day in Switzerland. So, I called downstairs, rented a nifty little Audi A3, and we took off in the direction of Lausanne at a satisfying 100 miles per hour. Well, it was satisfying for me, but apparently not for The Management, so my pleasure was short-lived. Speed limitation was enforced by marital rule of law, and we returned to a more leisurely pace. There is nothing quite like the threat of an indefinite suspension of conjugal rites to turn an aerodynamic Audi into a lumpy Lada.

We had no idea where we wanted to go – anywhere was fine, as long as it was off the beaten track. We didn't have much time and we wanted to make the most of it. It felt a bit like playing truant from school; we had escaped and were doing something that had been no part of our plan for the day. It was unexpectedly exhilarating.

Deciding that the concierge would have probably recommended the most predictable places to go, we ignored his advice and turned off the autoroute, heading blindly into a maze of pleasant back roads. The weather was spring showers with puffy white clouds, the mountains impressive, and every tree seemed to be sporting a thick blanket of pink or white blossoms. At one point, we came around a corner to be greeted with a picture-postcard sight of a herd of furry Bison-esque cows surrounded by hundreds of free-range chickens in an orchard of fruit trees under a canopy of blossoms. This was it – the picnic spot I had been looking for my entire life. Sadly, we had no picnic.

In the absence of an actual picnic, we discussed the etymology of the word, for which we must thank the French. The earliest use of *pique-nique*, was used to describe a group of people dining in a restaurant who brought their own wine. It is based on the verb *piquer*, which means "pick" or "peck", and the rhyming *nique*, which means "thing of little importance" or "trifle". After the French Revolution, picnicking became extremely popular in France; everyone flocked to the royal parks and peed on the topiary, just because they now could. The British love picnics, and they were responsible for the invention of sausage rolls, egg mayonnaise and wasps.

Having aimlessly cruised around for an hour or so, happily soaking it all in, we suddenly found ourselves in a stunning little medieval village called Romainmôtier. Set low in a small valley, it is well worth a stop, both in terms of its architecture and its setting. At its heart is a spectacular 1,000-year-old abbey, Switzerland's oldest Romanesque-style building. Nestling in the Jura mountains, on the river Nozon, the small medieval village is best explored on foot. Romainmôtier boasted a most unusual and rather Terry Gilliam-esque shop, called the Pectinarium. It sold the most dazzling and eccentric jams, jellies, and preserves, like raspberry-lemongrass and jalapeno-plum. Half an hour later, we were on our way again, loaded to the gunwales with jars of assorted preserves, unsure as to how we would safely pack them for the return.

It was quite extraordinary. We had set out from Paris for a bog-standard business trip to Geneva, but here we were, unexpectedly immersed in a memorable meander around the Swiss countryside. It was the perfect example of how, if one allows oneself to be just a little bit adventurous, something can happen that would otherwise not. You can effectively stimulate a *shift* yourself. In just a couple of hours, we had gone somewhere we had never been before, discovered a magical little village, and seen Switzerland at its most beautiful. Twenty years later, I still vividly remember this afternoon. I can recall the trees, and blossoms, and countryside in great detail; and in that memory is an element of the patina that has been gently polished into my soul. That simple afternoon has become part of me. How many times had we missed opportunities like this on previous bland, forgettable business trips? We would return to Paris, mission accomplished, but with a bonus. From then on, we would always try to find that gap in our schedule that would allow us to escape and experience something unexpected. Sometimes we would tack a day or two on the end of a business trip. Other times we would just take a walk, a drive or a detour, and see what happened.

Allowing ourselves to follow whatever little roads seemed to offer the most attractive scenery, we kept meandering through lush valleys and impossibly sweet villages until, quite suddenly and unexpectedly, we arrived at the Swiss border. This was odd because we were on the French side of the border, even though we were absolutely certain we had not left Switzerland. No, really, we were dead sure. There had been no indication at all of us ever having crossed anything even remotely resembling a border. Yet here we were in a small queue waiting to pass the checkpoint to go back into Switzerland from, apparently, France. The border guards gave our passports a cursory glance and waved us through. We had got all the way from Paris to the Pectinarium, without a problem. Maybe this odd little shop of curious conserves was indeed a Gilliam-esque shift in the space-time continuum? Had we perhaps been led unwittingly into another dimension, as if though the holes in a nice piece of Emmental? You just never know with the Swiss.

GERMANY
Best of Enemies

Early in the spring of 1945, Berlin ordered the relocation of all the Allied PoWs in prison camps across Europe. As the military situation continued to deteriorate and the Allies advanced inexorably across Europe, the Geneva convention required that all prisoners be removed from harm's way. However, the German High-Command planned to transfer those prisoners they considered to be of the highest value to Hitler's "Eagle's Nest" retreat in the Austrian mountains. There they were to be used first as hostages, then, if the Americans and the British attacked, as a last line of defence – as human shields.

One such high-value officers' camp was Oflag VII-B, just outside Eichstatt, a small city set in the lush, rolling fields, forests and hills of Bavaria. On Saturday April 14, at eight o'clock in the morning, 1,500 British officers marched through the gates, together with a number of guards. They travelled on foot, with as many of their possessions as they could carry, as well as a considerable amount of food and cigarettes. Many of the officers had been prisoners for several years and had accumulated quite a variety of personal odds and ends. This precious cargo of letters, photos, books, clothing, and anything of value that could be bartered, was balanced on an eccentric assortment of handcarts; ranging from derelict prams to home-made carts constructed from Canadian Red Cross crates, with tin soup plates doing duty for wheels. On leaving the camp gates, the column turned east on a small road that winds through gently rolling countryside, mostly following the course of a small stream. A dozen or so children accompanied the three-kilometre-long column, happily gambling alongside as they scrounged chocolate and cigarettes from the soldiers. They got off to a slow start, and, , by ten o'clock, the tail of the column was still inside the camp. After a mile or so, the vanguard halted in the valley just outside the small hamlet of Landershofen, to allow the tail-end to catch up. It was a crisp, blustery Bavarian spring day, and puffy cotton-wool clouds pushed across the sky. The officers sat on the road or lay stretched out in the odd patch of weak sun, smoking and indulging in good natured banter. Relishing the change of scenery and routine, they were in good spirits, and although the end of the war was imminent, there was still much talk of escape.

After resting for about ten minutes, they heard the throaty roar of an airplane, and an American P-51 Mustang fighter roared over the treetops, circling low to inspect them closely. After years of imprisonment, and far from home, they were overjoyed to see one of their own planes so close, and so completely unopposed. They cheerfully waved, and shouted greetings and encouragement. After a couple of circles, the plane flew away and they cheered its departure, convinced that help would soon be on the way. The guards looked on nervously, fidgeting with their weapons.

A mile across the valley to the south was another road running roughly parallel to the one they were on. Almost opposite the resting column, two German trucks, on seeing the Allied planes, had stopped, and the drivers had jumped out – presumably ready to make for cover. The column, still at rest, was abuzz with excited chatter and laughter when suddenly, with a deafening roar and the staccato crackle of heavy machine-gun fire, a flight of P-51s thundered over their heads and proceeded to strafe and bomb the two trucks the other side of the valley. The prisoners sat happily by the roadside watching the mayhem and cheering them on, thrilled the Yanks were putting on this little show for their benefit.

The Mustangs banked sharply and came around, heading back towards the column of cheering and waving British and Allied officers. Once again, the guns started blazing and, with horror, they realized that they were now the target. Fiery points of .55 tracer rounds ploughed up the field around them, as they scattered, guards and prisoners as one. Some scrambled to the left up a rocky hill; some to the right, into a ploughed field; others, frozen in disbelief and unable to make the leap of comprehension, remained in the road.

In a matter of seconds, it became a death trap. Without hesitation, several officers grabbed the children who had been walking alongside them. Some shielded children with their bodies, while others scooped them up and carried them to the cover of three shallow caves in the hillside that offered a small degree of protection. For the rest, there was no cover at all. After several years in a prison camp their nerves were not up to much, and their reactions were dulled.

There was a slight lull in the firing as the Mustangs roared overhead, banked up and over the hill and were gone. But to their horror, moments later a second flight of P-51s joined the first and started on the column in earnest. It was so sudden, so unexpected that there was nowhere to hide. As the roar of five Mustangs receded into dreadful silence, the acrid smoke slowly dissipated to reveal a road littered with the bodies of the dead, the dying, and the wounded. The cheers of encouragement had turned to screams and groans of pain, as the survivors ran to help their friends and fashion makeshift stretchers from whatever they could find.

After the attack, the camp commandant ordered the bodies and the wounded to be recovered and the march to be continued. This last order was ignored and the PoWs surged unchallenged back to the camp, where the true extent of the massacre become apparent. In front of the hospital block lay as many as 60 seriously wounded and 13 dead Allied officers. Among the guards, there was one dead and one wounded. The .55 ammunition had taken a terrible toll. Some of the bodies had literally been shot full of holes, an agonising sight even for battle-hardened soldiers.

When the march eventually resumed, as it had to, under cover of night, two British officers managed to escape from the line. Two days later, hunting for water, they arrived at the village of Böhmfeld, about 100 kilometres north of Munich. The village was divided. Some were die-hard Nazis; others felt they had been betrayed by Hitler and just wanted an end to the war. A group of French PoWs worked in the fields during the day, guarded by a detachment of German "home guard" soldiers. Narrowly escaping capture as German troops searched the village, the British officers met a French PoW who offered them a place to hide in his employer's barn.

At first, they were intent only on getting home alive after years of imprisonment, but the two escapees quickly became entangled in the life and struggles of the little Bavarian village. Disguised as French labourers, they were able to leave the barn and move about the village unchallenged. But there was danger on two fronts: the indiscriminate American bombardment was drawing ever closer, while ruthless bands of SS were prowling the woods nearby. The German villagers quickly turned to their new guests, hoping they could help save them from both.

Fearful for his life at the hands of the Americans, and with the end of the war imminent, the German Home Guard commander surrendered to the two British escapees. And so it happened that they found themselves – still miles behind enemy lines – in command of 60 armed German troops, several hundred French PoWs and with the fate of the entire village in their hands. Refusing rescue by an advance party of American soldiers, they held out for the last incredibly dangerous days of the conflict, protecting and guiding the unlikely group of war-weary people who now looked to them for leadership. Finally, in the ultimate condemnation of war itself, the German soldiers, French PoWs and half the villagers, all joined forces under the British Officers command to prepare to repel a ferocious attack by a band of die-hard SS.

One of those two British officers was my father, Ian Weston Smith. The other, Sandy Saunderson, was to become my godfather.

⋆ ⋆ ⋆

My father was a Captain in the 2nd Battalion, Scots Guards. He was born in Glasgow in 1917. His father died when he was five years old and his mother, a stern but principled woman, did her very best to give him a proper education and upbringing. He was educated at Fettes, the grim Scottish boarding school, about which he told us terrifying stories of being held upside down over the well of a spiral staircase and incarcerated in rat infested cellars. He was a thoughtful, careful, kind and considerate man, with strong principles, and a finely attuned sense of fair play. Extremely handsome, he had piercing blue eyes that twinkled when he laughed, and although he did not suffer fools, he found it easy to make friends. Enlisting in the Scots Guards in 1939, he was wounded in Ajdabiya in December 1941. On leaving hospital, he was appointed ADC[74] to General Oliver Leese, who had taken over the 8th army from Montgomery. He remained with Leese through the invasion of Sicily and was captured at Salerno in 1943, at the age of 26. He spent the rest of the war in Oflag VII-B.

Captain Ian Weston Smith, my father.

---

74 Personal assistant to a person of high rank in the military (as in this case), or to a member of a royal family or a head of state.

Captain Alexander Saunderson, my Godfather.

Alexander Saunderson – known to all as Sandy – was the same age as my father, and a captain in the Rifle Brigade. Born in Ireland in 1917, at the family seat of Castle Saunderson, he was once the target of the IRA, who attempted to kidnap him. Fortunately for Sandy, they were foiled in their attempt by his especially ferocious nanny, who was having none of this kidnap nonsense on her watch, and told them – in no uncertain terms – to go away. Before the war he had studied German and spent most summers in Germany. He heard Hitler speak, witnessed the Brown Shirts persecuting Jews and, as each year went by and his German became fluent, he saw the country he had come to love sliding increasingly quickly towards destruction. Sandy was highly creative, an excellent pianist, talented linguist, and thespian. Extremely gregarious, he was the life and soul of every party, and highly popular. In 1939, with war inevitable, he returned to England and enlisted. Promptly captured at Dunkirk, he spent nearly five years as a PoW, first at Laufen, and then at Oflag VII-B. He suffered from increasing ill health as each year passed. Throughout his incarceration, he kept the fact that he could speak fluent German to himself, as it was far more useful if that particular talent was not widely known.

* * *

My brother, Dominic, and I, had long been planning to take a trip in Bavaria to walk in the footsteps of my father and Sandy. More than that, it was an effort to retrace a piece of family history and, hopefully, to discover the details of these most remarkable events that took place in April 1945. Like many soldiers after the war, my father's experiences were intensely personal and traumatic. He was reluctant to discuss them with anyone other than his fellow soldiers. Occasionally, at the end of a good dinner, when the port bottle was on its second circumnavigation of the table and his guard was down, he would reveal small snippets, usually in the form of amusing anecdotes about Cairo or the prison camp. Humour helped cover the underlying pain of the unspoken curse of PTSD, and lost friends.[75] As he aged, he was slightly more willing to talk about his experiences, and would sometimes answer questions from us, or tell stories on request. Nevertheless, like an iceberg, nine tenths of what he endured remained below the surface.

Over the course of a few years, my father slid into the grips of a particularly cruel form of dementia, called Lewy Body Dementia

---

75 Post-Traumatic Stress Disorder was as prevalent as it is now, but its existence in the 1940s was not acknowledged.

(LBD), slowly slipping beneath the waters of hallucination and confusion. Very, very occasionally, he would have brief moments of lucidity. When I was sitting with him one day, not long before the end, he suddenly lifted his head, focusing his brilliant blue eyes directly on mine.

"I just want to thank you for everything you have done for me," he said. Immediately, his head dropped down, and he was lost again. He died about a month later, in June 2005. His ability to tell us more had diminished directly in proportion to our desire to hear it, until it was too late. Important pieces of family history were lost to us, and Dominic and I both deeply regretted that we had not been much more proactive in extracting it from him while he still had his wits about him.

However, from the detailed diaries both my father and Sandy had kept, we were able to piece together quite a bit about their escape, and the events of the ten days they were on the run. They both kept diaries, but being very different characters, it was extraordinary to read about the same set of events from two different perspectives. Combining them gave us a much more vivid account than just either on their own. Additionally, we had done a huge amount of research; we ferreted-out key people to help us, pored over historical records, maps of the area and photographs of the camp. We even tracked down the family who gave them shelter. But there were a lot of holes in the story. Some, we sensed, were deliberate; others simply omitted because they were not deemed to be important, or sufficiently entertaining. We had no idea what we would find when we finally shone a light on all these dark corners of history, but it was time to put all the pieces together and chase some ghosts in Bavaria.

And so it was, in June 2006, that my brother and I embarked on an unforgettable adventure.

Bound first for Munich, I took off from Los Angeles at 7:00am on the first leg of what was to become an exceedingly arduous journey. Six hours later, on arrival in New York, I presented myself at the gate for my flight to London and was naturally pleased to see it was on time. But as the minutes ticked by, and none of the usual pre-boarding activity could be seen, I grew apprehensive. There was the usual cluster of upgrade hopefuls, lurking like so many nonchalant vultures around a sickly wildebeest, yet nothing happened. Sure enough, there was a mechanical problem, and our 6:15pm departure became 7:15pm, which prompted renewed queuing activity by people suffering from connection panic. Suddenly it was 8:15pm and then 8:45pm. Connection panic became an epidemic, and several people began showing signs of hyperventilation and mild hysteria. One even asked to be taken off the flight altogether. Quite why you would suddenly decide that your trip to London wasn't worth doing if you were a couple of hours late is beyond me.

Finally on board and ready to go, the cabin staff discovered a woman who had arbitrarily decided she should sit in business class, even though she had clearly been assigned seat 896B. Apparently, she felt the delay was sufficient reason for her to be upgraded. So, in this day of book-it-yourself, carry-it-yourself, and feed yourself travel, she decided to upgrade herself. Excellent concept, I thought, and full marks for sheer bravado, but the eagle-eyed purser quickly rumbled her. Not wanting to give up without a fight, she steadfastly refused to move until the purser matter-of-factly informed her that she could sit there with pleasure, as long as it was clearly understood that when she got to London, her credit card would be missing $3,000 of credit.

Seat 896B was quickly occupied, the doors closed, cross-checks performed, and things began to hum in a satisfactorily mechanical way. It was 10:30pm by the time we at last experienced the thrill of a little G-force and, loaded to the gills, lumbered into the air. The first drink, they announced magnanimously, would be on the house. Just one? Before very long, I succumbed to the fractured sleep of transatlantic travel.

* * *

At the outbreak of war, the cavalry barracks built on the outskirts of Eichstatt, some 40 years previously, was repurposed to become a prison camp. Designated Oflag VII-B, it first housed Polish soldiers, and later thousands of captured British, American, Canadian, New Zealand and Australian officers. Set in the Bavarian countryside, with the River Altmuhl winding its way along one side, it was by far the most beautiful of all the PoW camps in Germany. Built on the hillside, the camp was about 250 yards long by 150 yards wide. Prisoners were housed either in one of the original three-storied barracks on the upper slope of a hill, or in eight more recently built concrete army huts on the flats below, in which about 800 officers lived. On the lower level were sports fields, including a football pitch, a tennis court, and gardens.

All but a few of the officers were the product of that venerable seat of upper class learning – the British boarding school. Consequently, the idea of being incarcerated with many other like-minded individuals for an extended period was something they were well used to, and little adaptation was necessary. With so many well-educated men gathered in one place, there were inevitably specialists from all walks of life, and no shortage of willing teachers. This incredible diversity of expertise could quickly and effectively be employed in the primary industry of the camp – escaping.

There was an escape committee, to whom all escape plans had to be submitted. They would review each application, and either approve or deny it depending on a number of factors: the feasibility of the plan; the danger of impacting escape plans already in progress; the number of men involved, the capacity of the escape industry to support such a plan with uniforms, disguises, documents etc.; the risk of discovery; and the chance of success. Consequently, escape attempts were brilliantly imagined, well-organised, carefully overseen and properly supplied with the necessary resources. The arrival at Oflag VII-B of one officer, whose civilian job had been as a tunnel engineer for the London Underground, was a game-changer for the escape committee.

The camp had accumulated a library of over 15,000 books, and prisoners organised all kinds of intellectual pursuits, from studying for law exams and other qualifications[76], to clubs that catered to such varied interests as bagpipe playing, highland dancing and bird watching. These also served as a good cover for various escape-related activities, masking noise, disguising detailed surveillance of guard's movements, or creating confusion and distractions when required. Ten British doctors and 16 medical orderlies were in charge of the health of the prisoners. Apart from a few mental cases, the health of the camp remained surprisingly good, despite cuts in their rations caused by the gradual Allied advance, and subsequent disruption of the German war machine. For the duration of the war, the supply of Red Cross food was for the most part regular enough to make up for the shortfall. Red Cross consignments and private parcels had allowed the prisoners to hoard adequate supplies of clothing, blankets, and other goodies.

A large vegetable garden was carefully tended, producing a variety of fresh produce in the summer. What was lacking from legitimate sources could sometimes be purchased on the black market with the help of German guards, many of whom were actively involved in black market trading as a way to supplement their own war rations. Everything from fresh bread, sausages and butter, to cameras, watches and even wireless parts were available – for the right price – and thus these goods found their way inside.

The purchasing power of British and American cigarettes was excellent and, as long as they kept arriving in the Red Cross shipments, the black market thrived.

The guards at Oflag VII-B were mostly former Russian front troops. They were good soldiers who did their work diligently and without undue malice. It was a delicate relationship, and prisoners became good at winning their trust, in return for which small

---

76 Sandy did a correspondence course while in prison, and escaped with a law degree from Cambridge.

favours were often granted. Guards were sometimes happy to talk about their previous war experiences, their families and home lives, exchanges that were generally welcomed by the POWs as they helped to create a more comfortable atmosphere.

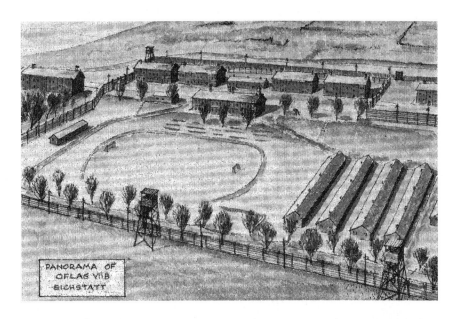

A view of Oflag VIIb, drawn by ex-PoW Frank Edwards in 1976.

All of this paints a rosy picture, and one might conclude that life in Oflag VII-B was really no hardship at all for these men, merely a temporary inconvenience. Indeed, compared to the deprivations and permanent dangers endured by their comrades on the front lines, they were well sheltered. The risk of injury or death was almost non-existent, unless they brought upon themselves by tempting fate. But for all the facilities, clubs, Red Cross parcels and occasional parole walks, there were constant hardships to be endured, both real and psychological.

In winter, the heating was completely ineffective, and they were bitterly cold all the time, often lying in their beds all day under a threadbare German blanket. After a while their bodies got used to the cold. Many people successfully taught themselves to knit, making hats, scarves and even pullovers out of wool scavenged from old socks and other clothing. But more than anything else it was a lack of food that occupied their minds daily, and hunger was their constant companion. The Germans kept them in this state deliberately, primarily because they hoped that if the men were very, very hungry, they would not think of much else, like escape. They were wrong. When you put 2,500 highly educated and well trained young men with diverse skillsets together in a temporary camp, and give them nothing to do, their imagination, ingenuity, and appetite for mischief and mayhem is boundless. The Germans had their hands full.

A view of the parade ground/sports field in winter,
with an ice hockey game in progress.

* * *

The miracle of flight lowered me gently onto British soil some ten hours after we had taken off, four and a half hours late. A request was made that "Passengers kindly remain seated to allow those with tight connections to de-plane first". This ensured that, as soon the seat belt light pinged off, 350 passengers simultaneously leaped into the aisle and dragged 500 pieces of hand luggage out of the overhead lockers with a perfectly reckless disregard for the fact that they may have shifted in flight. Four escalators, half a mile of corridor, a bus ride and a security checkpoint later I was told I was on standby for a BA flight to Frankfurt. What the hell, at least Frankfurt is closer to Munich than London. So, I shuffled obediently onto the plane, they shut the doors, fired up Messrs. Rolls and Royce, and we headed for Frankfurt.

Frankfurt required another terminal change, involving a train ride, a small decathlon, and some perplexing signage. The half-hour hop to Munich was, inevitably, delayed, but I arrived there at 8:00pm. I was supposed to have arrived at 12:45pm that morning. I took a deep breath and launched myself across the concourse towards Hertz, which was located about as far from the terminals as you could possibly put anything, without providing another aircraft to reach it. Collecting the car, I soon found myself blasting down the A9 towards Nuremberg. My car rental budget was not really up for too much fast-lane autobahn fun, so I had to content myself with a shot of vicarious pleasure, each time a BMW thwoooomed past me at 130mph, gently rocking my little Ford Fiesta in its slipstream.

After exactly 33 hours of beslubberingly awful travel, I finally arrived in Eichstatt at 10:00pm. Finding the hotel was not difficult, because Dominic was pacing up and down in the empty street outside it.

"What the hell happened to you?" he asked, not unreasonably.

"Five airports, four different aircraft, hours of delays and too much stress," I replied, dropping my bags on the pavement.

"Well, being a sleepy Bavarian town, they lock up at nine, so I was worried I wouldn't hear you arrive, and you wouldn't be able to get in. So, I thought I should wait out here for you."

"Well, I am sorry you have had to stand out here in the cold."

"That's OK, the architecture is fascinating, and I found somewhere for us to get a bite to eat."

Dropping my bag in a comfortable, teutonically furnished room, we popped around the corner to a small bistro. There was no one else there except a drunk, propping up the bar like a ruffled pigeon. We ordered a couple of beers and a steak from a jolly young waiter called Leo. He was running the place single-handed and appeared thrilled to be able to practice his English. The food was good, and the bill came to about 25 euros for the two of us. I was knackered so we headed for bed. Rather sweetly, the hotel had been meticulous in preparing for British guests, taping little temporary labels to the TV remote that explained its operation in English.

Dominic is three years younger than me, and in many ways very like my father. Extremely handsome, and with the same twinkly eyes, he is thoughtful, kind and considered, but capable of being be exceedingly witty, especially when writing letters to the *Telegraph*, which he does quite regularly. Possessed of great style, and good taste in art, furniture, and clothing, he does not care for small talk, but can light up a table and have everyone in hysterics when in the mood. One of his favourite pastimes is walking in the countryside, so he is extremely fit, and perhaps better prepared than I for what we were about to do.

After a few hours of sleep, punctuated only by the occasional mating calls of the local youth outside the window, Dom and I met in the breakfast room at eight. It clearly did double duty as a conference room and, judging by the deeply eccentric plastic flower arrangements, as an occasional wedding chapel. Breakfast was very German, with sliced meats, cheeses and a mysterious white substance labelled "krank". Giving the krank a wide berth we settled on some muesli, a rather good bread roll, some passable coffee and an orange juice. While we ate, we went over the day's plans, looked at maps and speculated over what was in store for us.

It was market day in the small, cobbled square outside the hotel, so after breakfast, suitably caffeinated, we took a quick stroll around. It was a pleasant April morning, not too cold, the sky punctuated with cotton wool clouds. The miniature city of Eichstatt is really quite lovely, centred around the cathedral and largely designed by the prominent architect Gabriel de Gabrielli, who was also responsible for significant parts of Vienna. Church clocks binged and bonged enthusiastically every fifteen minutes and people bustled about everywhere with bags of fresh produce stuffed into bags and baskets. The Germans are clearly big on Easter, and plush Easter bunnies. The damn things were everywhere, most of them a hideous combination of bawdy, fluorescent colours. The market was full of stalls selling flowers, nuts, delicious looking potatoes, and pots and jars of things with frightening German names.

At nine o'clock sharp, Helmut Reis appeared at our hotel. About 60 years of age, Helmut was as fit as a fiddle and a delightful man to boot. He had spent 25 years at the Police Cadet Training Academy that was previously PoW camp Oflag VII-B. Over the years, he had become the self-appointed camp historian, written a book about it, and guided numerous ex-PoWs around, many of whom had become friends. His English wasn't up to much, but we chatted fairly successfully in pidgin as we waited for our translator to arrive. Before long, a tall young man, with short hair, spectacles, and a brace of earrings in one ear, came striding down the street. Christian was a local English teacher who had kindly agreed to translate for us.

Making the five minute drive to the old camp, we parked and untangled ourselves from the tiny car. I was surprised to find myself standing in front of a building which felt very familiar to me. As I stood looking at the playing fields and the Commandants Quarters, I could hardly believe I was here, both in the present and simultaneously in the past. I found myself standing where my father had stood, all those years ago, under such extraordinarily different circumstances. It felt surreal. I took photos, but I knew that would never capture this extreme feeling of standing in a piece of my own history, as a time-traveller might. I put my camera away – and just let my eyes breathe in this staggering view. I wanted my eyes to understand the importance of what they were seeing. I wanted to take a mental picture, not just a physical one.

Even in the early days of spring, with the buds barely visible on the trees and hedgerows, the abundant natural beauty of the camp's setting was immediately clear. Beauty is not usually something one would associate with a prison camp; but with forested hills in the background, the rooftops and spires of Eichstatt nearby, and the River Altmuhl meandering past, it was an idyllic setting.

Now, there is not much left of the camp as it was then. Just the commandant's large house, the hospital building, the expansive playing field and parade ground. We imagined we could almost hear the snarky hubbub of the officers, and barked commands of the guards, as 2,500 British officers milled about the six-acre site. For these soldiers their captivity was a defining moment in their lives, one of mixed and conflicting emotions. It was a time of great camaraderie, laughter and hope, but also one of deep uncertainty, frustration, danger and suffering. This prison camp was a place where lifelong friendships and enduring memories were formed. My father and Sandy seemed to be very much present with us at that moment.

Helmut stopped at a patch of bare ground and marked the spot with his heel.

"The building is no longer here, but this spot is where the tunnel went down underneath the stairs," translated Christian, as Helmut spoke in German.

Helmut pointed up the hillside. "The tunnel sloped upwards for about 30 metres, before coming up in a hen house outside the wire, over there."

"I remember him talking about the hen house," said Dominic. "The tunnel was concealed under a false lavatory bowl, and I remember him mentioning the chickens, and how it was such a perfect place for the tunnel's exit to be hidden."

"Wasn't that the one the guards discovered?" I said.

"Yes," replied Helmut. "They discovered it during one if their routine checks, when they were probing the ground along the perimeter."

"It must have so very disappointing, after all those months of work, to have it discovered at the last moment," reflected Dom.

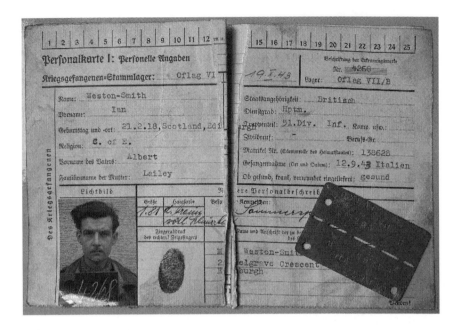

My father, not very happy about becoming a prisoner of war.

We walked around the rest of the site, quietly imagining what it must have been like, and I understood better than ever before how it had so profoundly affected my father's life.

Driving about a kilometre down the road, we arrived at the spot where American fighters, mistaking the column of marching British officers for German troops, had strafed them. A few years ago, a commemorative plaque had mysteriously been erected there in memory of the incident. Helmut said that it had been arranged by a local doctor named Braun, who had been ten years old in 1945 and, like many other children, had leapt at the chance to tag along with 2,500 chocolate wielding PoWs. When the American Mustang fighters screamed in low over the beautiful valley, sending shells ripping into the rag-tag column of unarmed British prisoners, Doctor Braun was one of those children whose life was saved by a British PoW. Many years later he erected the plaque in their honour. I had another strong time-traveller moment, able to vividly imagine the roar of the engines, and the sound of bullets thudding into the ground around me. Right here – this was where it actually happened. Of course, I had stood on the site of history many times in my life, as we all do when we visit a castle or some such monument. But the fact that this was not just any history made this different. For Dominic and me, this was *our* history. It was intensely personal, and the first of many deeply moving moments over the next few days.

After an excellent lunch, we set off to drive the route of the march and to try and determine the point at which they escaped. It was somewhat challenging as the roads had changed slightly and the account of their route was sketchy at best. We managed to estimate their escape point as being between the villages of Eitensheim and Gaimersheim but were confused because the small river they described crossing was definitely not there. In its place was what you would at best describe as a watery ditch. Giving the ditch the benefit of the doubt for now, we followed farm tracks across the hedgeless, rolling countryside, to try and find the small patch of forest in which they spent their first day hiding out. After comparing the map they used for their escape to the present-day ordinance survey map, we identified a likely candidate and set off in hot pursuit.

In most places these days, a well-used, ungated, farm track that is clearly marked on a map is pretty much fair game for driving down. However, in Germany it is apparently *verboten*.[77] Christian sat in the back giggling.

"Actually, we are not allowed to be doing this, you know."

"Really? Why not?" I said, as we bounced along.

"Well, the woods are *verboten*, for cars you know. I have never done this before!" he giggled, as we passed two lederhosen-ed hikers and received a disapproving look.

"But there are no signs, Christian. And even if there were, I doubt I could read them."

---

77 Forbidden.

Inspection by the camp Commandant. *(Photo: Bibliotheca Ananda, Col. Telly de Vielder)*

A football match. *(Photo: Bibliotheca Ananda, Col. Telly de Vielder)*

Inspection by the camp Commandant. *(Photo: Bibliotheca Ananda, Col. Telly de Vielder)*

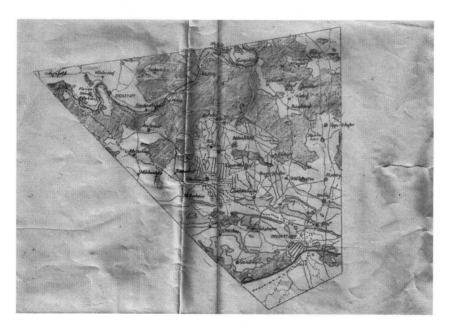

Escape map of the local area used by Ian and Sandy, drawn by the camp cartographer.

The parade ground/playing field in 2014. *(Photo: Richard Weston Smith)*

Dominic discussing tunnels with Helmut and Christian.

The roadside plaque, commemorating the friendly fire incident.

Parking at the edge of the trees and looking back, we could see the lay of the land for miles around perfectly, each village clearly identified by its church spire. Poring over the map, we discussed the routes they might have taken. It was starting to become clearer. We drove around a bit more, again taking a detour through the Böhmfelder Forest on unmarked tracks, much to Christian's delight. He found this imposed naughtiness by his British charges extremely amusing. The Germans are just so well behaved it's ridiculous.

"There it is!" exclaimed Dominic, as we exited the forest just outside Böhmfeld, "That's Böhmfeld! Amazing!" There indeed, for the first time, was the village itself.

The story of my father and Sandy's escape is far more about what happened in this village than about the escape itself. For that ten-day period of the war, the village became an ecosystem containing several opposing and allied factions. There were the villagers, some pro-Nazi, some not; there were the SS, who patrolled the woods through which we had just driven, dispensing ruthless injustice on their own citizens and instilling terror in all; there were the French ex-patriot farm workers – prisoners who did the jobs of the German men; there were the Americans who made occasional Jeep forays behind enemy lines, a la *Saving Private Ryan*; and lastly, there was the German "home guard" responsible for guarding the French.

It was, at that precise moment in the war, a very dangerous place to be, and the threat was not necessarily from the enemy. The German villagers were terrified of the SS, who would kill any German who put out a white flag. Without a white flag, the Americans would indiscriminately shell villages as they advanced, destroying entire communities. To cap it all off, the writing was on the wall, and the end of the war was imminent, so emotions were running high. A sense of self-preservation was starting to kick in. Into this little scenario walked two escaped British officers. What happened there is a story of humanity regaining control over insanity and saving a village and its inhabitants from destruction and death, in its myriad forms.

Returning to Eichstatt, we found ourselves immersed in the history of this beautiful, tiny city, and all that happened there. Already we had uncovered hitherto unknown parts of the story and seen significant places we had known nothing of, until today. Tomorrow, we would meet one of the major characters in the story, who knew more than anyone else about what happened in Böhmfeld.

I am convinced that in most places the sky, like everything else nowadays, has been watered down. But not, apparently, in Bavaria. The next morning, I awoke to a sky of the sort of blue I remembered from childhood summers. A blue that demanded you rush out beneath it and gaze upwards. Against this backdrop, the ochre, yellow, green and terra-cotta houses of Eichstatt glowed brilliantly around the square. The white of the cathedral and the clanging of the church bells provided dramatic punctuation.

In the square in front of our hotel, opposite the Rathaus,[78] preparations for the Easter bunny-fest were in full swing. A man

---

78 Town Hall.

carefully reversed a strange looking trailer into position. People put the finishing touches to handicrafts stalls full of garish bunnies, dried flower arrangements and dingly-dangly things of all shapes and sizes. Pots of daffodils were everywhere, brightening still further a scene that already boasted eye-popping colour. The strange trailer, satisfactorily positioned, suddenly began to unfold, transforming itself before my eyes into a huge circular fibreglass bierkeller, a pub on wheels. It had a roof, an integral sound system, seated about 25 at the bar and could probably pump Bavaria's finest faster than a fire tender at Frankfurt Airport. Meeting Dom in the breakfast room, we found the krank from the previous morning replaced by a bowl labelled "Quark".

There are two types of quark, one is a sort of soft, yogurty cheese. The other, a type of subatomic particle that, when found in large quantities, may even look like soft, yogurty cheese. Physicists think that quarks are elementary particles, which means they aren't made up of anything else except quark. There are apparently six different types of quark, known as "flavours" and this is where it all gets very *Alice in Wonderland*. These flavours are *up, down, charm, strange, top* and *bottom*. There seems to be some logic in the fact that down, strange and bottom are negatively charged, while up, charm and top are positively charged. Dominic and I decided this quark was less charm and more strange, especially at breakfast, so we avoided it.

On the way to Böhmfeld, Christian told us that he had made some inquiries and discovered that the "ditch" that had confused us the day before, used to be much more of a stream or small river. This information confirmed that we had found the place where they made good their escape from the line of march. We now had the starting point – crucial information we would need to accurately retrace their steps the next day. It was encouraging. We had set aside the day to go and meet the Halsner-Blobb family who had, at great risk to their own lives, sheltered my father and Sandy from the SS.

Frau Blobb was a devout Catholic, whose husband had been sent off to war. She and her young daughter Franziska were left to run the family smallholding, helped by French prisoners, who would do much of the manual labour. She hated the Nazis and longed for the war to be over. So strong were her beliefs, and her courage, that when her farm hand told her he had hidden two escaped British officers in her barn, she allowed them to stay. She knew full well that the consequences for her and Franziska, should they be discovered, would be a bullet in the head.

Böhmfeld had always been a purpose-built farming village and their house, like all the others along the main street, was immediately next to the road and backed directly onto the fields at the rear. After 1945, as the wartime population of 700 had expanded to 1,400, and the Audi factory at Ingolstadt provided alternative employment, many families had demolished their barns to make way for additional houses for sons and daughters. No sooner had we got out of the car than Jakob and Franziska Halsner came out to greet us enthusiastically. They were clearly delighted to see us. Jakob had a friendly face and a firm handshake. Franziska twinkled and beamed at us as she clattered away in German and hugged me warmly, her eyes brimming with tears. It was amazing to finally meet the woman who, as a young teenager, had played in the barn as my father and Sandy hid in the hay bales, terrified she might discover them, and precipitate their re-capture, and possible death.

Jakob herded us inside, as Christian adeptly juggled the translation of two simultaneous conversations. Coffee and biscuits appeared as we all wondered over old photos of Sandy and my father, slowly piecing together the history like a bilingual jig-saw puzzle. It turned out that they knew little of the detail that my father had recorded in his diary and were fascinated to hear the chronology of the ten days. Franziska explained that as she was only 13 at the time, she had been privy to little of what was going on. After a couple of days, she had been told that there were two men in the barn and a little later she had learned that they were in fact escaped British officers.

Franziska, rather timidly, asked a question of Christian.

"Franziska would like to know if you would be able to stay for lunch. It is only simple Bavarian cooking, but she would be honoured if you would."

"Please tell her we have come a long way to see her, and nothing would please us more than to stay for lunch," replied Dominic.

Franziska beamed, thrilled that we wanted to stay, and happy in the knowledge that ours was not a token visit. She wasted no time in heading to the kitchen, and from then on our conversation was punctuated with the sounds of preparation. We sat down to classic roast *schwein* with vast, soft, cream-coloured dumplings, with delicious Benedictine monk-brewed "Dinkel" beer.

After lunch they invited us to walk through the village with them, to better get a sense of it. Franziska and Jakob, keen to share their excitement, rang doorbells as we passed, and friends popped out from their houses to meet us and reminisce. One man clearly remembered Sandy and my father being in the village. A few doors down, a hysterically enthusiastic lady, with no teeth, and eyes that focused either side of the person she was talking to, had apparently become a good friend of Sandy's on his return visits to Böhmfeld after the war. I wondered she had perhaps taken a fancy to him. Jacob explained that there were specific houses we would avoid, as we would not be welcome there. I asked why, and he explained that they were the families who had been the Nazi sympathizers during the war. Clearly the divisions in the village still ran deep, even 60 years later.

We returned to the Blobbs' for more coffee and cake at the kitchen table. Their coffee was strong, and forced my afternoon jet lag back into its box for a while. We explained that next day we planned to walk the exact route of their escape, through the woods and across the fields to Böhmfeld. As we said our goodbyes, Franziska's eyes once again brimmed with tears, as did mine, and we knew we had made a friend for life.

Returning to Eichstatt at about five in the afternoon, we found that the Easter market was in full swing, as evidenced by the stream of people walking away from the town centre clutching virulent green bunnies and pots of primroses. Christian excused himself and Dom and I agreed that we simply had to sample a beer at the portable bierkeller. The beer was great, but the glorious sky of earlier had become overcast, and a cold wind had started whistling through the narrow streets. We drank up quickly and walked across to the hotel for a siesta.

The next morning, my eyes blinked open and I was immediately wide awake. Only jet lag can do that to me. I imagine it is how elephants feel when the vet administers the antidote to the tranquilizer that, moments before, had them out like a light. I opened the curtain to find that the day had dawned cold, rainy, and grey. Damn, on that day of all days, just when we were planning to walk several miles through open countryside and forest. I tried not to think of the soaking we were most likely in for.

As I approached the Café Paradis, to meet Helmut, an extremely large lady was coming towards me along the pavement. Both she and I unexpectedly turned into the café simultaneously, in one of those natty, Trooping the Colour[79] sort of moves. I had no choice but to take evasive action, ducking sideways to avoid – to use a naval term – being rammed. She roared with laughter and rattled something off in German as I allowed her to pass with a smile and she steamed into the café scattering people left and right. As I sat down, Helmut produced some photos and explained in his broken English that they were of the camp in late 1943. They had been taken by the guards and showed the tunnel that my father had helped dig, after it had been discovered by the Germans. This was terrific! Overhearing our conversation, Frau Bismarck (who had seated herself on a couple of chairs close by) joined in, keen to share our excitement. As it was at least an hour since she had had breakfast she had apparently popped in for some coffee and a slice of cake to

---

79 Over 1,400 parading soldiers, 200 horses and 400 musicians come together each June in a great display of military precision, horsemanship and fanfare to mark the Queen's official birthday.

ward off starvation until elevenses. The "slice" of cake in front of her was not appreciably smaller than the rubber tire-wedges used to restrain 747's. She seemed far more interested in the fact that I had come from California and kept interrupting our conversation with comments about her deep love of all things American, and San Francisco in particular. Her mouth worked like a cement mixer as she talked, displaying vast quantities of churning coffee cake as she rolled her eyes in delight and chortled. You try chortling, rolling your eyes and eating cake, all simultaneously ...

Saying our goodbyes to Helmut, we set off for Lippertshofen, in the rain. Having successfully identified the point where they ran from the line of march, we were now in search of the first hideout: a small copse of trees surrounded by fields. Before long, navigating the farm tracks to get into the right sort of area, we had identified a potential candidate. It was small, and if women had been working in the fields around it, Sandy and my father would have been well and truly pinned down for the day – as we knew they had been. What's more, it was due north of the point where they escaped the march. We knew that that was the direction they had headed, guided in the dark by only a compass. Dominic pulled out a folding telescope and, looking like Admiral Nelson, he scanned the countryside. Their route and this copse intersected; broad, tall trees confirmed its age. We approached, picking our way into the middle of it, and stood there in the dripping rain. On its southern edge the ground sloped away for about two miles, and we could clearly see the approximate area where they had crossed the river, moments after making their break. This, we agreed, was in all probability the very spot where they had collapsed, wet and exhausted, after a two-mile run across ploughed fields, on their first night of freedom.

Photographs taken by German guards after the escape. The
sophistication of its construction was thanks to a PoW who was an
engineer on the London Underground. The work that went into this
tunnel was immense, under the most impossible conditions.

Perimeter of camp behind buildings where the tunnel
started, showing hillside with the road above.

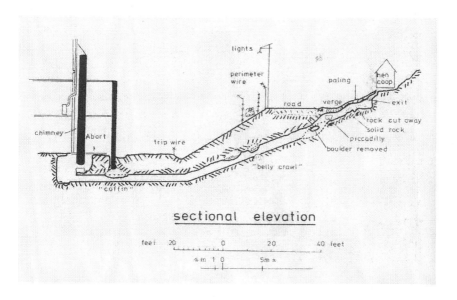

Sectional illustration showing route of tunnel

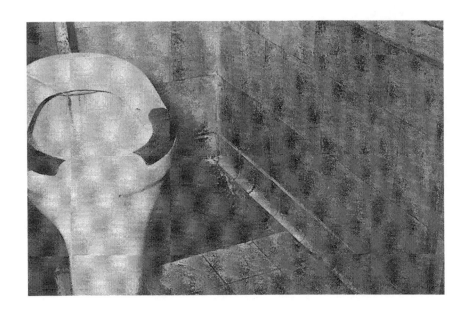

Toilet (*abort*), showing trap door in place and removed.

To retrace the route of their second night's walk, we moved a little further north and parked the car. It had stopped raining as we set off into the pine forest, all quiet and green above, soft moss underfoot; the first buds of spring just beginning to pop all around us. We had deliberately timed our trip to be at the same time of year as their escape, so the conditions would be approximately the same. For my father and Sandy, being in this forest must have given them the most incredible feeling of peace and freedom after the barbed wire and overbearing companionship of 2,500 others.

As we emerged from the forest, so did the sun, from behind puffy white clouds, and we speculated that there might be a little divine intervention in the meteorological department today. Out of the forest, we moved up onto the ridge overlooking Böhmfeld from where we could clearly see the forest north of the village, where they had spent their second night. Interpreting our father's use of the word "skirting" in his diary, we approximated the route they might have taken down the hill, below and out of sight of the village and up the other side to the safety of the trees. On the way we passed huge, neatly stacked piles of firewood, each log cut to the exact same length with Bavarian precision and the tolerances of a BMW piston.

Reaching the forest to the north of Böhmfeld took us just over two hours. We reckoned that in the dark, with my father's bad leg, Sandy's weakened condition and the slow and cautious progress of men taking care not to be seen, it must have taken them four or five hours. Due to time constraints, we decided not to delve further into the forest, but to see if we could retrace their steps into the village on the day when Sandy was nearly re-captured. So, we set off towards Böhmfeld, about three quarters of a mile to the south. Other than barn conversions, the northern edge of the village is pretty much identical to the way it looked in 1945. We know that when they reached the village and Sandy went into a house for water, my father had raked grass in a field where he could see up into the village street. He had described his perspective, as he looked up the street to where Sandy had gone. It was here where Abel, the Frenchman, recognised him as a fellow prisoner, and where my father stood and watched in horror as German soldiers went into the farmhouse he had seen Sandy go into. It was not long before we found ourselves standing on the very spot where this had all taken place, 62 years earlier. It was by far the most intense and emotional time-traveller moment of the trip so far. It was as if I was there with them that day. That end of the village was largely unchanged; no new buildings had been erected, so we were here at the very same time of year, and the street curved exactly as it had all those years ago. I was here, on the very spot where my father had stood, probably terrified, as he raked the grass and tried to look inconspicuous, wondering if at any moment he would be captured or shot. It was a quite extraordinary feeling.

Herr Blobb (left) while on leave. Abel (right) the mischevious
French PoW who worked on their farm and came across my father
in the field, and offered to shelter them in the Blobb's barn.

Frau Blobb, after the war, when Sandy visited Bohmfeld. She was in poor health.

(left to right) Franziska Blobb-Halsner, RWS,
Dominic Weston Smith, Jakob Halsner.

RWS with Franziska Blobb-Halsner.

Our boots clodded with mud, we called it a morning and rang Franziska and Jakob's doorbell, thrilled in the knowledge that we had, with 90% accuracy, not only retraced their steps but pinpointed two places where we knew, precisely, they had been. Once again, we received a warm welcome. Beer and the most delicious open sandwiches were immediately produced, and we eagerly demolished them as Christian translated the details of our walk. Franziska had apparently been having flashbacks all night. Jakob remembered that his father had told him about the note that my father and Sandy had given to Franziska's mother before they left, ensuring her good treatment at the hands of the Americans. Apparently, the American officer she presented it to was sufficiently impressed to promise her that she should be given a cow by way of reward. I wonder how he concluded that a cow was the appropriate compensation for risking certain death to hide British escapees. In the end, she never got the cow; the chaos of the end of the war proving too much of a challenge for the equitable distribution of farm animals. How extraordinary that our lives were so intertwined. Back then, with their countries at war, they had officially been enemies, but that was not how things had played out in the little village of Böhmfeld. They had become best of enemies, and the best of friends; and now, so many years later, so were we.

We said our goodbyes to Franziska and she gave me a lingering hug. A hug full of meaning. With promises of return visits and a final wave, Jakob drove us back to our car. Our families had shared a piece of history together that neither would forget. We were both fighting back the tears as we said goodbye. Tears for my father, and for our journey. His story had now become ours.

On the flight home, I reflected silently on this adventure. I knew that no matter how frustrating my journey there had been, it was nothing compared to what my father and Sandy had gone through over those 14 dangerous days in Bavaria. Reluctant as they both were to speak of what happened, it now felt as if Dominic and I had become a small part of their story. Something had undoubtedly shifted in us both – dislodged perhaps, becoming free. We had not just travelled, we had travelled back in time, making our own important and lasting connection to Eichstatt, Böhmfeld, and the brave Frau Blobb; and in doing so, we had proudly trodden in the footsteps of giants.

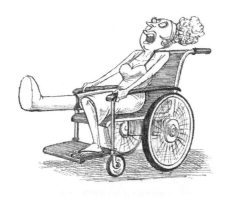

TURKEY
The Achilles Heel
of Istanbul

Snap! It had never occurred to me that one can actually hear the sound of an Achilles heel snapping. The Management and I were consulting together as to whether the cobblers shop she was looking for was farther on, or if we had already passed it, when she suddenly toppled off the 10-inch edge of the narrow pavement, landing in the gutter with a howl of pain. That is all it takes – a moment's distraction in unfamiliar surroundings and, in an instant, the next six months of your life are radically altered.

It was an innocent enough question, six months before, that had precipitated this trip: "Darling," I asked. "I thought we could cash in some air miles and go somewhere for your birthday. Where would you like to go?"

"Ooooh, well… I would love to go back to Istanbul, as I never really had the chance to see it properly."

Having travelled extensively in the course of her work there were many places The Management had been, but rarely had the leisure time to explore. Istanbul was one of them.

"OK, well we could…."

"Besides, you know those cowboy boots I need to get re-heeled?" she interjected.

"Er, yes."

"Well, Istanbul would be the perfect place to get them done properly."

"You mean we would be travelling from California to Istanbul… just to get your boots fixed?"

"Is that not a good enough reason?" she asked. "Besides, it's *my* birthday, and you asked me where I want to go, and that's where I want to go."

And so that was that.

It was one o'clock on a February morning – some five hours behind schedule – by the time we finally arrived at the Hotel Antik in the heart of Istanbul. In places, snow still lay on the ground from a recent fall. It had been a tiring journey, peppered with delays. At Heathrow, I had spent a long time at the information desk, which had turned out to be a study in advanced oxymoronics. I pointed out to the BA representative that the board showed our departure time was scheduled for 5:00pm. It further indicated that our gate would be announced at 5:15pm, which was after the flight would have departed had it left at 5:00pm which it clearly hadn't because the time was now 6:00pm. A look of bovine incomprehension was the only response I got.

First called Byzantium, then Constantinople, once capital of the Roman Empire, the great city of Istanbul straddles the Bosporus, its skyline studded with domes and minarets, at once ancient and modern, eastern and western. Churches and mosques stand among centuries-old bazaars and trendy new clubs and restaurants, as the calls of the muezzin float through the air. It is a fascinating, wonderful city, but not one designed for the disabled. A wheelchair is a rare sight, as every sensible disabled person in the city has long since moved to California, where the Americans with Disabilities Act makes their lives much more enjoyable. Come to think of it, it's not great for cars either, or pedestrians. There are no ramps, lots of stairs, irregular cobbled surfaces, and random drains and open holes everywhere. Drivers enjoy seeing how close they can get to pedestrians without causing injury – although it appears they don't mind very much if they do – and trams ting-ting their bells as they trundle, unstoppable, through the melee. I imagine this is also the reason why there are virtually no dogs or old people to be seen. There are a lot of cats, but they present more challenging targets than dogs and old people.

The Hotel Antik was a modest establishment, chosen more for its views of the Bosporus and the Blue Mosque than for the opulence of its accommodations. Our room offered a small fridge, a sofa, and a view onto the rear of a tenement block. Demolishing the inevitable homemade smoked salmon sandwich the Management keeps with her at all times when traveling, we popped an Ambien and fell into a wonderful, deep, jet-lagged sleep.

The next morning, woken early by the call to prayer, we rose quickly, excited to get out and explore the mysteries of Istanbul.

Breakfast at the Hotel Antik was disappointing. The orange juice had a taste unrelated to any known citrus fruit, and there was a vast selection of entirely inedible meats and cheeses that might have been pilfered from an expired Red Cross package. A bit of rummaging uncovered a bowl of passable yogurt and a fresh bread roll, but the coffee was undrinkable. The Management didn't fancy any of it, and announced she was off to get her cowboy boots re-heeled. Having brought them thousands of miles for precisely this purpose, she was not going to let a shitty breakfast hold her up.

So, left to my own devices, I discovered the terrace outside the breakfast room. Overlooking the Bosporus on one side and the Blue Mosque on the other, it afforded me a breath-taking view. It was a fabulous day, with the sky blue and the air cold, crisp and clear. I shivered slightly and pulled my jacket around me. "Cold enough to freeze the balls off a brass monkey," I thought.

This is a curious and often used British expression. The story goes that cannonballs used to be stored aboard warships in piles, held in a pyramid by a brass frame called a "munkey". In very cold weather the water spray would freeze on the balls. In extreme weather conditions, the combination of expanding ice and contracting brass could squeeze the cannonballs off the munkey and send them tumbling away. So, in very cold weather the British will stamp their feet and mumble, "It's cold enough to freeze the balls off a brass monkey". This is sometimes abbreviated to, "It's brass monkeys out there today." The veracity of this expansion/contraction theory has never been established because no university has yet managed to get funding to test it.

Anyway, a short time later I followed the Management, catching up with her on the cobbled street where she was having some problems with the sketchy directions she had been given by our surly receptionist. Moments later, the streets of Istanbul claimed another victim, and the City Public Works Department stencilled another stricken pedestrian icon on the side of their trucks.

I quickly picked her up and sat her on the edge of the curb to assess the damage. It wasn't good. She was in considerable pain, and walking was out of the question. I hailed a cab and instructed him to take us the 100 yards back to the hotel, which made him rather cross. The receptionist, largely unmoved by the sight of an injured guest, was unhelpful.

The Amerikan Hastanesi is definitely top of the list of hospitals you would want to go to if you are medically compromised in Istanbul. It is clean, friendly, and far more efficient than many hospitals I have encountered in my travels. Most importantly for us, the doctors spoke English. Within 60 minutes, the Management had been admitted, seen by an orthopaedic surgeon, X-rayed, had pain relief administered, and seen by the ortho a second time. At some American hospitals she still would have been sitting in the waiting room next to a victim of gang-warfare, reading a six-month-old copy of *Woman's World* and signing all sorts of forms that absolve both doctor and hospital if they cut off the wrong foot or let you die from some flesh eating bacteria that is camping out in their cooling system.

On inspection, the doctor, a lovely chap called Ozgur, pronounced it to be merely a sprained ankle and prescribed a soft cast and several days bed rest. The Management reacted to this in much the same way she might have if she had just been told she was going to spend the weekend handcuffed to a dead goat. I explained to the doctor that my wife was not the sort of person to travel halfway around the world for the purpose of celebrating her birthday in freshly heeled cowboy boots, only to sit in a poky hotel room with her leg up. Unless death were imminent, she would be gallivanting around the Grand Bazaar within minutes of being discharged. This caused him to reconsider.

"In that case, we do MRI." Somewhat surprised at this sudden and dramatic change of tack, we questioned him further. He admitted that there was a possibility there might be something going on that the X-Ray was not revealing.

"I have hunch," he said mysteriously, and disappeared before we could probe further, leaving me hoping he had indeed said "hunch" and not "lunch."

Within no time at all the Management was thoroughly de-blinged and popped into the centre of a magnet powerful enough to suck a Volkswagen in off the street. Unable to minister to her, I went to the glitzy hospital cafe for a revitalizing double espresso to pass the time as the MRI hummed, clicked, and buzzed about its business. A wheelchair seemed inevitable, so I placed a call to the guide we had booked for the day to ask him if he could locate one we might rent.

Forty-five minutes later, we all gathered around a lightbox for Ozgur to give us the low down.

"There is problem," said Ozgur, pointing. "See looky. You have hair fracture here."

Ah yes, we agreed, there it was.

"But this is not problem," he continued briskly, "Here you see Achilles – she busted, looky."

Sure enough, the MRI showed it clearly. There goes our holiday, I thought to myself.

In Greek mythology, Achilles was the greatest of all the Greek warriors, hero of the Trojan War, and the central character of Homer's *Iliad*. A hell of a tale, the *Iliad* is chock full of sex (straight, gay, cousin and deity), treachery, murder, mayhem, battle and betrayal. The legend goes that Achilles was pretty much invincible, but in good movie script tradition, he was killed by Paris, who shot him in the heel with an arrow. Who the hell shoots anyone in the heel? Later, legends came up with the idea that Achilles was invulnerable with the exception of his heel, because his mother, Thetis, had held him by the heel when she dipped him in the river Styx as an infant, as one does. This is the reason the term "Achilles' heel" is used to this day to mean a point of weakness, often in someone who, in all other regards, has the constitution of an ox. In the movie *Troy*, in which his acting was a wooden as the horse[80], Brad Pitt starred as Achilles. However, in a moment of supreme irony, Pitt ruptured his Achilles during a fight scene and filming shut down for three months.

---

80 But not a single woman in the world cared one jot.

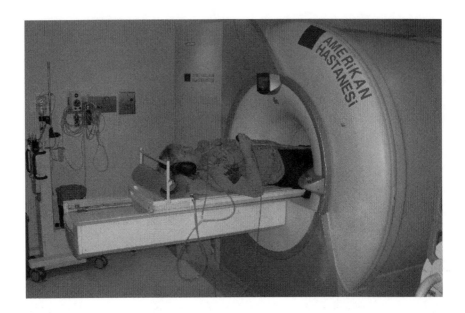

The Management, being MRI'ed

Moving from legend to medical science, the Achilles tendon is the longest, thickest tendon in the body; without it, we are rendered pretty much immobile. Found at the back of the lower leg, it attaches the calf muscles to the heel bone. It can handle a load of almost four times our body weight while walking, and nearly eight when running. Not many people know that. About 1 in 10,000 people per year suffer a snapped Achilles tendon, and this year the Management was one of them.

"You need surgery to fix," Ozgur said, delivering the message we least wanted to hear with a flourish inspired by the size of the bill he would doubtless give us afterward.

On cue, a charming lady with a clipboard, who had apparently been waiting for just this moment, appeared magically out of the shadows and told us that the operation would cost $10,000 and require us to stay in Istanbul for quite a bit longer than we had planned. Despite the efficiency and general cleanliness of the hospital, the Management shot me a glance that made it quite clear she would rather hack off her own leg with a rusty butter knife than undergo surgery in Istanbul. So, I paid our account, picked up a prescription for some large, bright pink Ibuprofen, thanked Ozgur profusely, and eased her gently into a cab.

Returning to the hotel we found our guide waiting for us with a wheelchair, and immediately discovered how wheelchair inaccessible the hotel was. The lift was barely big enough to fit both the Management and the chair. Squeezing her in, I shut the door and scooted up three flights of stairs as fast as I could to meet her on the third floor. By the time I got there, panting and red-faced, there was no sign of her at all, and the lights indicated the lift was going down. I raced back down the stairs to reception, skidding to a halt at the lift as the doors opened to reveal a man wearing a Fez. Shit, where the hell had she gone? I jumped into the lift and hit the button for the third floor. Racing along the corridor, I arrived at our room to find the door open and the Management having an altercation with a coffee table.

"Where the hell have you been?" she said, patience not being one of her strong points.

"Well, you disappeared, and when I caught up with the lift, had been replaced by a man in a Fez" I said, exasperated and out of breath.

"Yes, he helped me out of the lift – lovely man. What took you so long?"

Cancelling everything for the day, we spent a few hours commiserating with each other over the misfortune that had befallen our little celebratory trip. I proposed booking a flight and getting her back to LA for surgery at the earliest opportunity. The Management disagreed, adamant she was not going to let a broken Achilles impact our little holiday one bit. We would use the wheelchair and go ahead as planned. The pain was manageable, she said. I had some take-out brought in, which the Management advised strongly against, and refused to touch. I reflected, in the way that one does after some mishap has occurred, how it all would have been different if only the cowboy boots had been cobbled in California; then none of this would have happened. But that's just not the way life, or travel works, is it? Travel is like rolling the dice; you never quite know what you are going to get. Sometimes it's good, sometimes it's bad, you just have to be able to go with the shift.

The Management was, as is often the case, right; the take-out I had eaten the night before was trying to get back out again; by every possible route. Imodium was required. During the course of the previous 12 hours, we had discovered quite how difficult it was to navigate a slippery hardwood floor on crutches; how impossible it was to have a bath or shower; how much difference even rudimentary room service would have made, and quite how monumentally pissed off disabled people feel when battling an environment clearly designed with a cavalier disregard for their needs.

In a wise but uncharacteristic concession to her injury, the Management decided she would spend the morning resting, before taking on the streets of Istanbul in the afternoon. Lesser mortals, such as Brad Pitt, would have hired a couple of excitable nurses and stayed at home for a week. Very sweetly, she told me that she wanted me to be able to see the sights of this extraordinary city, without the impediment of a wheelchair, and that I should go with the guide for the morning. Setting off with Kurshatz, I quickly discovered him to be one of those people who cannot walk and talk at the same time. This was rather irritating, so I explained that I had an indisposed wife, a bad case of attention deficit disorder and limited time, so we had better get a bloody move on.

At the Blue Mosque, dusty beams of creamy sunlight streamed through high windows. I paused to take a photograph of Hakim the Hooverer, silhouetted dramatically against the windows as he methodically, solemnly, and entirely alone, vacuumed the three acres of carpet that covers the floor. Good idea for a Dyson commercial, I thought.

Next, we nipped down into the Roman Cisterns. Built in the sixth century during the reign of Byzantine Emperor Justinian the 1st, they could store enough fresh water for the city to survive 150 days of siege. Siege warfare is the passive-aggressive military blockade of a city or fortress and was, for thousands of years, common practice. So common, in fact, that building facilities such as Istanbul's cistern were all part and parcel of good city planning. The word siege is derived from the Latin *sedere*, "to sit". And that pretty much sums it up. The art of conducting and resisting a siege – taught in all the finest military academies –went something like this: The besieger would arrive, surround the city and set up camp, preventing anything and anyone from getting in or out. The besieged would lock themselves in and put some oil on the boil, to repel attempts at entry. There would be a bit of shouting and some demands would be made, then both sides would say "Fuck you!" and pretty much sit it out. Occasionally there would be some negotiation, or a bit of tunnelling, or some dodgy attempts at trickery involving wooden horses, but generally it was a long and very dull process. Both besiegers and besieged were banking on the other succumbing to hunger, thirst, disease, or boredom before they did.

The Romans were experts at laying siege and knew that water was critical to surviving one. Lots of water. So, they brought surplus old pillars to Constantinople from various parts of the empire, as well as leftovers from the construction of Hagia Sophia, and cleverly recycled them to build the cisterns. Avenues of columns and arches, now artfully up-lit, reflected in the still water beneath. The cavernous structure was like a hall of ancient mirrors: an underground, watery, temple-like structure made of mismatched marble, upside-down Medusa heads, assorted capitals and other Roman architectural detritus. I was enthralled.

Our tour of the Hagia Sophia was somewhat spoiled by a vast twenty-storey scaffolding structure that towered from floor to ceiling – part of a restoration project that had been going on for the previous 21 years. Considering the entire Hagia Sophia originally took only six years to build, I wondered at both the length of its restoration and the methods employed to motivate the workers.

A brisk walk took us from there to Topkapı Palace, former home of the Ottoman Sultans. I was keen to see the famous, emerald-encrusted Topkapı dagger, subject of the eponymous 1964 Hollywood heist film, based on Eric Ambler's novel *The Light of Day*. The dagger's handle is set with three massive Colombian emeralds, the size of pigeon's eggs.[81] At the end of the handle is an octagonal-shaped emerald, which opens to reveal a small watch; this is presumably so you can tell what time you stabbed someone. The sheath is made from gold, with enamelled flower motifs, and encrusted with diamonds. It is, quite simply, a masterpiece of murderous beauty.

"Hakim the Hooverer" tending to the carpets in the Blue Mosque.

Returning to the hotel, three hours later, I found the Management relaxed, having enjoyed a restful morning chatting, in Italian, with Mrs. Bulgaria, the maid. The fact that Mrs. Bulgaria did not speak a word of Italian seemed to have in no way diminished their evident enjoyment of each other's company. She was obviously in some pain (The Management, not Mrs. Bulgaria) but was putting on a

---

81 A pigeon's egg is about four centimetres long – larger than a quail's egg but smaller than a hens'. Does that help?

brave face. Determined to make the most of our trip, the Management announced that she wished to go out. Into the lift she went. I pounded down the stairs and met her at the bottom, fired up Kurshatz, who was busy chatting up the receptionist, and off we went.

I had never pushed anyone in a wheelchair before – at least not any great distance – so to warm me up, the Management decided we should take a practice spin around the Mısır Çarşısı (Egyptian Bazaar, or spice market), a smaller version of the Grand Bazaar. Completed in 1665, the building is part of the New Mosque, and the revenues obtained from the eighty-five rented shops inside it go towards the upkeep of the mosque. The ride quality proved to be smoother than expected, thanks to the polished marble flagstones. We were taken to a particular vendor of spices, Yacoub, who took pride in explaining the dazzling array of merchandise on display. Piles of saffron, cumin, garam masala, teas, Turkish delight, sponges and ground nuts were all available, and a heady aroma hung in the air. Several mixtures, flagged with signs that read, "Five times in the night!" promised either imminent carnal bliss or a complete nightmare, depending on your point of view. We crammed the wheelchair into the tiny store, sampling and sniffing as we negotiated prices and amounts with Yacoub. Finally, laden with exciting vacuum-sealed bags for friends, we headed back to the hotel. On arrival, Kurshatz announced that if we wanted his services the next day, his rate would be triple. So, we informed him we did not. This made the receptionist, through whom we had booked him, quite cross, and there was a highly animated exchange between them, in which it was clear we were not being complimented. We decided that henceforth the establishment would be better named the Hotel Miserable Weasel, due to its contemptuous disregard of any kind of customer service.

The Management was up and down a bit in the night, and the calls of the muezzin again woke us early. I flung open the shutters to see an apricot sun rising behind Istanbul. Pigeons flapped and wheeled from perch to perch and the beautiful wails of the muezzin, ancient and haunting, were an enchanting soundtrack to sunrise. With some trepidation I wondered what, given the hand fate had dealt us, the day had in store for us. Having been a producer before she became a film director, my wife naturally had a Plan B up her sleeve and announced that a new guide by the name of "Alp" would be joining us for the assault on the Grand Bazaar. Alp, she explained in an offhand sort of way, was a "shopping guide". There are no two words that strike greater terror into a man's heart than these, but considering her circumstances I felt I must put on a brave face, as she was. It turned out that Kurshatz was the boyfriend of Ms. Weasel, the receptionist, so we got an extra-frosty glare and she snatched the key from my hand when we went downstairs that morning.

Alp fell at the first jump by taking us straight to a leather shop that was up three flights of stairs with no elevator. Not a tall chap to start with, he quickly found his stature further reduced after this fundamental error of judgement. He followed this faux pas with a complete disregard for the realities of wheelchair perambulation, leading us off down a hill, over a curb, across two sets of raised tram-lines in between traffic, over another curb and finally up a step into a porcelain shop. In his defence, it wasn't entirely his fault, but that of the city itself. For me, this was the equivalent of an assault course, and it was almost impossible to deliver a comfortable ride; a fact I was sharply reminded of at increasingly regular intervals. Anyway, he was charming and chatty and much more helpful than Kurshatz, so we forgave him. Not finding anything to our liking, I wrangled the Management and her wheelchair into a cab, and we made tracks to the Grand Bazaar. Already, my hands were rubbed nearly raw from the spiky handle grips of the wheelchair. This was not a situation either of us were particularly relishing, but we had come a very long way to see this extraordinary city, and both felt strongly that we should make every effort to overcome whatever obstacles it presented. I was determined to try and figure out the best way to manoeuvre the blasted chair.

Deep into the bustling bazaar we went, the pitchmen outside each shop jumping on the novelty of a wheelchair-bound customer as we passed.

"Hey lady, what happen you?"

"Mister, you come in, rest here... and bring missus too!" (Yeah, like I wouldn't). Alp deftly led us to a little shop that we could never have found without him and which probably belonged to his uncle. It was full of antique fabrics that had been lovingly repaired, restored or cleaned, and we sat and sipped hot apple tea as Uncle Alp pulled out bolts of different shapes, sizes, colours and patterns and lay them out on the ground around us. Gaultier, Ozbek, and many other great names of fashion were, he assured us, regular customers, and his fabrics had graced the runways of the world. The Management was in her element, shrewdly choosing a unique, richly coloured strip of old silk with which to trim curtains.

Moving on, past shops selling endless designer goods of questionable provenance, we visited other fabric shops, jewellers, knick-knack stores, and so forth, before stopping for lunch at the restaurant in the centre of the bazaar. A couple of staff nimbly hoisted the wheelchair up some steps, and we were served a reasonably good meal by a waiter who had spent several years in Texas. He was keen to reminisce, until the Management politely suggested that we had not travelled 6,500 miles to Istanbul to discuss the merits of Dallas Fort Worth airport. He scuttled off, suitably chastened.

That afternoon, tired and with the Management in some pain, we returned to the Hotel Miserable Weasel to rest, and I put in an emergency call to a close friend who is general manager of a Four Seasons hotel in California, a bastion of eye-watering luxury. Explaining our unique predicament, and our frustration with the limitations of our current hotel, I asked if there was anything she could do to secure us more comforting and practical accommodations at the Four Seasons in Istanbul – preferably without the need for a second mortgage. She replied that, coincidentally, she had been the GM there for a time and would see what she could do.

In no time at all, we received a phone call from Tarik, the general manager, asking if we would like to be his guest for the remaining nights we were here, at a rate not far above what we were currently paying at the Hotel Miserable Weasel. Never have you seen two people disappear from one hotel and reappear at another so fast. It was almost teleportation.

No more than a few hundred yards away as the crow flies, we found ourselves in another world from the Weasel. We were met by a highly efficient Australian assistant manager, who whisked us to our room. There were no steps to speak of and the corridors were long, smooth and wide. We were shown to a vast room, with views of the tradesmen's entrance to the Blue Mosque on one side, and a stunning panorama of what appeared to be a cross between an archaeological dig and a hotel construction site on the other. In any other city in the world, the back door of a church and a construction site would not rate very highly on my list of desirable views; in Istanbul, it was utterly spectacular.

Nothing gets in the way of a bit of shopping.

Staff were abundant and the room capacious, with a bathroom as big as I had ever seen. No one batted an eyelid when I asked for a small waterproof plastic stool and a large roll of cling-film – they are trained to be deadpan in the face of the strangest requests. I am sure that if I had requested a stuffed parrot, a Kalashnikov and a bag of potting compost, they would have replied: "Certainly Mr. Weston Smith, would that be hollow point or regular ammunition?"

* * *

Built as the Sultanahmet Prison in 1919, the hotel is a fine example of Turkish neoclassical jail architecture. Its pointed arches, ornate tiles, domes and enclosed courtyard are watched over by imposing guard towers. Sultanahmet Prison was located next to the city courthouse; Graham Greene mentions it in his 1932 thriller novel *Stamboul Train*. Several famous artists and political figures were held there from time to time, including Mihri Belli, a communist leader; Orhan Kemal, a novelist; and Aziz Nesin, a controversial humourist who published more than 100 books. Obviously not so funny to some.

You can see elements of the original prison structure throughout the hotel, including some wooden doors, and marble pillars that still display carvings made by inmates a century before. I kept thinking I heard the wailing and moaning of ghostly prisoners, but it always turned out to be the Muezzin calling the faithful to prayers, a sound I was still unused to, but enjoyed immensely. The exercise yard, which for decades was the realm of wretched, shuffling humanity, has now been transformed into an exotic pool area with Philippe Starck chairs and the sound of tinkling fountains instead of jingling keys. I wondered how many fingernails had been extracted in what is now, ironically, a centre of excellence in fingernail pampering: the Spa. On that subject, I learned that the iconic film *Midnight Express* was actually shot entirely in Greece, a fact that has done much to cool Greco-Turkish relations for the last thirty years. It caused a precipitous decline in the Turkish tourist industry immediately after its release. The Turkish spoken in the film is apparently delivered with such a strong Greek accent, it is almost incomprehensible to the average Turk.

The team of concierges and porters immediately swung into action, anticipating our every need as they embarked on a service endurance trial, the likes of which they had never previously delivered. They performed, I might add, with flying colours. The concierge called Turkish Airlines and got us the best seat for an injured *left* leg, found where we could get a Velcro boot for the flight, sent out for bandages, aspirin, six extra pillows and more boot repairs.[82] A hairdresser was arranged, and the stool and cling film used to good effect in the shower. The Management emerged an hour later transformed by this procedure, glowing like a satisfied conductor after a particularly good performance.

The Harbourmaster greeting Kirsten on the dock at Yeniköy.

---

82 Those boots were going to get re-heeled, if it was the last thing Kirsten did.

We spent the next few days basking in this magic garden of service, trying to restrain ourselves from going overboard on the room service menu. All in all, it was a wonderful treat and made an enormous difference to The Management. Her patience with the Hotel Miserable Weasel had been stretched waff-er thin by the time we left. Despite her injury, and guided by the expert concierge, we now spent our time taking well-planned excursions. We visited restaurants with stunning views of the city at night, took the ferry up the Bosporus to lunch at Yeniköy, a charming fishing village, and visited the bazaar several more times. As it turned out, there was almost nothing we were unable to do because of the wheelchair, a fact that says a lot more about the Management's cast-iron fortitude than it does about the wheelchair accessibility of Istanbul. Her snapped Achilles would simply have to wait for some attention until she returned to California.

On disembarking from the ferry at Yeniköy, the Port-Master was so impressed to see a lady in a wheelchair come bumping down the gangplank that he insisted we take a photograph of him personally welcoming her. This proves my theory about the rarity of disabled people in Istanbul.

This trip was not at all what I had expected, but we had rolled with the punches. the Management had once again proved her cast-iron fortitude in the face of challenges that would have made lesser mortals weep. In four days, I had become an expert wheelchair perambulator, developing extraordinary muscles in my forearms, and hand calluses like an Abyssinian goat-herder. Despite the injury, we managed to see a great many things in Istanbul, and really had a terrific weekend. Our return flight was long and tedious so I won't dwell on that, and it was eight months before the Management could walk unaided again. We both agreed that we would like to return to Istanbul and experience this magnificent city again – just without the bloody wheelchair.

BRAZIL
A Medium Risk
of Extortion

Excited to be planning my first business trip to Rio de Janeiro in July 2018, I did some scuffling about on the Interweb to get a sense of what to expect. The first risk assessment I came across pulled no punches:

Overall travel risk: High
General kidnap and ransom: High
Express Kidnapping: High
Crime and civil unrest: High
Extortion: Medium

Oh, only a medium risk of extortion? Well, that's fine then. And what the hell is "Express kidnapping"?

Some further investigation revealed that one of the problems with kidnapping is that it usually takes a tedious amount of time, requires a fiendishly criminal level of intelligence, a lot of detailed planning, and has a high likelihood of military retaliation. An IRA kidnapper once called the wealthy father of a hostage, saying that they were holding his 20-year-old son, and wanted a million dollars for his safe return. "A million dollars!" exclaimed the man. "Don't be ridiculous! He's a bloody nuisance, you can keep him," he said, then hung up. That is a true story. If the victim is tremendously wealthy, which is usually a prerequisite, then the chances are reasonably high that the family will have a number of ex-SAS soldiers on speed-dial, and you might soon be on the receiving end of a flash-bang grenade and come around with a boot on your neck, looking up the barrel of a Heckler & Koch.

Express kidnapping is an opportunistic method of abduction well suited to those less patient criminals wishing to avoid the SAS experience and looking for a fast buck. In many parts of Latin America, express kidnappings are known as *Paseo Millonario* (millionaire tour). A victim is usually chosen on the spur of the moment because they are wearing ostentatious accessories, walking out of a Prada store, or look like Paris Hilton. It goes like this: Mr. Prada hails a cab and gets in. Once on the way, the driver stops, three accomplices suddenly jump in and stick an assortment of weapons in his face. All sorts of ghastly threats involving his earlobes and kneecaps are made, and Mr. Prada is then taken on a tour of the city's ATMs. At each, he is forced to withdraw as much as allowed, until every card, and everyone, is exhausted.

The aviation project I was leading for my company – that's all I can say, it was a stealth project – would need security for a team of people who would soon be coming down to Brazil, so I called an international security company to get their take on things.

"We can provide you with comprehensive support, tailored to your needs," I was assured, "from drivers and armed security personnel, to convoy protection and escort vehicles."

"Well, I am neither part of a United Nations delegation, nor Jeff Bezos," I replied, imagining trying to sip on a Caipirinha while surrounded by men in dark suits talking to their wrists. "Could you just recommend the best way for me to get around Rio to a few meetings, without too much fuss and gunfire?"

"Certainly Mr. Weston Smith. At the very minimum we would suggest a driver, trained in ambush avoidance, with an armed bodyguard riding shotgun, who can accompany you between the vehicle and buildings. That would cost $1,200 per day, but you have the option to upgrade to a fully armoured saloon car for an additional $750." This was the first time I had ever heard anyone using the term "riding shotgun" literally, and quoting a price for it. There must be a better way. I thanked him and hung up. I said nothing to the Management about any of this in case she had a complete sense of humour failure, and booked my ticket before objections could be raised.

Settling down into my Executive Goat compartment on American Airlines, I hoped my 20-hour journey from London, via Miami, would be uneventful. It was not. Some hours after leaving Miami, I stood up to go to the loo. I looked around for a place to temporarily put my laptop, where it would be both out of the way and accessible.

To one side of the window, there was a shallow lip and a half inch deep groove, close to where the shelf of my cubicle met the wall of the cabin. It conveniently enabled me to lean the laptop up against the wall, without it sliding flat. It was a nice groove, a well-placed groove, a groove so perfect, I felt sure it must have been conceived for exactly this purpose. Having checked with my fingers that the groove had a solid bottom, and was not a gap, I used it a couple of times when I was rearranging things and it performed admirably.

Dinner was served, so having propped my laptop up in the groove once more, I tucked into my meal, scrolling through trailers for a film I might want to watch later. As I finished my main course and my plate was cleared away to make room for some cheese, we hit a little turbulence. Bump... wobble. Nothing too alarming. Then there was another little one, and the most extraordinary thing happened. I heard a soft scrape/whoosh sort of sound – a bit like an automatic door opening on the Starship Enterprise – and, out of the corner of my eye, I saw my laptop slide down into the groove as if by some invisible mechanism and vanish. It took no more than a second, and it was gone. Where there had, moments before, been my laptop, there was now just cabin wall.

I blinked. I tried to process what had just happened. I stared at the spot where the laptop had been, wondering vaguely if perhaps I was imagining things. I reached out and tapped the spot, expecting – hoping – I might possibly touch it and then know it could be retrieved. I stood up and leaned in to try and look down into the groove, but the curve of the cabin wall and the inconvenient position of my eyes in my head prevented me from getting close enough. Becoming more frantic, I probed urgently with my fingers along the length of the groove, in the unlikely event it had moved sideways. But all the time the groove felt as solid as it had when I first checked it out. Slowly, I began to understand the turbulence had created enough of a jolt-and-twist in the cabin fittings to momentarily separate the bottom of the groove from the wall, allowing the laptop to slip down into the depths. Leaping out of my seat, I searched the lower reaches of the cubicle, in case there was some way I could access a hatch. There was nothing.

I pressed the call button. *Ping.*

A flight attendant slid silently into view. "My laptop has been eaten by the plane" I began, explaining in detail the whooshy-bit and subsequent disappearance.

The friendly flight attendant was sympathetic, poking and prodding in all the same places I had.

"How odd, I have never seen anything like this before," she said.

"Me neither," I replied gloomily.

"Let me ask the purser if he has any ideas on how to dismantle the seat and get back there."

"Jolly good." I replied, thinking this was highly unlikely, but at that point I would have happily asked the nun in row 79B to help, if I thought there was even the slightest chance she might have experience in the disassembly of interior fittings on a 777.

"Hi, I'm the purser," said the purser moments later. "Let me have a look." So, he had a look.

"I have no idea how to get it out Mr. Weston Smith. I am so sorry. We will have to get the maintenance tech to take a look at it when we land in Rio." My hopes of quick retrieval were dashed and a whole raft of unpleasant and inconvenient scenarios emerged, related the collapse of life as I knew it into a laptopless abyss. They were both very apologetic and left to go and wrangle some ice cream. I could overhear a lot of chat in the galley about the man in 7A and the quite extraordinary thing that had happened to his laptop. A head popped around the curtain to check me out, perhaps to see if I was weeping inconsolably. It was quite the event among the crew. I heard that pinging sound the crew intercom makes when they want someone at the back to pick up. Word spread like wildfire and several cabin crew from Goat Class stopped by to commiserate. One suggested a strong drink might help, and kindly brought me a scotch, of the strength one would likely want upon hearing news that your dog has to be put down. I had to ask for some water to dilute it.

Flying over the Amazon for the first time was quite an experience. Although it was a night flight, I was acutely aware that below me were thousands of miles of impenetrable forest. Roughly the size of the 48 contiguous United States, the Amazon rainforest covers 40% of the South American continent. Within its boundaries lie bits of no less than eight South American countries: Brazil, Bolivia, Colombia, Ecuador, Guyana, Peru, Suriname, and Venezuela – as well as a bit of France, in the form of French Guyana. The river itself is made up of over 1,100 tributaries, 17 of which are longer than 1,000 miles.

I touched down in Rio early in the morning the next day. I was going to meet up with Julian, a friend and colleague who had flown in from California. He loved adventure and was a terrific travelling companion. Julian and I came from similar backgrounds. We had both emigrated to America, we both had dual British/American nationality – and we both lived in Santa Barbara. We shared a desire for punctuality, had a similar sense of humour and often referred to each other as "Carruthers". Over the previous three years we had spoken on the phone almost every day and criss-crossed the world together on business. On the way we covered a plethora of subjects and, despite his far greater intellect, he was always open to my ideas and intrigued by a different angle or opinion. If I did not understand some technical detail, he would patiently explain, and was complimentary when I suggested something he had not considered.

He had an unusual fondness for Kit-Kats, which he would consume at every opportunity with a look of rapture. Julian would travel with an astonishing amount of technical gadgetry. No sooner had we arrived in the airline lounge than he would unpack the better part of a small electronics shop, and in minutes there would erupt a spaghetti junction of cables, chargers and adaptors. There he would sit, with an ever-present San Pellegrino and Kit-Kat, surrounded by a star-field of blinking, coloured lights, happily fiddling with a spreadsheet or some complex formula related to the behaviour of gas at altitude. Even on board an airplane, Julian would require a constant stream of information normally available only to the pilots and would attach his own GPS antenna to the window, occasionally stopping by my seat to brief me on some exciting landmark far below. When in Sydney, there was unspoken agreement that we would climb the harbour bridge. In Durham for a business meeting, the engineering marvels of the Cathedral had required a thorough investigation. He had great intelligence, wit, good humour and endless curiosity, all wrapped up in a cheerful passion for his craft.

As I had expected, on arrival in Rio, things began to deteriorate further. I had thought, perhaps a tad optimistically, that a laptop-rescue specialist would immediately appear, unscrew something, and return my laptop in moments. Instead, the purser adopted the tone of voice used to calm hysterical passengers.

"Now, don't worry Mr. Weston Smith, we have called maintenance and reported the problem, and they are on their way, but you must disembark, as must we. Just have a word with the gate agent," he said as he smiled and patted me on the shoulder. "They will be very happy to take care of it for you. Thank you for traveling with American Airlines!" I could tell instantly that a large, hairy buck was being passed, as I was swept out of the plane and up the jet-bridge by an ebb tide of passengers behind me. The gate-agent was clearly at the end of a long shift, and no known form of joy was currently anywhere within her emotional grasp. She would rather have sucked on a dead bat than taken care of anything for me, as had been promised.

"Sir," she began, with an inflection suggesting the next words she would speak could be roughly translated as please fuck off. "If the crew have reported it, the matter will be turned over to maintenance and you can claim the item from lost property. I suggest you call them." She picked up the phone, to emphasise that our conversation was at an end. Knowing that retrieving an object from the Mariana Trench would be considerably easier than getting my laptop back from the lost property office at Rio de Janeiro airport, I moved on to plan B.

The next hour was spent pleading with the staff in the Club lounge to find out if my laptop had been retrieved and prevent it by any means whatsoever from being directed to lost property. Fortunately, having summoned every ounce of charm I could muster, I found a kindly soul who was prepared to take on my case, make calls and chase it down. Eventually, having done everything possible, I left it with her, on the assurance that she would get it delivered to my hotel. I had my doubts.

* * *

Rio de Janeiro, home to more than six million people, lies on the Tropic of Capricorn, on the east coast of Brazil. It is famed for its Copacabana and Ipanema beaches, barely-there bikinis, Sugarloaf Mountain and the 38-metre-tall Christ the Redeemer statue on top of Mount Corcovado. The city has also gained a reputation for its sprawling shanty towns, known as favelas, and the noisy, flamboyant, and inestimably fabulous Carnival Festival, considered to be the world's largest annual gathering of pickpockets.

We were met by Duncan. A man of indeterminate nationality, Duncan spoke perfect English and fluent Portuguese with a touch of a South African accent. He had lived in Rio for many years and owned a transportation company that had been recommended to me by a friend at the British Embassy in Brasilia. They assured me that Duncan was all I would need. He had started out by providing transport for American sailors on shore leave. It turned out that when you let a thousand young sailors from an aircraft carrier loose, in no time at all they are partying all over the city, and more than just transport is required. Duncan soon became their minder, making sure they stayed away from the wrong parts of town, picking them up when they were hog-whimpering drunk at two in the morning, and safely returning them to the ministrations of their commanding officer. This prevented many unfortunate diplomatic incidents, some only just.

Over time, the owners of those bars frequented by the sailors got to know Duncan and would call him to come and collect his charges when things got a bit wild. Soon, he had the contract for the entire U.S. fleet as well as the British Navy. He was a gentle, good-natured man, discreet and exceedingly knowledgeable. His services were both affordable and very professional.

The road from the international airport into the centre of Rio very much sets the tone for the city. Perhaps I had been influenced by pictures depicting the glamor of Copacabana Beach, but I was surprised to discover Brazil is an incredibly deprived country, comparable to India, with extreme poverty alongside great wealth.

"The bottom line is that security here is highly nuanced. It depends on who you are, where exactly you are going, what your route is and many other factors," said Duncan, deftly avoiding a pothole. "For instance, you should only take an Uber in Rio for short distances in the centre of town and never between the airport and Hotel. The reason is the Uber drivers use GPS, but they aren't security trained and don't necessarily pay attention to where all the favelas are. They can easily drive you into a hot-spot."

He went on to describe a recent newspaper story about a British couple from Kent, who had been on holiday with their three children. Due to translation difficulties, they drove right into the middle of a favela, where they were approached by a gang and told to get out of the car. They refused, and the gang opened fire, hitting the mother twice. She survived, but it could have been a lot worse, and these stories were not uncommon.

"Most crime is opportunistic," he said. "Don't walk on the street holding your phone, don't wear a watch or jewellery, don't wear a jacket. Take a backpack, not a briefcase, and dress down – way down – to blend in."

"What about the police?" Julian asked.

"The Feds are OK, but the State police are as likely to rob you as anyone else," said Duncan.

As I pondered being robbed by the police, dilapidated warehouses and factories flashed past, walls exploding with graffiti-like tattoos, most of it the territorial markers of gangs. Duncan pointed out the first Favela as we travelled past, afforded only a slight margin of safety only by our forward momentum. You would not want to break down here.

Favelas are located in or around the country's large cities, especially Rio de Janeiro and São Paulo. Some of the best-known are those that cling to the steep hillsides in Rio de Janeiro, highly visible sores of poverty and crime on the landscape of an otherwise beautiful city. From the 1940s to the 1970s, Brazil experienced a great wave of migration from the countryside to the cities, where work was more available, but land was scarce and expensive. Squatters would occupy vacant land and build shanties made of whatever materials they could scrounge or steal. In Rio, such land was usually on steep hillsides, as it was inaccessible and unsuited to construction, although with breath-taking views. To this day, crowding, unsanitary conditions, poor nutrition and pollution are all commonplace, along with crime managed by gangs immersed in illegal drug trafficking. Police presence is sporadic, and spirited gun battles are common. The Brazilian government has, from time to time, tried different approaches to dealing with favelas, from programs to wipe them out entirely, to efforts to improve regulation, infrastructure, and housing. All without much success. The 12.6 million people who live in favelas are simply a law unto themselves, and in desperate need of proper housing.

As the freeway swept on into downtown, I was captivated by the view. Rio is, without question, one of the most beautiful cities I have ever visited. It makes Cape Town look like a dowdy aunt, Hong Kong a poor cousin. It is absolutely stunning. In addition to its position on the coast, lapped by the warm waters of the South Atlantic, its geological construction sets it apart. Gigantic towers of rock with domed tops rise up out of lush green vegetation, separated by residential areas, parks and lagoons. These dramatic, granite behemoths are the result of tectonic forces and the power of erosion; amid this bustling city they play a key role in creating a safe haven for the many endangered animals and plants. Their steep-sided forests have rich supplies of water and soil to support thick, lush tree canopies, creating an environment that is host to a vast array of specialized vegetation. One thing I noticed immediately, which is uncommon in cities, is the way the landscape constantly changed as one wound through it, so that you see the city from an entirely different perspective every couple of minutes.

The freeway transitioned to tree-lined avenues, brightly lit tunnels and the perimeter road of the Rodrigo de Freitas Lagoon, where the Olympic rowing events had been held. We were almost in Ipanema. I have always preferred small boutique hotels, and on this occasion I had chosen the Ipanema Inn, one block off the famous beach. Rather hilariously, considering its exotic reputation, the name Ipanema derives from the Tupi language words *ipá* (pond) and *nem-a* (stinking), but it couldn't be further from that today. It is one of Rio's most expensive districts to live in, with world-class restaurants, shops, and cafés, yet it manages to retain a down to earth, relaxed, friendly feel, largely driven by its predominant beach culture. Every Sunday, the roadway along the promenade is closed to traffic, allowing local residents and visitors to stroll, bike, jog or roller-skate beside the ocean. Ipanema beach is divided into segments delineated by *postos*, or lifeguard towers. Stalls and bars sell coconut juice, beer and traditional cachaça along its length, while vendors wander everywhere, trying to sell a range of cheap souvenirs. Rio has its fair share of dangers, but no more so than a lot of major cities. Of course, one needs to be smart and alert, and to stay clear of infamous dodgy areas, but life generally goes on as usual. The same can be said of Johannesburg, Buenos Aires and Glasgow. Little old couples walk hand in hand through tree-shaded neighbourhoods, lovers sit in the parks, and the nearly naked sunbathe with little fear of being assaulted.

We arrived to find our hotel was modest but very comfortable and the staff incredibly welcoming. We availed ourselves of an explosion of tropical fruit for breakfast while discussing our plans for the day.

"Well, it's Sunday, we have a day off, and we are in Rio," I said. "Do you feel like doing some exploring?

"Ooh, yes! Absolutely" said Julian, who had been waiting for this moment. "What do you say we see the Christos?"

"Yes, madness not to," I said, scooping another spoonful of luscious, aromatic passion fruit onto my yogurt.

"There's a marvellous funicular, called the Trem do Corcovado, one takes to get to the top. It's by far the most fun way to get there!" explained Julian, who had clearly worked this all out during the flight.

"It's a rack railway, using the Riggenbach system, that winds steeply through the rainforest. It was invented in 1863 and was very clever at the time – still is, actually, which is why they still use it." Julian was on a roll, I could tell. He picked up a croissant to illustrate.

"You see, a system of cogs move along a ladder in the track, enabling the train to go up and down very steep gradients."

"With a bare minimum of hysterical screaming?" I added.

"Exactly! You know, originally, this one was steam-driven, but in 1910 it was electrified. The first electric railway in Brazil!" Julian was inordinately fond of anything mechanical, so that pretty much settled it.

Within minutes of polishing off six massive passion fruits and a papaya, we were waiting outside the hotel for our car, like a couple of excited schoolboys.

Towering over 2,000 feet above the city of Rio, the statue of Christ, or The Christos, has become a cultural icon of both Rio de Janeiro and Brazil. In 2007, it joined Machu Picchu, the Great Wall of China and the Roman Colosseum, as one of the New Seven Wonders of the World. Sitting on top of Mount Corcovado, in the Tijuca Forest National Park, the statue overlooks the entire city of Rio. At 98 feet tall and with outstretched arms reaching to 92 feet, it is almost as wide as it is tall. After World War I, the Roman Catholic archdiocese in Rio and a group of locals became concerned the community was drifting slightly to the left of disinterested of Christianity, and it was hoped that by placing a massive statue of Jesus on top of a mountain overlooking Rio, it would put an end to the "increasing godlessness" in the country. It was decided that the statue be placed on the summit of Mount Corcovado so it would be visible from anywhere and everywhere, and thus represent a way of "reclaiming Rio" to Christianity. I am not sure how successful this has been, but it is undoubtedly a fabulous landmark (skyscraper, even) to behold. Many flock to marvel at it, but its religious significance is likely lost on many of them.

Many famous bottoms have sat on the well-worn wooden benches of the Trem de Corcovado, including Alberto Santos-Dumont,[83] Albert Einstein, Diana, Princess of Wales, Pope Pius XII and Pope John Paul II. A "Double-Pope" is an impressive and much sought-after achievement for any attraction. The Grand Canyon and the London Eye would give their eye-teeth for a Double Pope. But it occurred to me that this modest little train to the Christos may lay claim to an even greater accolade. This may well be the only spot in the world that has the tourism triple crown — a Double Pope, an Einstein and a Lady Di.

While I was absorbed in the rainforest, vegetation, Double Popes and bird life, Julian, always bristling with technology, was happily calculating the drag-coefficient of a Riggenbach tram on his laptop. Arriving at the top, we eschewed the available lift and took to the stairs with enthusiasm. Julian was an avid hiker and could out-climb a mountain goat. I had been running three miles a day on doctor's orders, so temporarily had thighs like pistons. Reaching the top of the steps, our mouths dropped open in sheer amazement at what lay before us, and we stood panting gently while we took it all in. The whole of Rio was spread before us, like the opening panorama of a feature film that unexpectedly gives you goosebumps. The azure sky and dark blue sea blended on the horizon in a perfectly airbrushed backdrop. To the east was Sugarloaf Mountain, the beaches of Copacabana and Ipanema strung out from it like a necklace between

---

83 Santos-Dumont is a national hero in Brazil, where it is believed by many that he preceded the Wright brothers in demonstrating a practical airplane.

hills, along to the peaks of the Two Brothers mountain in the west. In the foreground lay the huge De Freitas lagoon. Never have I seen a city as spectacular, on a day so perfect. If ever there was an entirely appropriate moment to use the word awesome, this was it. Although busy at the top, the view eclipsed the crowd and we spent a happy half hour with our eyes on stalks before returning by tram, and back to the hotel for a siesta.

* * *

Not many people know that, just a short way outside Rio de Janeiro, on an Air Force Base in the town of Santa Cruz, is the world's only remaining original zeppelin hangar. It was originally designed to handle airship operations for the Graf Zeppelin and the Hindenburg and, at 58 metres tall, it spans the length of three football pitches. The gigantic hangar was constructed in pieces in Oberhausen, Germany, then shipped across the Atlantic. From Rio it travelled from the port on a railway purpose-built by British engineers, to be reassembled in Santa Cruz. The first zeppelin to travel to Brazil left from Friedrichshafen in Germany on May 18, 1931 and landed in Rio on May 25. Our business in Rio was regarding a global aviation project, so Julian and I were scheduled to visit the base with the military attaché from the British Embassy in Brasilia.

I rose at dawn and set off on a run along Ipanema beach. Visitors to Rio are advised not to go anywhere near the beaches after dark, as it would be inviting assault, robbery, extortion, violence and probably express kidnapping. But at dawn the streets and beaches were eerily empty and perfectly safe; even muggers and kidnappers have to sleep sometime. A few keen coconut salesmen were starting to unload their stock for the day, and a handful of fellow joggers made their way along the esplanade, admiring the beautiful dawn light on Ipanema.

Duncan had arranged one of his drivers for us, explaining that the expressway from Rio to Santa Cruz can be very dangerous as it passes through, or close to, about five favelas. Although we were unlikely to be a target ourselves, it was entirely possible to get caught up in the random crossfire of someone else's battle. Firefights with the police often spilled over onto the expressway, and cars could often be hit by stray bullets. The gangs are so organised, and well-armed, that they are even equipped with ground-to-air missiles to shoot at police helicopters. Guns, he insisted, were useless against the firepower of gangs and law enforcement, and waving one around would only increase the risk of having everyone shoot at us. He assured me that careful planning and his well-trained security driver would go a long way towards ensuring we did not find ourselves in a tricky situation.

Though we spent most of the drive imagining bullets and mortar fire raining down upon us, it was uneventful.

"Do you know why the band Led Zeppelin chose that name?"

"I have no idea, Julian."

"Well, in 1968, when Jimmy Page told some friends that he was going to form a new band, Keith Moon, the drummer of The Who, made some snarky comment about it sinking like a "lead zeppelin". Jimmy Page rather liked the simile.

"But why the spelling?" I asked.

"Aha. Yes… that was because he was worried people would mispronounce it, so he dropped the 'a'." Julian was always full of extraordinary information. When Led Zeppelin's eponymous, bestselling, debut album was released on January 12, 1969, the cover depicted the *Hindenburg* bursting into flames.

As we got closer to Santa Cruz, we could see the gigantic zeppelin hangar dominating the landscape.

"It cost a million dollars to build in 1936, which was a lot of money at the time," explained Julian. "In the end, it was only used four times by *Graf Zeppelin* and five by *Hindenburg*, before the airship industry came to a screeching halt when the *Hindenburg* went up in flames. In 1999, the hangar was listed as a Brazilian National Heritage Site."

We reached the gate, where our credentials were checked, and we were let in. Pulling up outside the commanding officer's building, we were met by a full guard of honour, who crisply saluted us. I think being with the British defence attaché to Brazil, a charming, brilliant navy captain by the name of Kevin Fleming, might have had something to do with the formality of our welcome.

After an hour of meetings, the commandant asked if we would like a tour of the hangar. Absolutely nothing can prepare you for the extraordinary sight on entering this giant structure. The sheer scale of this unique part of aviation history is almost impossible to comprehend until you walk in its cavernous interior. At 900 feet long, the *Graf Zeppelin*'s 776-foot would fit comfortably inside. Today, a medium sized reconnaissance aircraft was parked down the far end for maintenance. It looked like an Airfix model. A volleyball game was going on in one corner and along its length, several people rode about their business on bicycles.

Flying at an average speed of 73 miles per hour, the *Graf Zeppelin* made nearly 600 flights, covering almost one million miles, and offering 24 passengers at a time the most luxurious air travel available. Her elegant, aerodynamic design was a masterpiece of lightweight engineering. Covered in a fabric skin that had been impregnated with aluminium powder to repel radiation and ultra-violet light, the *Graf Zeppelin* gleamed and sparkled in a way that black and white photographs could never effectively capture. Almost as long as the *Titanic*, it was the first airship to circumnavigate the world (in 21 days), fly to the Arctic, and cross the Pacific Ocean non-stop. It cruised at only 650-feet, allowing the passengers a fabulous view of land or sea beneath. In the gondola that hung below its huge body the accommodation was opulent, featuring a lounge with large arched windows, a cocktail bar with wooden inlays and Art Deco upholstered furniture. A corridor led to ten passenger cabins capable of sleeping 24, and a pair of washrooms. Like sleeper trains, the cabins could be configured as sitting rooms during the day and converted into bedrooms at night. The galley served three hot meals a day. Given the service offerings on major airlines now, reading about this golden age of travel just makes one want to weep.

The *Graf Zeppelin* was able to carry impressive amounts of cargo, mail and luggage. Some passengers even took their cars aboard with them to bring across the Atlantic. It was a beast to park. The ground crew lit a fire to provide smoke for the Captain to judge wind speed and direction. Trimming its ballast, the airship approached the mooring nose-down, descending at 100 feet per minute – faster in windy conditions. As with when a boat comes in to dock, the Captain would reverse the engines at the critical moment and order lines thrown out. Whereupon up to 300 crew on the ground would grasp the ropes and hang on for dear life, while the nose was secured to the morning mast. What could possibly go wrong?

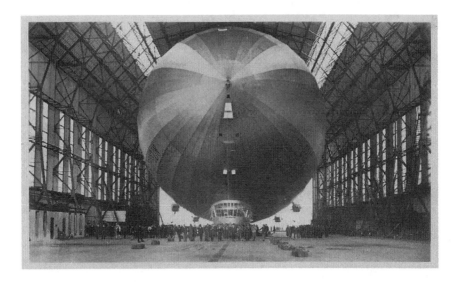

The Graf Zeppelin, possibly in the hangar at Santa Cruz. (PD-US)

Julian and I, along with our friends from the British Embassy, were given a tour of the hangar, escorted by our 20-strong entourage of officers from the base. Apparently, this was the highlight of their day and they were damned if they were going to miss a second of it. Always one to keep things interesting, Julian suddenly said to the base commander, "I would very much like to climb up onto the roof of the hangar; would that be possible?"

When asking someone in a position of authority for something that was unlikely to be granted, Julian always lowered his voice and adopted a mischievous smile, while his eyes twinkled. This was designed to make his victim feel that they were somehow already part of his plan, and therefore it was more difficult for them to refuse. I looked up at the roof he was referring to, almost 200 feet above me, and gulped. "Let me see if I can arrange it," replied the base commander and fired off a volley of Portuguese at his staff. Several phones were whipped out and brief conversations ensued. "OK, we can do this," said the commander. "But to make you safe, we must wait for the Bombeiros" – the base fire department. Julian beamed like a Cheshire cat.

Just a portion of the gigantic Zeppelin hangar at Santa Cruz.

Having been built in the early 1930s the hangar was no spring chicken. I had seen a similar, smaller one, in Tustin, California that had been built in the 1940s and it had been in a fairly poor state of repair. I craned my neck, tracing our possible route to the top. Towards the centre of the hangar were steep steps and ladders that ascended up to a landing about 75 feet off the ground. From there, a long, narrow, curving gangway stretched upwards, following the line of the roof, until it reached the apex, where there was a wooden catwalk that ran the entire length of the hangar.

Within about ten minutes, half a dozen men and women from the base's fire department arrived, carrying climbing harnesses, hard hats, huge carabiners and thick coils of rope. For a moment I imagined, in horror, that we were somehow going to be hauled to the top. Those fears proved to be unfounded, but were quickly replaced by worse ones as they explained that the wooden catwalks were old and unstable, and some of the ladders dangerously rusted. Past a certain point, we would need to be attached to secure points and obey their instructions at all times. It was agreed that Julian, myself and Kevin, the British military attaché, would all climb to the roof. Two Bombeiros would accompany us, as well as Adriana, a fighter-jet pilot who was to act as our translator.

Adriana was small and slightly built, with attractive brown eyes, flowing brown hair and an olive complexion. Long held stereotypes made it hard to imagine her flinging a fighter jet around at something over the speed of sound, dispensing missiles with ruthless efficiency. But the base was home to the Brazilian equivalent of the Top Guns, and despite her diminutive appearance, she was one of the Brazilian air force's elite pilots. I gazed at her with unfettered admiration as she helped me climb into my harness, before handing me a hard hat and checking me thoroughly to make sure everything had been secured properly.

We set off up the ladders, the Bombeiros in front and Adriana behind. Up and up we climbed, about ten flights, until we reached the landing. Looking down, our group below already seemed tiny, yet we were only halfway. Now we had to negotiate the first catwalk. At around 150 feet long, it was very disorienting because it was curved, so it climbed quite steeply upwards, at the same time as moving forward toward the centreline. It was smooth but with ridges every two feet, to stop one slipping. I tried not to look down, but it was hard to watch where your feet were going without doing so, and the first tentacles of fear began to creep over me. I grasped the handrail even tighter. Reaching the level catwalk at the apex of the hangar was both a relief, and scary in a different way, as I could now look 900 feet across the length of the hangar and 200 feet down at the same time. I used to think that being scared was a black/white thing, but now I was realizing there were not only shades of grey, but an entire colour spectrum of fear. I had no idea there were so many complex nuances to being scared shitless. Adriana asked us to wait while the Bombeiros strung a safety rope for us to clip on to. This gave us time to look about and consider our circumstances for a moment, which was not actually very helpful. Here we were, 200 feet in the air, on a catwalk with an undetermined number of loose or missing boards. The group we had left behind now looked like ants far below. I imagined the entire catwalk groaning, before disintegrating and crashing to earth in the manner of the *Hindenburg* itself, sending us screaming to our death on the concrete beneath. Julian, happy as a clam, and quite unaffected by all this interior altitude, distracted me by making me take photos of him.

The Santa Cruz Zeppelin Hangar, Brazil, 2018. *(Photo: Kevin Fleming)*

The view from part way up the sloping ladder to the spine.

A view along the spine catwalk.

Our military escort, far below looked like ants.

Captain Kevin Fleming and Julian Nott, with the
gigantic hangar doors in the background.

RWS being instructed in how to ascend a rusty ladder. *(Photo: Kevin Fleming)*

Before too long, the ropes were set, and we got the all clear to move. Our instructions were to stay 20 feet apart and avoid putting too much weight on any one section at the same time. We were called forward, one by one, gingerly watching where we stepped. Every now and again there was a missing board, or one with a hole in, which gave me little confidence in those that remained. There was little between us and certain death, as if we were crossing a gorge on a decayed suspension bridge, a raging torrent far below. I felt as if I was having an Indiana Jones moment, without the music, or Harrison Ford. At the end of the catwalk, almost above the giant doors at one end, was a vertical ladder, with a trapdoor at the top, and it became clear that this was where we were headed. Adriana had very specific instructions.

"Climb up this ladder very carefully. You will see that these rungs here and here, are rusted," she said, pointing them out. "Do not step on them." Julian, who knew everything about the hangar, explained that we were climbing up to the observation platform on top of the roof. He went first, followed by Kevin, then me. Adriana watched us like a hawk, while one of the Bombeiros stood at the top to give us a pull-up through the trapdoor. I got to the first rusted rung and found myself in a position where it was really hard not to put your foot on it. The rungs were spaced quite widely, so it became a bit of a contortion to skip one altogether. If this has rusted through, I wondered, what else had?

Climbing out on to the top of the hangar, I found myself in a small octagonal structure, about eight feet in diameter, with windows all around and a wooden roof. The floor had sheets of plywood laid haphazardly across it, signifying something structurally amiss. Some of the windows were broken and cracked. Around the outside perimeter ran another catwalk. As an observation post for weather and incoming zeppelins, the view was spectacular. In one direction you looked right down the external spine of the hangar to the vanishing point of the other end, 900 feet away. If you were certifiably insane and had a death wish, there was a catwalk that ran the entire length of the roof, in which I could see many broken or missing boards. To the right was the town of Santa Cruz, and to the left the runways. Some way off in the other direction was the sea, where a Hercules was busy practicing throwing pallets of equipment from its rear door. It was extraordinary to stand here and imagine the gigantic bulk of the Graf Zeppelin manoeuvring into position for a mooring, all those years ago.

After a considerable number of photos had been taken, we began the trek back down again. As you might expect, the descent was harder than the ascent, and much of it was undertaken slowly, backwards, and with a far greater sense of abject terror than on the way up. But before too long we were reunited with our entourage and climbing out of our harnesses. Despite my delight at being back on *terra firma* and my underlying fear, I was extremely glad I had made the climb, and it will remain an unforgettable experience. Our generous and gracious hosts had laid on a lunch for us and we spent a little more time with them to conclude our business, before posing for a group photograph and running the gauntlet of favelas back to Rio.

In May 1937, the dangers of dangling beneath a large bag of hydrogen destroyed the dreams of the nascent global airship industry. The Hindenburg exploded in a ball of flames which killed 36 people during a bad landing in Lakehurst, New Jersey.

Helium is the ideal gas for airships, as it offers maximum lift and the greatest safety. But it was expensive and largely unavailable to Germany. Not many people know that the reason the Hindenburg used flammable hydrogen instead of inert helium is that the U.S. Government refused to supply helium to foreign countries. The U.S., who were the world's sole supplier, considered helium to be a strategic resource, signing into law the Helium Act of 1925 which banned its export. The entire helium supply in America has been managed by the U.S. Government almost to this day. Only in 2020 was the helium supply gradually wrestled away from government control and transferred to the private sector.

Helium is an extraordinary, and finite natural resource. Colourless, odourless, tasteless, and non-toxic, you cannot manufacture it and it occurs only in nature. It is abundant in space, as it is constantly being created by nuclear fusion of hydrogen in stars, but there is very little of it hanging around on earth, especially when people waste it in stupid party balloons. Usually found underground, often as a by-product of natural gas, it must be extracted and purified, at considerable cost. In 1903, large helium reserves were found in natural gas fields in the United States, which remains the largest supplier in the world today. The few other countries that produce decent quantities of helium include Qatar, Russia, Poland, Algeria and Australia. In its liquid form, helium is the coldest substance known to mankind (–269 °C or –452.2 °F), which explains why the single largest use for helium is supercooling the magnets used in MRI machines. Welding and scientific research are the two other major uses. It is also increasingly used in the space industry to clean reusable rocket motors. Party balloons come very low on the list.

Flying over Rio in May 1930. *(Brazilian Public Domain Photo)*

One can imagine that airships might have had a much brighter future if helium had been available, as the Hindenburg would not have burst onto flames.

Returning to Ipanema, I breathed a huge sigh of relief on finding my laptop had arrived as promised, with only a single tiny scratch to show for its foray into the bowels of a 777. Well done, American Airlines, well done.

Ipanema's fame is largely due to the Brazilian bossa nova and jazz song, "The Girl from Ipanema". A global hit and Grammy award-winner in 1965, the song was inspired by a beautiful 17-year-old girl living on Montenegro Street in Ipanema. Each day, she would stroll past the Veloso bar-café, on her way to the beach. Sometimes she would come in and buy cigarettes for her mother. She was noticed by the composers, who felt she embodied the spirit and beauty of a young Rio girl. The rest is history. The girl's name is Helô Pinheiro, and she is still alive and living in Ipanema to this day.

Julian and I wandered out to get something to eat at a delicious local fish restaurant. On the way back, in a park close to the hotel, there was a free concert going on with an excellent band. The Park was packed with families, children, grandparents, food stalls, bars, general frolicking and fun. After spending so much of my time overly concerned about being mugged or shot at, it was revealing that such a friendly, safe, family event could happen at night in the middle of Rio, with no need for security of any kind. Perhaps I had been overreacting slightly. Ipanema was a lovely neighbourhood and my attitude to Rio was beginning to change. There might be a medium risk of extortion, but there was a far greater risk of enjoying oneself enormously.

In memory of Julian Nott
1944 – 2019

Known as the founder of the modern ballooning movement, Julian was one of its most creative and innovative exponents. During his lifetime, he set or broke 79 World Records and ninety-six British Records, including exceeding 55,000-feet in a hot air balloon. In 2014, Julian designed the balloon that enabled Alan Eustace to break the record for the world's highest parachute jump, from an altitude of 135,890-feet. At the age of 72 he set a world record for the highest documented tandem skydiving jump, from 31,916-feet. He was involved in developing balloons capable of operating on other planets, and had flown a working prototype of a balloon he designed to land on Titan, Saturn's largest moon. The Smithsonian Air and Space Museum, which has one of his record-setting pressurized capsules on display, described Julian as, "A central figure in the expansion of ballooning, as an organizer, pilot, and most of all as arguably the leading figure to apply modern science to manned balloon design."

When he died, Julian had been flying the experimental balloon he had invented to change the course of balloon history, using a new system in which conventional ballast is replaced with cryogenic helium. After a successful test flight, he landed the balloon, with its pressurized cabin, on the side of a mountain at Warner Springs, north of San Diego in California. Some hours after the landing, as he was inside the cabin packing up, it broke loose and tumbled down the mountain with him inside, causing injuries from which he did not recover.

www.nott.com

JAPAN
Poison and Perfection

The Asians have been crazy about cherry blossom for more than a millennium. In fact, they have been doing a remarkable variety of things for more than several thousand years. They were busy blowing things up and inventing lavatory paper, matches, porcelain, fireworks, and guns, while we in the west were still banging rocks together. But Japan is an ancient culture of contradictions, and the flip side of all the explosions and ferociousness is sensitivity, artistry, symbolism and tradition.

The fragile little blossoms of the cherry tree, called Sakura, are a perfect example of this. They can be found in literature, art, poetry and theatre, suggesting a relationship that runs very deep. Representative of life, death, friendship and renewal, their brief annual appearance has become a national event, rolling across the country like breaking surf, from Okinawa in January, to the most northerly island of Hokkaido in early May. Every year is different, so all eyes are on the official Cherry Blossom Forecast, to make sure you know exactly when the pink wave is going to sweep across your neighbourhood.

This is the point when everyone gets very excited and begins planning their picnic. Vast quantities of sake and beer are hauled into public parks, castles and other much loved cherry blossom viewing spots, and an enormous national piss up commences. It all starts off quite well-behaved and formally, but the Japanese can really tip it back. So before too long it morphs into a huge party under the Sakura trees, with a steady snow of pink petals falling on the woozy revellers beneath. The song and dance continues into the night, when lights in the trees throw a soft pink glow on the remaining inebriated bodies below, and the petals continue their soft descent to laughter and shouts of "Kampai!"[84]

In 2019, for the occasion of our 35th wedding anniversary, the Management and I decided something special was called for. After cashing in some air miles and booking a room at one of our favourite

---

84 Kanpai or Kampai means "Empty the cup" and is the Japanese equivalent of "Cheers!"

hotels in the world – The Okura – we headed for Tokyo. It is a city we both unconditionally adore but had not visited for some 20 years. Over the years, so much of our travel has been on business that we would only occasionally be able to grab a day or two at the end of a trip for ourselves. These moments, when we were able to travel on our own terms and have the time to do what we wanted, were always exciting.

From experience, we knew that the best way to get from Narita into Tokyo was on the airport bus, as it is comfortable, efficient, and offers huge windows to soak in the views. The invisible weight of jet lag was countered by the excitement we felt at being back in this magnificent city. We arrived at The Okura to find little had changed but the uniforms of the bell-staff. On our previous visits, the women had been immaculately dressed in kimonos, but now they wore classic bell boy outfits, reminiscent of Wes Anderson's *The Grand Budapest Hotel*. In fact, there is a lot about this hotel that brings Wes Anderson's movie to mind. A team of four bell-staff bowed constantly and scurried enthusiastically around the bus, first setting out a little step to help us dismount, then taking our luggage tickets from us in their smartly gloved hands. This was done in traditional Japanese fashion, using both hands together to show care and respect in receiving the item, in the same way you might receive a piece of papyrus from the tomb of Ramses III. Clucking warnings about an approaching vehicle, they directed traffic and guests simultaneously with a wonderfully exaggerated hand semaphore, all the while assuring us that we should worry about nothing more.

Walking into the magnificent lobby with its giant mural depicting cranes, one just has to stop and drink it all in. The central ikebana display, changed each month for more than five decades by the Sekiso-ryu flower arranging school, was for this month the most massive arrangement of cherry blossoms I have ever seen. More tree than flower arrangement, it erupted from the middle of a pond, every bough, twig, flower, and petal magnificently, delicately, perfectly alive.

In most hotels, checking in is nothing more than an annoying but necessary interruption on the way to the room. Not so at The Okura. Here it is a pleasure. Every guest is welcomed as royalty, not in an obsequious, superficial way, but with genuine care, attention, friendly efficiency and sincerity. It is something to behold, and the hotel industry worldwide could learn a lot from The Okura – and indeed the Japanese hospitality industry in general.

Check-in complete, managerial staff bowed like a herd of zebra at a waterhole, just to be sure not a shred of doubt remained in our minds that we were fully and completely welcome. We were whisked up to our room with our bags and had a cup of green tea on the boil within just a few minutes of stepping off the bus. Green tea – for me the quintessential taste of Japan.

The next morning, I picked up the phone and asked room service for some cream for our coffee, and two warm croissants. It is my experience, even in most good hotels, that if you call down for the simplest thing, you are told it will either be "30 to 45 minutes" or "right up" (which means 30 to 45 minutes). On our previous visits to The Okura, we had always found that a request for some small thing from housekeeping would appear within minutes – sometimes moments – of you putting the phone down. We decided there must be someone stationed in a cubby hole on each floor, who could bounce out and fulfil requests with amazing speed. Sure enough, less than ten minutes later, there was a knock on the door. Over the next couple of days, we recorded the following:

> Order croissants and cream: 10 minutes or less (without exception)
> Remove breakfast table: two minutes
> Provide additional hotel shampoo: two minutes
> Collect, gift-wrap, and return a bottle of wine: fifteen minutes
> Tea with egg mayonnaise and cucumber sandwiches: twelve minutes
> Collect laundry: one minute

If you called down to reception and said you needed a barn owl stuffed, the in-house taxidermy department would probably have it back to you, nicely mounted with an engraved plaque, in less than the time it takes an average Hilton to organize a Club Sandwich.

It is increasingly rare nowadays to receive perfect service, unless you are the Pope, or George Clooney. Many people in Hull[85] live their entire lives without ever once experiencing it. But in Japan, the service is equally excellent for everyone, at every price point. It is a matter of Japanese honour and pride not just to serve you, but to serve you attentively, quickly, efficiently, politely and deferentially – regardless of whether you are buying a Bulgari necklace or a small bag of parrot food.

In most cities, one must go out and create experiences for oneself – you visit a museum, go shopping, take a trip down the river, or go to a restaurant. In Japan, the simplest, most mundane thing becomes a memorable, enjoyable experience, without having to make the slightest effort. This is the perfect expression of my theory of travel – that you just have to let it wash over you. Don't try too hard. One day at The Okura, the Management decided she would like to find a patisserie and buy a couple of little cakes for tea, as one does. A call was duly placed to the concierge, and the question was asked. To our surprise, there was immediate confusion. First, about understanding exactly what we wanted, then about actually determining the location of such an emporium (heaven forbid they should get either wrong). A lot of background chatter went on, then we were told they would call us back. Five minutes later the phone rang – they wanted to check they had all the details correct. Ten minutes later, with apologies for taking so long, they called to tell us that a managerial meeting had been convened, advice had been sought, phone calls made, maps checked, opening hours confirmed and the answer was ready for presentation to us, at our convenience if we would do them the inestimable pleasure of stopping by the concierge desk. Nowhere else in the world would so much be done, by so many, to find a patisserie

---

85 Constantly voted as one of the UK's "Crap Towns". Sorry, Hull, you will have to try harder.

for so few. I just wanted to hug them all. The patisserie itself was its own memorable experience. A kaleidoscope of exquisitely decorated little cakes stretched the width of the shop. A kimono-ed lady bowed and smiled as we indicated the ones we would like. Her excitement at being able to serve us was palpable. The arrangement of the little cakes in a presentation box, lined with tissue paper and little cardboard separators, was done with the utmost care. Finally, now almost as excited as her, we were handed a package fit for royalty, and almost ran back to The Okura to have a cup of tea.

And so it was not entirely surprising that the Management spent most of her time in the hotel (when not actually asleep) at the concierge desk or on the phone to them. All the researching, arranging, cancelling, and reviewing was accompanied by a lot of bowing. At all times, there were a dozen or so staff positioned strategically around the lobby, whose sole purpose in life was apparently to bow enthusiastically every time you looked at them. It is possible they were also trained to extinguish fires, administer first aid and immobilise intruders, but we never saw them put any of these ancillary skills into practice. I think I would go so far as to say that the only place you will ever experience someone bowing to you over the phone – a voice bow – is at The Okura.

Venturing necessarily but reluctantly from the hotel's comforting embrace, we were reminded how uniquely wonderful and strange Japanese taxis are, with their white-gloved drivers, automatic doors and ornate doilies covering the headrests. Attempting to open the door manually, something we westerners are quite used to doing, results in a flurry of disapprobation from the driver. One must let the automatic door opener do its duty, without let or hindrance.

There is one thing that you simply *must* do in Tokyo. No one will ever tell you this, nor is it in any tourist guide or brochures, but I think it is one of the great cultural moments in the Japanese day: The opening ceremony of the Mitsukoshi department store. It is important to get there about fifteen minutes early, so as to secure a good position at the front of the small crowd that gathers. Eight immaculately turned-out staff mill around just inside the glass doors, looking anxiously at their watches. Behind them, four more stand at attention behind the customer service desk. There is a building sense of excitement as The Eight (as we named them) line up in front of the doors. One of them looks at their watch again and issues a command. They bow deeply, in unison, to the waiting customers outside, before stepping forward to unlock the doors. As the door is opened, I make a move to start in… but no, no! I am stopped by an upheld, white gloved hand. Apparently, I must be patient. Back in line go The Eight, as the customers jostle and shift their weight from one foot to another, like anxious racehorses at the starting gate. The excitement is electric. Suddenly, there is a loud pre-recorded chiming, as an invisible clock strikes ten, in Big Ben-esque tones. The Eight all bow again, in a deep sustained swoop that is held until the last chime, at which point they pop up. Neatly transitioning into a well-practiced, sweeping hand movement accompanied by a deft sideways heel-spin, they welcome customers in. Mitsukoshi is open for business. Remarkable, but the best is still to come.

The Management and I trip keenly in, whereupon the row of customer service ladies give us a synchronized bow. We bob our heads and smile in return. Continuing toward the escalator, the staff lining the passage left and right all bow in sequence as soon as you get within six feet of them. "*Ohayō gozaimasu!*" (Good morning!). There are dozens of them, and they are all bowing like a fine wave breaking on Rincon Beach. Rather enjoying all this, and feeling every minute increasingly like George Clooney, we take the escalator up nine floors. At the bottom of each escalator are staff to bow and wish you well on your ascent. At the top are gathered the staff from that floor, to bow and welcome you to their humble floor. At the very top floor, when we can go no further, we pause to grab an espresso and I estimate we have been bowed to by over 60 people in three minutes. Never in my life have I felt so deeply appreciated. It's a brilliant way to start the day and explains why Clooney always has that look of smug satisfaction on his face.

Leaving Mitsukoshi, feeling both caffeinated and revered in equal measures, we look for a taxi. I hail several, but they don't stop. A friendly Aussie explains I am trying to hail the wrong ones. Since we were last here, taxi drivers seem to have adopted a marvellously confusing light system that is entirely unintuitive, and at odds with the rest of the planet. If a taxi is vacant, the light on top of the car will be off, but they'll also display a red light in the front of the car with kanji for ku-sha or "empty car" (a green light means occupied). Go figure. I think it must have been devised by a descendant of the man who came up with the street numbering system in Tokyo. Houses are numbered in the order they were built, which makes finding a particular house or building an astonishingly time consuming and difficult task. Long ago we learned never to get out of a Tokyo taxi until you set eyes on the number you are looking for.

Yoshi, an old friend, had invited us to join him for dinner. An accomplished impresario, local "fixer" and producer for foreign film companies; Yoshi is a gentleman, a quintessential host, and one of our favourite people on the planet. Educated in America but from an old Japanese family, he is wise, gentle, witty and huge fun. Whenever we saw him in Tokyo, he would always host a wonderful dinner at a traditional Japanese restaurant, and this evening was no exception. We were ushered into a private room with tatami mats and treated to a long procession of exquisitely prepared and presented dishes. As we relaxed at the end of the meal, I noticed that Yoshi had in front of him what looked like a cup of sake with a piece of tree bark floating in it. By way of explanation, Yoshi said only that it was a "special type" of sake.

"Very good! Would you like one?" he asked, without providing further details. Always adventurous, I accepted and about five minutes later my own tree-bark sake was sitting in front of me. I took a sip. It was not what I had expected: slightly fishy and not at all in the expected range of aromatic tree bark.

"What exactly is in this, Yoshi?" I asked, poking the tree bark suspiciously with my finger. "Ahhhh!" he responded, clearly relishing the denouement with a grin. "It is Fugu in sake, called Hirezake! You like it?"

Fugu, or pufferfish, is the second most deadly vertebrate in the world.[86] Pufferfish are just chock-a-block full of Tetrodotoxin (TTX), a neurotoxin 1,200 times more deadly than cyanide and for which there is no known antidote. Just one of the little buggers contains enough TTX to kill thirty adult humans. Symptoms typically develop quickly and are an encyclopaedic compendium of nastiness: tingling of the lips and tongue is rapidly followed by more tingling in places that really shouldn't tingle, hypersalivation, sweating, head-ache, weakness, lethargy, incoordination, tremors, paralysis, purple discoloration of the skin, inability to speak and swallow, seizures, nausea, vomiting, diarrhoea, abdominal pain, respiratory failure, paralysis and death are to be expected – and that's just the short list. The victim, although completely paralyzed, may be completely lucid until shortly before death, usually within four to six hours.

So, generally speaking, the pufferfish delivers a much more unpleasant death than even Vlad The Impaler himself could have dreamed up. One might expect that anything this deadly would advertise the fact with a colourful array of "stay away" spots or "don't fuck with me" fins. But instead, it looks pretty drab when compared to the overall colour scheme of reef fish, preferring to warn off preda-tors by inflating itself with water to look like a surprised football. It's a bit like puffing up one's cheeks to ward off a gang of moped-mug-gers – not a particularly effective way of saying, "Stay back or I will kill you."

Now most of us in the western world have heard of the pufferfish and know that in the hands of a very skilled chef it is possible to remove the naughty bits and eat the flesh without dying in a puddle of bodily fluids next to the Aga.[87] But if you dig a little deeper, there

---

86 The first is the very tiny, and deceptively sweet looking Golden Poison Dart Frog of the Amazon.

87 An Aga is a type of stove, popular in Great Britain, that is always hot and has an ancient, mercurial temperature gauge that is almost impossible to read. It

is a whole lot more to both the history and general weirdness of the Japanese's love of Fugu. Amazingly, the therapeutic uses of pufferfish eggs were mentioned in the first Chinese pharmacopoeia, the *Shen Nong Ben Cao Jing*, sometime around 2500 BC. Here, although classified as having "medium" toxicity, the eggs could have a "tonic" effect when used at the correct dose.

The German physician Engelbert Kaempfer, in *A History of Japan* (1727), described how the fish were commonly used for the purpose of committing suicide (there was a lot of that, then), and how the Emperor had sensibly decreed that soldiers were not permitted to eat them. Captain Cook recorded the first known case of TTX poisoning affecting Westerners in his log from September 7, 1774. Cook stated that his crew ate some local "tropic fish" (pufferfish), then fed the leftovers to the pigs kept on board. The crew got a bit of a scare with numbness and shortness of breath, but the pigs were all found dead the next morning. The crew had clearly survived a mild dose of TTX, but the leftovers consisted of the most toxic bits – the skin, ovaries, testicles, and liver – so the poor piggies didn't stand a chance. Pork was off the *Endeavour's* menu for the rest of the trip.

So, let's explore the interesting, ancient idea of it being a "tonic", rather than something that needs two years training to prepare in a way that won't kill you in the most mind-buggeringly ghastly way. Plenty of people get sick from it and a handful die each year, but people love living a little dangerously, so it remains a popular, if risky delicacy. It turns out that the reason for this is because a teeny-tiny bit of neurotoxin makes you quite high and, as we know, lots of people will accept a slight chance of full-body paralysis for a bit of good old-fashioned euphoria and some tingling. The crew of the *Endeavour* probably got quite a nice high. The really die-hard Fugu fans (pun intended), actually get a bit shirty if the chef does

---

requires ten years of training to learn how to cook on it. An Aga is always on, ensuring that your kitchen is nice and cozy throughout winter. During summer, it makes you feel like you are living in the crater of an active volcano. It's a posh British thing.

a technically perfect dissection of the fish. For them, removing all traces of TTX also takes all the fun out of Fugu. So, here I am, with a fun Fugu fin gently seeping TTX into my sake.

"It's delicious!" I tell Yoshi. "Although somewhat fishier than expected." He beams at me happily.

Wait! Is that a slight tingling I feel?

One evening, before we leave, Yoshi meets us in Shinjuku, to take us to a tiny bar in the Golden Gai, an area of Tokyo. Once known as the red-light district, it is now appreciated for its original architecture and over 200 miniature bars and restaurants, all connected by six narrow alleys and a subset of passages that barely accommodate one person at a time. Most buildings are barely 10-foot wide, with a tiny restaurant or bar on the bottom, and another on top, up an impossibly steep and narrow flight of stairs. Each bar caters to a specific clientele, attracting artists, musicians, writers, academics and celebrities, and although scruffy looking, it is not cheap. It's well to do patrons like exclusivity. Seating only half a dozen customers at a time, only regulars are welcome at many of these tiny establishments.

The Management and I followed Yoshi as he guided us through the maze of passages, until we reached a tiny door, behind which was an equally miniscule staircase that rose almost vertically. Reaching the top, we found ourselves in the smallest bar I had ever seen. The room was about ten-feet by ten-feet, with a tiny bar that seated six. There were two people already there, one of whom was the owner, Nobu, Yoshi's friend. The place felt immediately full. Nobu greeted us warmly and drinks were immediately poured. Nobu was a successful entrepreneur and ran the bar purely for fun. It was his hobby. He had one employee who opened up around 9:00 pm and managed things, but most nights Nobu himself came in sometime after 10:00 pm and ran the bar himself. It was not hard, for six people, most of whom were his friends. We chatted away happily in broken English. The song "Games People Play," by the Alan Parsons Project boomed over the speakers, and as fingers tapped on the bar, we instantly felt a bond. We told Nobu that we happened to know Alan, and that he lives in Santa Barbara.

"Aaaaaahhhhhh! You know Alan Parson?" boomed Nobu, his face lighting up[88].

The other man at the bar, who has been quiet until now, suddenly piped up excitedly

"Alan Parson Project! Excellent! Excellent!" Nobu turns the music even louder and sploshed more whiskey into my glass as we launched into a conversation about our favourite tracks. It's amazing how one connects with people in different cultures by finding the strangest little things in common.

We visited three more Lilliputian bars and I had no idea where we were. In the second bar, which served food, we met a charming young Italian named Alberto. He was with two female Japanese friends. We got to talking. It turned out he had chosen to leave Italy and come to live in Tokyo because it is absolutely at the forefront of virtual and augmented reality design. He was studying for his PhD under an esteemed Japanese professor in the field. As an artist, film-maker and technologist, he was working on VR stuff that will likely blow our collective minds when we see it in five years' time. It seemed every little corner of The Golden Gai was stuffed with interesting people. It was a late night, but when we left to head back to The Okura, Yoshi bade us farewell saying he was just going to head back to Nobu's... for a nightcap.

* * *

Across Tokyo, the cherry blossoms were in full bloom, in all their synchronised, pale pink perfection. We had timed it perfectly. Close to The Okura is the Imperial Palace, right in the centre of Tokyo. Beside its ancient moat bloom the most spectacular old cherry trees, their long boughs drooping down to Sakura-kiss the water, high rise office blocks standing tall in the background. It was stunningly beautiful, wandering the paths on our last day, coming unexpectedly

---

88 To get accurate pronunciation, replace all the L's with R's.

on quiet corners, where an explosion of Sakura had burst quietly against the aged stones of a dynastic guardhouse.

So much of travel is hectic and can be tiring. The shifts can be unexpected, surprising, harsh. But Tokyo demonstrates that another sort of shift is possible – a gentle, calming shift. Simultaneously ancient and futuristic, formal, and informal, Tokyo is a city that comforts and delights me, a place where I can feel at peace, and yet entirely invigorated at the same time. It is a city that is obsessed by perfection in every form, at once steeped in the most ancient of traditions and yet sitting on the bleeding edge of technology, art and entertainment. Sometimes travel is not about visiting somewhere new but revisiting somewhere you have been before. You might be lucky and discover a totally different side to it.

In short, I love Japan.

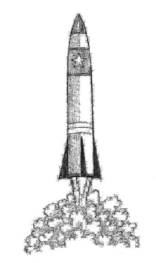

THE FUTURE

An Orbital Perspective

So, what does the future of commercial air travel hold? Well, who else would you expect to find on the bleeding edge of aviation but Richard Branson, who was responsible for founding the commercial space line Virgin Galactic in 2004. Until then, the only way you could possibly get into space was if you joined NASA at birth or hitched a ride on a Russian Soyuz rocket for an unimaginable amount of money. That all changed with the promise of Virgin Galactic. Rides into space, to experience four minutes of zero G's and a view of the earth – only previously seen by 550 odd people – were suddenly available to purchase for about $250,000 (return).[89] Virgin took the commercial space tourism route, working on an air-launched system designed by the legendary aerospace engineer, Burt Rutan.

At the same time, and with extraordinary speed, Space X came after the NASA business – sending cargo and people to the International Space Station. Under the wild, crazy, rollercoaster brilliance of Elon Musk, Space X began reinventing everything NASA had been catatonically unable to change for decades. They focused on the innovative and economical re-use of spent boosters, landing them with pinpoint accuracy on floating barges, which everyone agreed was pretty badass. Now, Musk has set his sights on Mars.

While there was a lot of noise coming from these two contenders, a third equally brilliant and determined billionaire – Jeff Bezos – was quietly designing and building his own dream. His company, Blue Origin, now also takes tourists into space using a ground launched, re-usable rocket. However, Blue Origin have for some time been building a bigger rocket called New Glenn that will likely take a chunk out of Space X's market in the not too distant future.

Unlike Musk, both Branson and Bezos are initially aiming for the tourist market. Now I know $250,000 seems like an insane amount of money, but there are many thousands of people in the world who routinely fork out these kinds of sums to take the family on a break

---

89 Over 600 advance tickets were sold.

– just not you and I. Branson's private island in the British Virgin Islands, Neckar, is available to rent, from $80,000 per night for up to 34 guests – that's over a half a million a week. For the one per cent, the "ultimate vacation" is not within our comprehension. The choices are ever-changing: there is a one-day trip to Antarctica, for which a family can board a Gulfstream Private Jet in Cape Town and head south for about eight hours of exploration. Ending in a gourmet dinner, the entire trip lasts less than 24 hours and will set you back $195,000. On Fiji's private Laucala Island, there's a $44,000-per-night villa where guests can enjoy secluded luxury. Suite 5000 at the Mandarin Oriental, New York, is located on the hotel's fiftieth floor. The walls are lined with an exhibition of New York City-inspired art, and the living room stocked with records that follow the city's music scene back to the 1930s. You will need $36,000 per night to stay there, and plenty of people do. So, for the not so few this is all in a day's vacation. So, when Branson started Virgin Galactic, he knew full well there were plenty of customers out there, and more importantly, what they could help create.

Virgin Galactic's goal is to send four passengers and two pilots, up to 53 miles above the earth in SpaceShipTwo, several times a week. It's been a hard slog, because nothing this insanely complicated is easy. Tragically, in 2014 the VSS Enterprise crashed, with the loss of a pilot's life. But in July 2021 they finally made it happen. The launch site is the gorgeous, purpose-built Spaceport America in New Mexico, designed by acclaimed architects Foster & Partners. Jeff Bezos followed with his first launch only a couple of weeks later, slightly higher, and with M&M's. Importantly, both have a vision far beyond just tourist flights for the 1%.

Those who ridicule the idea of spending such a massive amount of money for a flight to space just don't get it; if you look back at aviation history this has *always* been the way it works. In fact, it is *essential* if humanity is to thrive and grow. Exploration has always required money, and space exploration is no exception. The Kings and Queens of Europe paid handsomely to fund expeditions to new worlds, in the hope their investment would pay off in the form of great riches and new discoveries. Before aircraft were able to, the Zeppelins made hundreds of transatlantic crossings during the late 1920s and 1930s, and their passengers were all very wealthy indeed. Likewise, seats on the first transcontinental and trans-oceanic flights of commercial aviation, flown by great airlines like Pan American Airways, were occupied exclusively by the super-rich. The passengers were all wealthy business owners, celebrities and high-ranking government employees – they were the only ones prepared to pay a king's ransom to reach far-flung places quickly. The wealthy single-handedly funded the expansion of commercial aviation. Without the huge amount of money paid for tickets in the early days, air travel would simply not have become as readily available as it is now, when people consider it their inalienable right to fly to Mykonos for a stag weekend. The same will apply to spaceflight. If our children are ever going to take to space regularly, like our generation have taken to the air, it will be thanks to the likes of Branson, Bezos and Musk.

* * *

As we mere mortals increasingly and inevitably shake off the bonds of gravity and travel into space, we may experience perhaps the most life-changing shift in flight it is possible to achieve. Astronauts describe the profound effects of seeing the earth from space for the first time. They describe a state of mental clarity and self-awareness that is now referred to as the "overview effect", in which they were overwhelmed by a sense of the fragility of Earth, and a sudden understanding of the unity and coherence of life, the universe and everything.

One of the Apollo 8 astronauts commented:

"When we originally went to the moon, our total focus was on the moon. We weren't thinking about looking back at the Earth. But now that we've done it, that may well have been the most important reason we went."

In 2008, astronaut Ron Garan was clamped to the end of the robotic arm of the International Space Station as it swept him in an arc over the station and back:

> As I approached the top of this arc, it was as if time stood still, and I was flooded with both emotion and awareness. But as I looked down at the Earth – this stunning, fragile oasis, this island that has been given to us, and that has protected all life from the harshness of space – a sadness came over me, and I was hit in the gut with an undeniable, sobering contradiction.
>
> In spite of the overwhelming beauty of this scene, serious inequity exists on the apparent paradise we have been given. I couldn't help thinking of the nearly one billion people who don't have clean water to drink, the countless number who go to bed hungry every night, the social injustice, conflicts, and poverty that remain pervasive across the planet.
>
> Seeing Earth from this vantage point gave me a unique perspective – something I've come to call the orbital perspective. Part of this is the realization that we are all traveling together on the planet and that if we all looked at the world from that perspective, we would see that nothing is impossible[90].

The race to see who will be the first to launch "tourist astronauts" into space has been won. It's risky, dangerous and expensive, but they will be the first in a new generation of non-astronaut astronauts to experience not just the view to end all views, but the ultimate life-changing travel experience. History will record 2021 as the year everything changed.

* * *

---

90 Excerpt from Ron Garan's *The Orbital Perspective: Lessons in Seeing the Big Picture from a Journey of 71 Million Miles*, published 2015.

Although it is entirely possible that the first hotel in space will be a Virgin Hotel, from whence you may still be able to send a postcard, not many people know that Richard Branson is driven by a vision broader than just space tourism. Apart from a brief time when the Concorde was operational, we have been traveling around our planet at roughly the same speed for decades. But in 2019 and 2020, Virgin Galactic announced partnerships with both Boeing and NASA to develop safe, efficient, and environmentally responsible "High-Mach" vehicles. A High-Mach vehicle is one which travels at between Mach 2 and Mach 5[91]. SpaceShipTwo reaches just over Mach 3, making it the first crewed, High-Mach, commercial winged vehicle – and the perfect stepping-stone. Using existing technologies and experience, Virgin and others want to begin development of a new class of high-speed, point-to-point aircraft. The real holy grail here is hypersonic intercontinental travel. Hypersonic is a speed of Mach 5 and higher, or more than five times the speed of sound. NASA's X-43 was the fastest aircraft ever flown. It used a rocket engine to provide an initial boost, then an air-breathing hypersonic jet engine called a scramjet to reach 7,300 mph, nearly ten times the speed of sound. But one experimental aircraft does not an airline make. However, Branson knows that if he can design a plane to take you to the edge of space and back at 2,600mph, the next logical step is to launch commercial flights from London that would skim through the lower edge of space and land in Sydney three hours later. That, would be a Wright Brothers moment. Don't hold your breath though – having the vision is the easy part; turning it into reality is much, much harder.

The Wright Brothers made the first controlled, sustained flight of a powered aircraft on December 17, 1903. For many years afterwards, flying was insanely dangerous, difficult and expensive. People then thought it was all pointless and superficial. But today, here we are, fuming when we are told we cannot hop on a plane to Alicante for

---

91 The speed of sound varies with altitude and air temperature, but as a rough guide, Mach 2 is 1,500mph.

the weekend. I marvel at the fact that in just a little over one lifetime we have come so far. From that first brief hop on the beach at Kitty Hawk, North Carolina, to humankind's first steps on the moon, we are now on the verge of space tourism, short-distance vertical take-off-and-landing taxis and traveling from one side of the planet to the other in a mere three hours. Technology has achieved a remarkable track record of making the unimaginable commonplace. I know we tend to take it all for granted, but you and I are watching history being made. Something to consider, next time you are bored of the in-flight entertainment.

EPILOGUE
The day travel stopped

The Management leaned over and whispered loudly at me.

"That bloody man on my left keeps coughing!"

"Which one?"

"That Italian or Spanish one over there. He coughs literally every few minutes, and…" she added by way of condemnation, "… it sounds like a dry one. Did you hear it? I think it's completely unacceptable."

We were some way into our flight from Madrid to London Heathrow, and on the verge of an in-flight diplomatic incident. It was March 3, 2020, and Covid-19 was exploding all over northern Italy. We had just spent a long weekend with friends in the hills of Ibiza and were making our way back to England to hole up and see how things developed. This was likely to be the last flight we would take for a while. The prospect of strapping ourselves into an aluminium tube with 400 random people and buddy-breathing our way back to Los Angeles was rapidly losing its lustre.

"Bloody man! What does he think he is doing? It's so incredibly selfish – I mean we don't know where he's been… and he may have bloody Covid and be giving it to the entire plane."

"A-huuh. A-huuh," went Coughing Man, for emphasis.

"See what I mean!!" exclaimed the Management, her eyebrows doing somersaults, almost apoplectic at this Olympic display of super-spreader behaviour.

"Here you are, darling," I said, handing her a mask. "Pop this on then."

"Faydo beeble-saps and ramble clams," she said very crossly from underneath it.

"I am sorry darling I can't understand a word you are saying." I beamed sweetly and returned to my book. She turned again to Coughing Man, glowering at him in the hope he would spontaneously combust.

Super-spreaders like Coughing Man moved across the world, unwittingly – or uncaringly – infectious. Politicians waffled (except in New Zealand), people suffered, and doctors and nurses struggled to stem the rising tide. But despite their heroic and selfless efforts, too many died, mostly alone, or with a loved one on FaceTime as their only comfort. Businesses, restaurants, and cinemas closed their doors. Hoarders hoarded, roads emptied, and food ran short. People stayed all day in their pyjamas, and fashion companies turned to making masks, the new must-have accessory. Many small business owners watched the success they had striven to reach for so long slip from their grasp at the last moment. Few would recover their momentum; their dreams of independence and success dashed on viral rocks. Even large businesses declared bankruptcy. The Internet slowed to a crawl, bearing the weight of our collective surfing, streaming, shopping, and searching. The Amazon river of packages broke its banks, flooding the land with little brown boxes.

Hotels closed their doors, resorts were shuttered, taxi drivers and tour guides stayed home, their self-employed income evaporating like a hundred million popping balloons. Hundreds of planes of every description, their interiors still and dark, lined the perimeter of airports from LHR to LAX and SYD to JHB. Many would never fly again.

The fleet of 747s operated by British Airways were, one by one, flown to scrapyards in Wales, Spain, and Gloucestershire to be broken up. For so long the Queen of the Skies, more than one 747 pilot had tears in their eyes as they shut down the engines for the last time, the great aircraft a sudden, unexpected victim of Covid. Many pilots and crew went home jobless.

This was the day our world changed overnight; the day we all took a forced break in our travelling; the day it began to dawn on us that we were in a full on pandemic. But, although times were hard and loved ones died, some good emerged alongside the suffering.

In lockdown, people busily Zoomed and cooked and baked and gardened and sang from their balconies and clapped for their carers and wrote books and learned a language or played a musical instrument, and did all manner of other things they had never done before but had wanted to do all their lives. Neighbours helped neighbours, and families and communities came closer together, in the way that only happens in a crisis. The roads were empty of cars and belching trucks, the air devoid of aircraft, the seas vacant of pleasure craft. Dolphins frolicked in the suddenly clean canals of Venice and, with humans gone, wildlife began roaming the streets of eerily empty towns and cities. The Himalaya were visible from Delhi for the first time in decades, and satellite images showed pollution and smog to be at the lowest levels in living memory. Although only briefly, we demonstrated quite how quickly we can collectively impact our environment for the better.

For me, these images of clear skies, pristine waters, and roaming animals appear so fresh and remarkable and utterly wonderful. For a moment it brought to mind the memory of sitting on horseback in the rainforest of North Queensland, very slightly high, after eating that sandwich into which I had slipped a single magic mushroom. Everything looked like it had been colour corrected to the "vivid" setting. The massive fronds were impossibly green, the parrots explosively red and Vantablack. Everything was alive, vibrant and singing in a way I had never seen before. The only way I can think to describe it is like the feeling you get as you see, hear or experience something that causes you to momentarily tingle all over. At that moment the tingling was not in me, but in everything I could see. Seeing these images of a suddenly, unexpectedly clean world I could no longer reach was an extraordinary, hyper-real moment that brought my life's travels into sharp perspective. Now this is a bit extreme, but could we ever travel with something resembling that enhanced sensitivity for everything we experience? Maybe not, and taking magic mushrooms is not something I recommend you do without medical supervision, but we could definitely try harder to soak in every gorgeous second, allowing travel to do its' business of changing us, of reaching into the centre of our being and gently polishing our souls.

Now, as I conclude this book, with myself in lockdown, I have gone full circle and find myself unexpectedly back where I started, in the small village in Oxfordshire where I grew up. We can go nowhere except on essential journeys, and the valid reasons for those are few. So, this is an opportune moment to reflect on what travel means to us, and how we should never take the privilege it affords us as a right.

Ralph Waldo Emerson may have famously said, "It's not the destination. It's the journey," but, for me, it was beloved American celebrity chef, author, and travel documentarian, Anthony Bourdain, who said it best.

> "Travel isn't always pretty. It isn't always comfortable. Sometimes it hurts, it even breaks your heart. But that's okay. The journey changes you; it should change you. It leaves marks on your memory, on your consciousness, on your heart, and on your body. You take something with you. Hopefully, you leave something good behind." – *Anthony Bourdain*

For me, this is the central idea to travelling perfectly, the idea that things not only shift in the baggage lockers over our heads, but deep within us, as we allow unexpected experiences, people, and places to change us. We *should* come back changed. The idea that we also would leave something behind with the people we encounter along the way is a charming one that makes this concept so beautifully balanced.

For me, these are the things that have done much to make me who I am, and this is why we should embrace travel – warts and all. We should be present, in the moment, everything tingling with appreciation. Most importantly, and I cannot emphasize this enough, you should keep a simple diary of your travels, in which you can record each evening – briefly – before bed; the small but wonderful details of the day that will otherwise quickly elude you, never to return, as you travel inexorably forward in time.

By the time you read this we will have set out once again, desperate to scratch the itch we have been unable to reach these many months of lockdown. Travel will have changed forever. The G-forces of flight, the waves against the bow, the sway of the train, and the mountain-trail beneath our feet will be back, but with them will be temperature checks, masks, sanitizer and who knows what else. There will still be delays and disruptions, widespread crowds, discomfort, dodgy curry, antibody tests and packets of Imodium. The experience of travel will be mostly the same from a physical standpoint but, I hope, cerebrally different. Will we be changed by our vacation from vacations? Will our appreciation of all we encounter be more finely tuned? Will we be less dependent on the number of likes we receive? Let us try. Let us live the moment more fully, take fewer posed photos and selfies. However we get there, be it on the slow boat, the fast train, or hypersonic to Sydney, we need to remember to unplug, and allow our senses to feast on the special moments, remarkable people, extraordinary places and glorious memories with which travel endows us.

Thank you for coming with me on my journeys. Where to next…?

THE END

A PERSONAL NOTE

Nowadays, unless you are a celebrity chef or an abdicated Royal, it is nigh-on impossible to get a book published through an actual publisher, who would do useful stuff like marketing. This is the reason we all publish on Amazon, where reviews are the beating heart of any book. I hate to ask, but if you enjoyed this book, please be five kinds of fabulous and write a nice review. Being a first-time author, a complimentary review will tell others this is a book worth their time and money, and you will have abundant good karma as a result. It only takes seconds, and you can go about your day knowing you have paid it forward. Thank you.

A MESSAGE TO ALL MEN

Prostate cancer is a killer hiding in the shadows, and it is my duty to help shine a light on it. What you don't know could kill you, so this is a conversation that not only must be heard, but must become commonplace. I consider this my version of an urgent public service announcement, so pay attention. Lives will be saved, possibly yours or that of someone you love.

Regardless of your own sex, you should really be aware of how prostate cancer can sneak up on a man – possibly your partner, your friend, your brother, your father – and unceremoniously tip his world upside down. I believe each of us has a responsibility to be aware of issues affecting those we love. In recent years, breast cancer has achieved a tremendous surge in awareness and, as a direct result, more women than ever are being diagnosed sooner, and successfully treated to make a full recovery.

We men don't like to talk about our prostate, even among ourselves; let alone to our partners or, heaven forbid, a doctor. This is because anything that might question our abundant fertility, or our ability to get an erection like a prize stallion, is pretty much still taboo. It strikes to the very heart of our masculinity. Get a grip, I say. Women endure far worse indignities on a regular basis, involving an array of medieval instruments and extensive scuffling about. Be thankful you don't have a vagina, which is exhaustingly high-maintenance.

For heaven's sake men, just get an annual blood test and save yourself from a thorough rummaging by a six-armed robot, and other indignities, not least of which is death. And ladies, if there is a man in your life over the age of 45, exert whatever pressure is required to make sure he does,[92] because it is a well-known fact that most men

---

92 Yes, you know exactly how to do this.

would rather have their nipples chewed off by a badger than go and see a doctor about their dangly bits.

For more information:
www.prostatecancer.co.uk
www.pcf.org

ACKNOWLEDGEMENTS

Numerous friends have urged me to put finger to keyboard over the years but the first, and most persistent, was Ginny Wheatley. Without her urging I would not have started writing, and this book would never have seen the light of day. Many others took up the cry, including Dominic Wheatley who encouraged me to write an entirely different book – sorry Dom, maybe next time. Lockdown gave me the opportunity and the motivation to get it done, and my wife, the Management, put up with me tapping away for days, weeks and months. When the crucial first draft was ready, a raft of friends and family around the world stepped up to read, critique and correct, so an equally heartfelt thank you goes out to them all: Phil Bowen in Queensland, Harry Eversole, Robert Schlueter, Arabella Weston Smith, and Bob Wallace in California, Russ Setzekorn in Texas, Kathleen Kinney in New Zealand, Pamela Brice and Ollie Mace in Scotland, Pagan Hopkinson, Rachel Sherwood, Shane Martin and Freddie Weston Smith in England. Some of you did some major heavy lifting, correcting my grammatical errors, political incorrectness, and general rambling. Last, but not least, my editors, Malcolm Croft, and Hugh Barker, who left no paragraph unturned in their quest to make this a better book. With your collective advice, all of you have left your mark on this book, and I am incredibly grateful for your guidance, wisdom and encouragement. Thank you.

FURTHER READING

Gavin Young: *Slow Boats to China*

Bruce Chatwin: *The Songlines*

Tim Butcher: *Blood River*

Geoffrey Kent: *Safari: A Memoir of a Worldwide Travel Pioneer*

Bill Bryson: Absolutely everything he has written

Douglas Adams: *The Meaning of Liff*
(a small book that makes me cry with laughter)

Anthony Bourdain: *No Reservations:
Around the World on an Empty Stomach*

Nicholas Schmidle: *Test Gods: Virgin Galactic
and the Making of a Modern Astronaut*

Ron Garan: *The Orbital Perspective: Lessons in Seeing
the Big Picture from a Journey of 71 Million Miles.*

ABOUT THE AUTHOR

Richard grew up in England. As a child, he was allowed great freedom, and generally had to create his own entertainment. Being a poster child for Attention Deficit Disorder, this was never diffic … *"oh look, a badger!"* He could bicycle anywhere he wished without a helmet, fall out of trees, set fire to stuff (occasionally himself), upset tadpoles, shoot things with an air rifle (occasionally himself), and frolic irresponsibly through fields and woods in a way that would now be thoroughly disapproved of and quite possibly illegal. He first got a taste for travel when he was sent to Australia at the age of 17 to survive working on a cattle station. Against all odds, he did, and by age 23 he had travelled through India, and, in 1982, settled in Johannesburg, where he married his wife, Kirsten. Working in corporate marketing allowed him to travel throughout Southern Africa. He moved in 1989to California, where he and Kirsten set up a marketing services company, Brainstorm Creative; their client list is a Who's Who of the Fortune 500, including Virgin, Nike, Apple and BMW. Richard has been writing for years for his clients but has never attempted to write a book about himself before. However, like many people, knew that a book about his life was lurking within him, desperate to break out. He enjoys writing, humour, travel, brightly coloured socks, cooking Italian food, and making proper British marmalade. His work has enabled him to travel the world continuously and extensively, and he and Kirsten now live between Santa Barbara and England. They have three children and almost permanent jet lag.

Made in the USA
Middletown, DE
04 September 2021